James Watt's historically grounded account of Gothic fiction takes issue with received accounts of the genre as a stable and continuous tradition. Charting its vicissitudes from Walpole's *The Castle of Otranto* to Scott's Waverley novels, Watt shows the Gothic to have been a heterogeneous body of fiction, characterized at times by antagonistic relations between various writers or works. Drawing on diverse archival materials, he describes the various kinds of classification of Gothic fiction made by writers and readers of the time. Central to Watt's argument about the writing and reception of these works is a nuanced understanding of their political import: he discusses Walpole's attempt to forge an aristocratic identity, the loyalist affiliations of many neglected works of the 1790s, the subversive reputation of *The Monk*, and the ways in which Radcliffean romance proved congenial to conservative critics. Watt concludes by looking ahead to the fluctuating critical status of Scott and the Gothic, and examines the process by which the Gothic came to be defined as a monolithic tradition, in a way that continues to exert a powerful hold.

James Watt is a Junior Research Fellow at St Catharine's College, Cambridge.

CAMBRIDGE STUDIES IN ROMANTICISM 33

CONTESTING THE GOTHIC

CAMBRIDGE STUDIES IN ROMANTICISM

This series aims to foster the best new work in one of the most challenging fields within English literary studies. From the early 1780s to the early 1830s a formidable array of talented men and women took to literary composition, not just in poetry, which some of them famously transformed, but in many modes of writing. The expansion of publishing created new opportunities for writers, and the political stakes of what they wrote were raised again by what Wordsworth called those 'great national events' that were 'almost daily taking place': the French Revolution, the Napoleonic and American wars, urbanization, industrialization, religious revival, an expanded empire abroad and the reform movement at home. This was a literature of enormous ambition, even when it pretended otherwise. The relations between science, philosophy, religion and literature were reworked in texts such as *Frankenstein* and *Biographia Literaria*; gender relations in *A Vindication of the Rights of Woman* and *Don Juan*; journalism by Cobbett and Hazlitt; poetic form, content and style by the Lake School and the Cockney School. Outside Shakespeare studies, probably no body of writing has produced such a wealth of response or done so much to shape the responses of modern criticism. This indeed is the period that saw the emergence of those notions of 'literature' and of literary history, especially national literary history, on which modern scholarship in English has been founded.

The categories produced by Romanticism have also been challenged by recent historicist arguments. The task of the series is to engage both with a challenging corpus of Romantic writings and with the changing field of criticism they have helped to shape. As with other literary series published by Cambridge, this one will represent the work of both younger and more established scholars, on either side of the Atlantic and elsewhere.

For a complete list of titles published see end of book

CONTESTING THE GOTHIC

Fiction, Genre and Cultural Conflict, 1764–1832

JAMES WATT

PUBLISHED BY THE PRESS SYNDICATE OF THE UNIVERSITY OF CAMBRIDGE
The Pitt Building, Trumpington Street, Cambridge CB2 1RP. United Kingdom

CAMBRIDGE UNIVERSITY PRESS

The Edinburgh Building, Cambridge CB2 2RU, UK http://www.cup.cam.ac.uk
40 West 20th Street, New York, NY 1001–4211, USA http://www.cup.org
10 Stamford Road, Oakleigh, Melbourne 3166, Australia

First published 1999

Printed in the United Kingdom at the University Press, Cambridge

Typeset in Baskerville 11/12.5 pt [VN]

A catalogue record for this book is available from the British Library

Library of Congress cataloguing in publication data
Watt, James.
Contesting the Gothic: fiction, genre and cultural conflict, 1764–1832 / James Watt.
p.   cm. – (Cambridge studies in Romanticism : 33)
Includes bibliographical references and index.
ISBN 0521 64099 7 (hardback)
1. English fiction – 18th century – History and criticism. 2. Horror tales, English –
History and criticism. 3. English fiction – 19th century – History and criticism.
4. Gothic revival (Literature) – Great Britain. 5. Culture – Political aspects – Great Britain.
6. Romanticism – Great Britain. 7. Literary form. I. Title. II. Series.
PR858.T3W38   1999
823'.0872909'09033 – dc21
98–42850   CIP

ISBN 0521 64099 7 hardback

For my parents

Contents

Acknowledgements

This book derives from my PhD thesis, which benefited greatly from the guidance of my supervisor, Nigel Leask. I would like to thank my examiners, Simon Jarvis and Gary Kelly, along with Alun David, Paul Hartle, and the anonymous readers who commented on my typescript on behalf of Cambridge University Press. Thanks also to my editor, Josie Dixon, and my copy-editor, Jan Chapman, as well as Keith Burroughs, Andrew Cowan, and Neil Cowles, who provided technical assistance throughout. I am grateful to the Master and Fellows of St Catharine's College, Cambridge, for electing me to a Junior Research Fellowship, enabling me to continue my work in the Romantic period. Above all, I would like to thank my family and friends for their constant backing during the course of this project.

Introduction

Though the genre of the Gothic romance clearly owes its name to the subtitle of *The Castle of Otranto*'s second edition, 'A Gothic Story', the elevation of Walpole's work to the status of an origin has served to grant an illusory stability to a body of fiction which is distinctly heterogeneous. Face-value readings of the preface to *Otranto*'s second edition have encouraged the idea that Walpole issued a manifesto for a new literary genre, the emergence of which was coincident with a revival of imagination in an era that privileged rationality. As I will argue, however, any categorization of the Gothic as a continuous tradition, with a generic significance, is unable to do justice to the diversity of the romances which are now accommodated under the 'Gothic' label, and liable to overlook the often antagonistic relations that existed between different works or writers. The project of this book is to reconsider the so-called Gothic romance from a historical perspective, and to focus in detail on the functioning of specific works, so as to provide the basis for a more nuanced account of the way that the genre was constituted in the late eighteenth and early nineteenth centuries.

A historically grounded study of Gothic fiction must begin by acknowledging that the genre itself is a relatively modern construct. The Gothic romance as a descriptive category is the product of twentieth-century literary criticism, and specifically of the revival of interest in late-eighteenth-century romance in the 1920s and 1930s. If it is difficult to be certain as to why there was a surge of interest in writers such as Walpole, Radcliffe, and Lewis in this period, it is nonetheless important to recognize the influence of the works that initially labelled and described 'Gothic' fiction, such as Edith Birkhead's *The Tale of Terror* (1921), Eino Railo's *The Haunted Castle* (1927), J. M. S. Tompkins's *The Popular Novel in England 1770–1800* (1932) and Montague Summers's *The Gothic Quest* (1938). Though these writers often appealed to the aura of romance in a defensive tone, their labelling of the Gothic supplied the

initial foundation for subsequent critics to make larger claims about the
importance of the genre as a whole. Arguably the most powerful
exploration of the significance of the Gothic has been provided by
David Punter's groundbreaking study *The Literature of Terror* (1980).
Punter reads the Gothic as a materialist genre, a literature of self-
analysis which emerged at a stage 'when the bourgeoisie . . . began to try
to understand the conditions and history of their own ascent'.[1] In a
period of industrialization and rapid social change, according to Punter,
Gothic works insistently betrayed the fears and anxieties of the middle
classes about the nature of their ascendancy, returning to the issues of
ancestry, inheritance, and the transmission of property: 'Under such
circumstances, it is hardly surprising to find the emergence of a
literature whose key motifs are paranoia, manipulation and injustice,
and whose central project is understanding the inexplicable, the taboo,
the irrational.'[2]

Following Punter, many critics have invoked models of generic
tradition in order to support sometimes expansive claims about the
nature of the anxieties disclosed by the Gothic. It is important to remain
sceptical about the explanatory power of such theories of the Gothic,
however, since they are liable to become reliant upon a 'her-
meneutically circular process' whereby, in the words of Jacqueline
Howard, individual works are interpreted 'in such a way as to produce
the generic frame against which [they are] being read'.[3] The term
'Gothic', as Chris Baldick has stated, is now established 'as the name for
one sinister corner of the modern western imagination',[4] and this
increasingly dominant sense of the Gothic, chiming as it does with the
postmodern suspicion of Enlightenment values, continues to exert a
powerful influence on those approaching eighteenth-century Gothic
fiction for the first time. Yet despite the resonance of the Gothic as a
metaphor, and the privileged access to repressed material which Gothic
works are now seen to offer, it is also important to take into account the
range of literal meanings which the term held in the late eighteenth
century, and to recognize in particular the way that the Gothic was
constructed as an idealized pseudo-historical period or a locus of exemplary virtue and valour. Only a small number of romances after *Otranto*
actually characterized themselves as 'Gothic' works,[5] but it is difficult to
incorporate these into an account of an interrogative, 'bourgeois' genre.
If the past exerts a coercive force on the present in Clara Reeve's *The Old
English Baron: A Gothic Story* (1778), for example, it does so in order to
redeem the aristocratic family at the centre of the work, and to stress the

legitimacy of its hero's status as the nobly born heir to the Castle of Lovel. Reeve subordinated the role of sensation or suspense to a didactic purpose, as I will go on to argue, yet her work has been dismissed and virtually ignored because of its failure to live up to a normative critical standard of what a Gothic romance should look like. At the outset, therefore, it is important to underline the fact that the unitary genre upon which many readings of the Gothic rely is a twentieth-century creation. Though the description of genres, movements, and traditions serves an important purpose in literary history, this must be accompanied by a focus on the consequences of such acts of definition, and literary criticism must be sensitive to the more nuanced kinds of classification that were made by writers and readers of the Gothic romance in its historical moment.

Most of the works which literary history has classified as 'Gothic' actually described themselves by way of the larger category of 'romance', a term given prominence in the period by the expansion of scholarly research into the question of national and cultural origins. What we now know as the Gothic, according to Ian Duncan, was 'the first English prose fiction to call itself "romance" with a certain generic intention, distinguishing itself from the novel and the representation of contemporary life'.[6] Though many accounts of the genre's emergence, encouraged by Walpole's second preface, have read *Otranto* as an empowering fictional manifesto, it is nonetheless difficult to isolate a *single* 'generic intention' underwriting the rise of the Gothic romance. The status of the Gothic as an assimilative literary hybrid was foregrounded even at its acknowledged point of origin, indeed, when Walpole claimed that *Otranto* was a *'blend* [of] the two kinds of Romance, the ancient and the modern' (my emphasis).[7] This book will be less interested in trying to define the parameters and preoccupations of the genre as a whole, therefore, than to locate the Gothic in the context of the revival of romance in the second half of the eighteenth century. The history of prose fiction in this period, as Katie Trumpener has recently argued, is one of 'dislocations, bifurcations, and disengagements as much as it is of continuity and accretion', a history whose 'complex dynamic of development' necessitates both local and relational analysis.[8] In the light of this claim, I want to explore some of the connections between the Gothic and other forms of contemporary fiction, and examine neglected as well as canonical works, in order to assess the diverse range of possibilities which the category of romance offered to various Gothic works and their writers.

The Gothic romance, as Gary Kelly has stated, 'was not so much a coherent and authentic genre as an ensemble of themes and formal elements which could be taken over and adapted in whole or in part by other novelists and writers'.[9] While *The Castle of Otranto* clearly helped to establish the vocabulary of character-types and plot motifs which later writers exploited, it is nonetheless important – despite the superficial similarities between subsequent Gothic works – to be aware of the different ways in which these common elements were deployed. Though it is the self-described 'literary offspring' of *Otranto*, *The Old English Baron*, for example, significantly rewrote Walpole's work: by setting its action in England, rather than Mediterranean Europe, by toning down the extravagance of *Otranto*'s supernatural machinery, and by restoring its hero to his true aristocratic status and to the seat of his ancestors, Reeve's work, as I will go on to argue, offered an earnest moral fable rather than a frivolous claim on the attention of the leisured reader.[10] Just as it is important to recognize the differences in meaning between various deployments of a 'Gothic' lexicon, so too is it important to take account of the other diverse materials which such romances assimilated.[11] *The Old English Baron*, for example, not only rewrote *Otranto*, but also displayed its affiliations to the existing genre of the historical romance, exploiting the remoteness of romance in order to appeal to the exemplary value of English medieval history. Other works in the tradition which I will identify as 'Loyalist Gothic' similarly opted for Samuel Johnson's definition of romance as 'a military fable of the middle ages',[12] whereas a canonical 'Gothic' work such as Matthew Lewis's *The Monk* (1796) accentuated the sensationalism of a range of sources, including German ballads and folk-tales, and offered a daring or rebellious ideal of authorship. Ann Radcliffe, by contrast, privileged the 'feminine' (but not necessarily feminist) associations of romance, in order to reward her heroines with an idyllic refuge from the threats posed by the outside world; more than any other 'Gothic' writer, she sought to dignify or elevate romance by subsuming elements of higher literary genres, and appealing to the prestigious discourse of aesthetics. As I will finally argue, this project of legitimizing the romance for a larger audience was continued and extended, in turn, by Walter Scott's Waverley novels, synthesizing romance and history in order to create a further literary hybrid.

One way of explaining the diversity of what we now know as Gothic fiction, as I have suggested above, is to look at the manner in which certain works both appealed to the vocabulary of the genre and defined the possibilities offered by the characteristic historical and/or geographical otherness of romance. This focus on different constructions of the potential provided by the 'Gothic' lexicon and by the remoteness of romance must then be complemented by an examination of the ways in which contemporary critics and reviewers themselves discriminated between Gothic works. 'Terror' or 'Terrorist' fiction began to be loosely classified towards the end of the 1790s,[13] and along with Jane Austen's famous parody *Northanger Abbey* (written in the late 1790s), a number of 'recipe satires' in the period defined such fiction in terms of an easily repeated set of conventions and devices. This characterization has been held up by literary critics throughout the twentieth century as evidence that the Gothic romance was a monolithic genre: 'a standardized, absolutely formulaic system of creating a certain kind of atmosphere in which a reader's sensibility toward fear and horror is exercised in predictable ways'.[14] Contemporary summaries of romance ingredients were never simply descriptive, however, since readings of the sameness of Gothic fiction, and attacks on commercial publishers such as the Minerva Press, were always motivated by much larger concerns about the regulation of cultural production and the disciplining of readers – especially women and the lower classes. Numerous critics dismissed the modern romance as a whole, of course, and writers were often condemned for pandering to a debased popular appetite, yet many reviewers who were able to devote space to the discussion of individual works also drew more nuanced distinctions between different romances, and recognized concerns and priorities that extended beyond the desire to generate fear and horror. While some form of supernatural agency was regarded as an essential component of terror-fiction by contemporary satirists, most critics who considered individual works at any length nonetheless understood that different treatments of the supernatural varied greatly in terms of their tone and register. Late-eighteenth-century writers generally acknowledged the frivolity of the pantomime-style arms and armour in *The Castle of Otranto*, for example, and Walpole's romance was indeed associated as often with the *Arabian Nights*, or the tales of Count Anthony Hamilton, as it was with other canonical Gothic works. Critics and reviewers of *The Monk*, a work most famous for its representation of Satan, inferred that Lewis was primarily concerned to establish a reputation as an *enfant terrible* in the literary field. Ann Radcliffe's romances, by contrast, were much more frequently discussed in the context of suspense techniques, but they were exempted from the stigma of mass-production that satirists attached to most other contemporary productions; conservative critics seized upon what they found congenial in Radcliffe's work, such as its rationalization of the supernatural, and regularly made the claim that Radcliffe was the founder of her own 'school' of romance.

The dual focus on the motivation and reception of individual works, outlined above, enables the modern reader to appreciate that 'Gothic' fiction was far less a tradition with a generic identity and significance than a domain which was open to contest from the first, constituted or structured by the often antagonistic relations between different writers and works. The individual chapters of this book will substantiate this claim by offering detailed case studies of specific authors, works, and publishing phenomena, and by addressing along the way some of the established views about the status of the Gothic as an interrogative or transgressive genre. Following the historical method advanced by Jerome McGann, I assume that all of the novels and romances which I discuss have 'two interlocking histories': 'one that derives from the author's expressed decisions and purposes, and the other that derives from the critical reactions of the [work's] various readers'.[15] By remaining alert to the fact that writers such as Walpole, Reeve, Lewis, and Radcliffe had different agendas, and by paying attention to the subsequent reception and functioning of their works, the chapters which follow will approach the relations between these writers and works from a historical perspective, so as to provide the basis for a more rigorous account of the Gothic romance as a contested social space.

A revisionist account of the Gothic genre must begin, as almost every critical study of the Gothic does, by considering the status of *The Castle of Otranto*. In order to counter the reputation which *Otranto* has acquired as a work which heralded the eruption of 'unreason', my first chapter locates Walpole's romance in the context of the 'aristocratic' identity that he sought to construct by way of all his diverse works and projects. As I argue with initial reference to the eclecticism of Strawberry Hill, Walpole resorted to the category of Gothic as a means of stating his privileged ability to amuse himself however he chose. The eccentricity of *Otranto*, in turn, similarly needs to be viewed in the light of Walpole's apparently overriding concern with maintaining a non-accountable position in the field of cultural production. Though Walpole's two prefaces framed *Otranto* in a seemingly defensive way, there is little other evidence to suggest that he was anxious about the immediate reception of his romance. Instead, as I argue, Walpole presented *Otranto* as a source of absurd and extravagant novelty, which was calculated both to amuse a leisured audience and mystify those uninitiated readers without the necessary powers of discrimination to appreciate the nature of the work's invention. My reading of *Otranto* is substantiated by a focus on the different claims that Walpole made about the work, especially in his correspondence, and by a discussion of Walpole's other works in the period, which similarly revelled in the mechanics of deception. This description of Walpole's 'position-taking' is complemented, in turn, by a focus on the way that *Otranto* was read and reviewed, both by its initial audience and by critics writing later in the century. Several recent critics have read Walpole's romance as an allegory of class-relations and historical nemesis, but writers in the late eighteenth century – whatever they thought of the work – almost unanimously acknowledged *Otranto*'s status as a frivolous diversion. Though *Otranto* continues to be credited as the origin of terror-fiction, therefore, Walpole's contemporaries recognized that his construction of 'fancy' and 'imagination' was a class-specific one, and they largely rewarded him with the distinction which he sought.

This reading of Walpolean frivolity was endorsed by the first work to present itself as an imitation of *Otranto*, Clara Reeve's *The Old English Baron*. Despite her claim to have 'written upon the same plan' as Walpole, however, Reeve – as I have already indicated – defined the possibilities of romance and the Gothic in a markedly different way. My second chapter claims that Reeve's work was the forerunner of what I term the 'Loyalist Gothic' romance, a critically neglected yet significant line of works which were particularly prominent in the 1790s and early 1800s. From around the time of the British defeat in America, as I explain in detail, the category of Gothic was widely redefined so as to denote a proud heritage of military victory. In the context of this increasingly powerful loyalist discourse, I argue that the majority of works after *Otranto* which called themselves 'Gothic', along with numerous other 'historical' romances, served an unambiguous moral and patriotic agenda. These little-known works rely upon an English medieval setting, and locate their action in and around a real castle, identified primarily as the symbol of a stratified yet harmonious society. Loyalist Gothic romances refer to real historical figures from the pantheon of British patriotism, and depict the defeat of dubiously effeminate or foreign villains. Most importantly, such works privilege the didactic potential of romance, and allow the supernatural only the benign role of punishing usurpers and restoring the property claims of rightful heirs. Though Loyalist Gothic romances are in effect structurally bound to describe an act of usurpation, therefore, this act is nearly always presented as a *fait accompli*, and such works concentrate instead on the purging of corruption, staging the providentially inspired process by which legitimate hierarchies are re-established.

Despite the aura of subversion that still surrounds the genre as a whole, nearly all of the romances which actually called themselves 'Gothic' were unambiguously conservative. My third chapter proceeds from this finding in order to investigate the historical basis for the perceived notoriety of the Gothic romance, outlining some of the reasons why certain works were condemned so violently. In general, it is fair to say that the majority of critics in the period found the content of specific novels and romances to be far less important in itself than the 'context' of their production and reception. Works that described themselves as translations or imitations of German fiction were seen to be increasingly suspect as the 1790s progressed, since anything 'German' was guilty by association with the deluded revolutionary idealism attributed to the Illuminati, or to writers such as Schiller and Kotzebue. The escapist fiction published by commercial presses, such as William Lane's Minerva, was widely censured, in addition, because of the way that it was seen to feed the demand of an undisciplined yet ever-expanding reading public. In the light of this focus on the supposed effects of prose fiction in the 1790s, I consider the reputation of perhaps the most prominently scandalous work in the period, *The Monk*. Lewis's romance is still viewed by many as an archetypally 'Gothic' one, and has often been held up in order to exemplify the transgressive status of the genre as a whole. Yet although *The Monk* was ultimately condemned, like many other works in the period, because of the way that it was seen to 'circulate' so promiscuously among a large and diverse audience, the content and method of Lewis's work were atypical. Focusing on *The Monk*'s usage of source materials and its cynical narratorial commentary, I develop my account of the contested status of the Gothic in the period by describing the way that Lewis defined his work against other current romance paradigms. Lewis eschewed the emphasis on legitimacy and property favoured by the Loyalist Gothic, and amplified the suggestion of impropriety that was only implicit in the work of a writer such as Ann Radcliffe. Even though several works written in the early nineteenth century were clearly affiliated to *The Monk*, it remains difficult to substantiate the view that either Lewis or his work was representative of a larger genre; in a brief discussion of other works by Lewis in the 1790s and early 1800s, I claim instead that he went on to try and maintain the profile he had attained with *The Monk*, casually defying critics and reviewers in the process.

Whereas Lewis's work was consistently controversial, the romances of Ann Radcliffe were virtually exempted from criticism altogether. My fourth chapter deals with the specific nature of Radcliffe's popularity, and describes the way in which her work was celebrated by conservative critics for providing a legitimate release or transport from the problems of the present. Radcliffe integrated certain Gothic motifs with both the format of the *Bildungsroman* and the heroine-centred focus of contemporary romances such as Sophia Lee's *The Recess* (1783–5). During her lifetime, Radcliffe was widely praised for the affective power of her work, while – more recently – many critics have concentrated on the way that Radcliffean romance foregrounds the consciousness of the persecuted heroine. Despite the suspense which Radcliffe's work provides, and the obvious interest her romances offer to feminist or psychoanalytic criticism, however, it is important to recognize that the regulatory strategies which her work also supplied made her writing particularly attractive to those reviewers who were suspicious of most other contemporary fictions. From *A Sicilian Romance* (1790) onwards, as I argue, Radcliffe offered forms of supplementary material which were calculated to dignify or elevate the reputation of romance itself. Radcliffe sought to temper the absorption that her work fostered in its readers, by appealing to the discourse of aesthetics, and by providing long and digressive passages of natural description enhanced with references to current theories of the sublime and the beautiful. Most famously, Radcliffe framed the role of sensation and suspense in her work by explaining away the supernatural, a move which was widely equated with a rejection of 'delusion' and a recovery of the rule of law. In *The Italian* (1797) especially, Radcliffe clearly took account of the criticism levelled at contemporaries such as Lewis, and sought to reinstate some of the more innocent properties of the romance genre. Contemporary commentators endorsed the 'exceptionalist' status of Radcliffe's work, I go on to argue, by appealing to her biography and to her profile as an author; critics presented information about Radcliffe's distance from the taint of the present in order to claim that her works could be safely consumed by whoever read them.

Radcliffe's reputation in the 1790s and early 1800s was sustained by the critical consensus that her work provided a legitimate form of 'transport' in a period of obvious national crisis. Despite the initial acclaim with which Radcliffe's work was greeted, however, the praise it received was significantly qualified, and authoritative male critics emphasized that Radcliffe was only successful in a minor and relatively unimportant genre. From the early nineteenth century onwards, indeed, the criteria by which Radcliffe's works were judged became more and more demanding. My fifth and final chapter deals with the subsequent status of Radcliffean romance, and of 'the Gothic' in general, via the retrospect offered by Walter Scott and the Waverley novels. After a brief discussion of the reception of Scott's early poetry, inspired by the success of Lewis, I focus on the diverse ways in which Scott positioned himself and his work in relation to the field of prose romance. As a critic and as a novelist, Scott defined the bulk of contemporary fiction in terms of confinement and limit, so as to clear a space in which he could emerge – anonymity notwithstanding – as a revitalizing presence. Although, as I argue, Scott's digestion of the Gothic romance was less complete than some accounts of his groundbreaking impact assume, the Waverley novels were initially celebrated because of the way that they synthesized romance and history, and offered the best of both worlds. During his lifetime at least, Scott was widely praised for putting paid to the perceived immaturity of the Gothic romance, since his own works were regarded to be both more romantic and more historically plausible than those which had preceded them, and since his novels served to draw their readers away from the private absorption fostered by romance and reconnect them to the communal space of history and public life.

Such an 'evolutionary' reading of the Waverley novels, of course, is clearly liable to impose an artificial closure on any account of the Gothic, and to imply that the Gothic romance somehow eventually gave way to the true genius displayed by Scott's work. An account of the genre which proceeds from Radcliffe to Scott, moreover, has to bypass a great deal of what happened to the Gothic in the early nineteenth century, and ignore the influential ways in which the vocabulary of the genre was constructed by writers such as Mary Shelley, Charles Maturin, and James Hogg. Pressure of space dictates that this book has little to say about the 'wave of neo- and retro-Gothic experiments' heralded by *Frankenstein* (1818), *Melmoth the Wanderer* (1820), and *Private Memoirs and Confessions of a Justified Sinner* (1824), and little to say about – to give just a few examples – the subgenre of the 'Irish Gothic', the connections between the Gothic and the emergent 'Godwinian' novel, or the revival of German literary influence in the tales published by *Blackwood's Edinburgh Magazine*.[16] If omissions inevitably result, however, there is nonetheless a compelling case for using Scott's work to frame an account of the functioning of Gothic romances in the period under discussion. This is not simply because the Waverley novels hastened the decline in critical favour of writers such as Ann Radcliffe, although this was certainly the case during Scott's lifetime, but because of the subsequent fluctuations in the relative standing of Scott and the Gothic. Towards the end of the nineteenth century, for example, the Waverley novels were increasingly conflated with a feminized notion of romance or relegated to the status of children's literature, while in the early twentieth century, as I stated at the outset, the Gothic was steadily rehabilitated – and defined and labelled as a genre – precisely because of its escapist aura, and its association with the non-realist co-ordinates of romance. By concluding in this way with a discussion of the immediate reception and 'after-life' of the Gothic and the Waverley novels, I aim once again to draw attention to the very different ways in which these works have functioned for their various readers, and to underline my initial claim about the status of the Gothic romance as a modern construct. Only from this point of departure can modern criticism develop a properly historical account of the Gothic tradition.

CHAPTER I

Origins: Horace Walpole and The Castle of Otranto

In mazes monastic of *Strawberry Hill*,
Sir Horace first issu'd the marvellous pill;
His brain teeming hot with the chivalrous rant, O!
Engender'd the *Giant*, and *Castle Otranto*:
A stupid, incongruous, blundering tale,
The *rank* of whose writer alone caus'd its sale;
Since, had Leadenhall's *Lane* seen the work, I'll be bound,
To possess it he would not have proffer'd five pound
                    'Anser Pen-Drag-On, Esq', *Scribbleomania*, 1815[1]

To this day it is by no means easy to be certain what Horace
Walpole really meant to write, or thought he was writing in
The Castle of Otranto
                    George Saintsbury, *The English Novel*, 1913[2]

I

While literary critics have often signalled their confusion about the
meaning of *The Castle of Otranto*, they have nonetheless been virtually
united in seizing upon the second edition's subtitle, 'A Gothic Story',
and locating the work as the point of origin for a whole genre. It is still
widely assumed both that Walpole's preface to the second edition
offered the manifesto for a new kind of writing, and that the tale itself
paid the first fictional tribute to an emergent Gothic aesthetic and an
'unreason' which had been 'silenced throughout the Enlightenment
period'.[3] If it is initially hard to argue with the common-sense statement
that Walpole was the 'father' of the Gothic romance,[4] however, it is
important to be sceptical about the functioning of this model of pater-
nity, since such a point of departure is liable to underwrite a seamless
narrative of a far from stable genre. *Otranto* was a self-consciously
groundbreaking work, of course, but it is hard to credit its status as an
origin with much explanatory power, since such a label begs too many
questions about *Otranto*'s own context of production, and more

specifically about its relations within this larger matrix: where, for example, did *Otranto* originate?; why did it announce itself as a *Gothic* tale? *The Castle of Otranto* must be discussed in terms of its author's attempt to distinguish himself from other writers of fiction and provide novelty for a particular audience, therefore, but the meaning and influence of the work ultimately need to be considered relationally, and addressed in the context of the overall system of its 'field of production'.[5] What I want to do in this chapter, as a result, is to look at *Otranto* alongside Walpole's other works or projects, and in terms of the antagonistic relations that made up the different fields in which he intervened, so as to assess the priorities of his self-definition, as well as some of the attendant anxieties. *The Castle of Otranto* was the first self-described 'Gothic romance', and 'the first modern attempt to found a tale of amusing fiction upon the basis of the ancient romances of chivalry',[6] but any focus on its newness must also be accompanied by an awareness of the contest over the keywords 'Gothic' and 'romance' among Walpole and his contemporaries, in order to explain the positions he tried to claim. Beginning with a discussion of Strawberry Hill, often cited as an analogue for *Otranto*, the first half of what follows will address the diversity of Walpole's work, and argue that he sought to fashion an 'aristocratic' identity – not simply reducible to his privileged *social* position – in all of the fields (architectural, antiquarian, literary) in which he operated. The second section will look more specifically at *Otranto* in the context of Walpole's concern with self-presentation, and focus on the two prefaces alongside the narrative, so as to situate the diverse comments that Walpole made about his work, and describe what he meant by the 'Gothic' subtitle. This chapter will argue that Walpole constructed the Gothic as a form of private and recreational class property, to which he was able to lay claim because of the status he had forged for himself as a licensed risk-taker. *Otranto* differed so much from the Gothic romances published by the Minerva Press, as the writer of the first epigraph implies, that it could only have been written by someone with the ability to consecrate 'stupid' and 'incongruous' material; as I will argue in this chapter, only a contextualizing approach can begin to address George Saintsbury's question about what Walpole 'really meant to write, or thought he was writing'.

Any account of Walpole's recourse to the Gothic must first of all recognize the range of meanings which the term held in the eighteenth century. The term 'Gothic' requires particular attention now because it was invoked in so many different contexts in the period in question, and used variously to describe (for example) styles of architecture, a form of print or type, and anything connected to the Goths themselves, as well as anything generally medieval, or even post-Roman. The term demands detailed critical attention, moreover, since it was not only invoked in a neutrally descriptive way, but served in addition, especially in the decades after the Glorious Revolution of 1688, as a contested category within debates about the nature of economic, political, and social change: the Gothic was constructed both as a distant, non-specific, period of ignorance and superstition from which an increasingly civilized nation had triumphantly emerged, and as a (similarly distant) fount of constitutional purity and political virtue from which the nation had become dangerously alienated.[7] This 'public' profile of the Gothic can be further complicated by looking at the associations of the Gothic with gendered forms of private diversion. Harriet Guest, for example, has argued that by the mid eighteenth century, 'the pleasure of Gothic' for many male writers was 'bound up with its furtive and feminine opposition to the social and fraternal virtues of public life':[8] writers such as Richard Hurd (in *Letters on Chivalry and Romance*, 1762) and Thomas Warton (*History of English Poetry*, 1774) combined a historical approach to literary criticism with an investment in the Gothic as a locus of creative or poetic plenitude, set against the values of modernity and commercial society. To complicate this brief narrative of the Gothic still further, it should also be recognized that 'modern' versions of the Gothic emerged, in the field of architecture especially, which frivolously rejected classical standards, but at the same time necessarily embraced (because they were partly dependent upon) mercantile expansion: 'The economics of gathering commodities', as James H. Bunn has argued, 'induce[d] a subsequent aesthetics that self-consciously point[ed] to the occlusion of native foundations', as heterogeneous elements (Gothic, Hindu, Chinese) were combined to form new architectural hybrids.[9]

Such an introductory narrative is unable to say much about why Walpole invoked the Gothic in the first place, at Strawberry Hill, or why he called *Otranto* a 'Gothic Story', but it does emphasize both that this resort to the Gothic existed within a much larger contextual frame, and that accounts of Walpole as a creative innovator need to examine the available meanings of the terms he used. Concerned primarily with the field of architecture, Charles Eastlake's influential work *A History of the Gothic Revival* (1872) stated what has since become a common view, that 'Walpole's Gothic . . . served to sustain a cause which had otherwise been well-nigh forsaken.'[10] This claim is misleading, however, since different varieties of Gothic architecture, the domain in which Walpole initially made his reputation, were already very popular by the late 1740s when he began to 'improve' Strawberry Hill. As recent histories of the so-called Gothic Revival have shown, this architectural work encompassed restoration on a large scale (as at the Duke of Argyll's Inveraray Castle), and garden buildings (such as the Temple of Liberty, built for Lord Cobham at Stowe), as well as a host of smaller decorative or ornamental projects.[11] This latter form, the 'modern Gothic', attracted an especially large amount of contemporary recognition, and taste-forming magazines like *The World*, to which Walpole contributed, debated the meaning of its apparent ubiquity. Drawing attention to the ambiguity of the 'Gothic' label, William Whitehead in 1753 disputed the claim that there was anything in this modern fashion 'congenial to our old Gothic constitution', and instead interpreted the popularity of 'decoration' as a negative tribute to 'our modern idea of liberty, which allows every one the privilege of playing the fool, and of making himself ridiculous, in whatever manner he pleases'. Whitehead claimed, indeed, that the Gothic was in the process of being superseded, so that even 'the good people in the city' were reducing everything to another 'prevailing whim', according to which 'every thing is Chinese, or in the Chinese taste'.[12] In the light of such commentary, Walpole's project clearly needs to be viewed as a response to contemporary trends rather than as a completely novel experiment. Walpole defined his work at Strawberry Hill against the popularity of the modern Gothic, and he exaggerated the fidelity of his project to 'ancient' models. Strawberry Hill copied details from topographical works, and imitated parts of Canterbury Cathedral, Westminster Abbey, and York Minster, in addition to incorporating arms and shields of Walpole's family and ancestors; according to Michael McCarthy, Walpole – unlike most of his contemporaries – was interested in introducing 'historicism into the gothic revival'.[13] Yet despite this apparently faithful attention to detail, Walpole performed the imitation of 'historic' models in a self-consciously fictional and insubstantial way and openly admitted to his use of 'paper' (papier-mâché) in the building of his retreat.[14] While the exterior of Strawberry Hill was superficially faithful to venerable architectural models, Walpole also played up the fact, as in his 'Description' of 1784, that its interior decoration was heterogeneous, and nothing more than 'an assemblage of curious Trifles'.[15] Walpole frequently conceded that his 'folly' offended recognized standards of taste, and, to quote Dianne S. Ames, he made 'a virtue of what others [would] deem a fault'.[16] Though he seemed to distance Strawberry Hill from the 'impurity' and whimsy of the modern Gothic, therefore, Walpole drew attention to the inadequacy of its imitation of ancient models and deliberately exaggerated the accretive logic of the 'modern' style in his villa's interior, displaying his privileged ability to circumscribe its decorative excess.

Walpole's desire to improve Strawberry Hill mystified even some of his friends, among them Horace Mann who declared himself 'totally at a loss' as to how to help Walpole in his search for 'fragments' for the mock castle: 'Why will you make it Gothic? I know that it is the taste at present but I really am sorry for it.'[17] If the 'tone' of Strawberry Hill was ambiguous for the uninitiated, however, Walpole informed his regular correspondents that it was merely a 'play-thing house . . . out of Mrs Chevenix's shop', which he would not even try to defend by rational argument.[18] Walpole often referred in his correspondence to how he 'played the fool', but – in concert with friends such as John Chute and Richard Bentley on his 'Committee of Taste' – he continually displayed a habituated knowledge of higher, public, or classical standards so as to permit a degree of non-accountable privacy. Walpole made it clear on different occasions that he was aware of the gulf between 'the rational beauties of regular architecture' and 'the unrestrained licentiousness of that which is called Gothic',[19] yet he was keen to emphasize that he knew how to circumscribe his pleasure, and authorize the irregularity of Gothic *bricolage*. In many of his letters of the 1750s and the 1760s, Walpole revelled in the incomprehension of visitors to Strawberry Hill, especially foreigners, and displayed a sense of delight in his ability to indulge in what was ostensibly bad taste. Walpole described the 'trumpery' that surrounded him in a letter to Henry Conway in February 1756, and gave a list of items that he had bought from 'Mrs Kennon the mid-wife's sale' ('Brobdignag combs, old broken pots, pans, and pipkins, a lantern of scraped oyster shells, scimitars, Turkish pipes, Chinese baskets, etc., etc.'), which he intended to pass off as 'the personal estate and movables of my great-great-grandmother'.[20] As Eastlake astutely recognized in 1872, Walpole was first and foremost a 'collector of curiosities' who was influenced much more by an idiosyncratic love of 'old world associations' than by any 'sound appreciation of artistic design':

In this spirit he haunted the auction rooms, and picked up a vast quantity of objects that were destined by-and-by to crowd his villa at Twickenham.

Nothing to which the faintest semblance of a legend [was] attached was too insignificant for his notice. Queen Mary's comb, King William's spur, the pipe which Van Tromp smoked in his last naval engagement, or the scarlet hat of Cardinal Wolsey, possessed for him an extraordinary interest.[21]

Eastlake went on to claim that Walpole (albeit inadvertently) formed 'the nucleus of what . . . promised to become an important Mediaeval museum'. Despite such projections of a historical sense on to his collecting habits, Walpole nonetheless paid little attention towards assimilating his miscellaneous 'trumpery' within a historical or social-historical framework. Certainly in his work at Strawberry Hill, the past was chiefly a site of amusement and diversion for Walpole, as he stripped the Gothic of the 'public' meanings referred to above and redefined it in terms of decorative heterogeneity and idealized association; as 'every true Goth must perceive', Walpole wrote in 1794, the rooms of Strawberry Hill are 'more the works of fancy than imitation'.[22] Though, for example, Walpole called one of the rooms at Strawberry Hill the 'Star Chamber', he did so merely to trade upon what a nineteenth-century writer referred to as a 'horrible name of fearful associations', since the chamber was in reality 'only an innocent little room, with green walls powdered with little stars, like a modern French paper'.[23]

Strawberry Hill became an almost instant tourist attraction, and Walpole eventually had to issue tickets so as to regulate the number of visitors he received. Rather than overstate the 'historicist' impulse of Walpole's project, it seems most accurate to position Strawberry Hill and Walpolean Gothic within a context of aristocratic display and conspicuous consumption. 'Gilly' Williams wrote to George Selwyn in October 1764, for example, that he could 'figure no being happier than Horry', since '*Monstrari digito praetereuntium* [the desire to be pointed out by those passing by] has been his whole aim. For this he has wrote, printed and built.'[24] Walpole for his part gleefully described the profusion of identities which Strawberry Hill enabled him to assume, telling Henry Conway in 1755 about his mimicry of baronial status:

> When I am in my castle of Bungay
> Situate upon the river Waveney
> I ne care for the King of Cockney.[25]

In the same way that the 'extreme fashions' of the eighteenth century were 'symptomatic of the lengths to which the rich were prepared to go to proclaim their wealth [and] their rank',[26] as Neil McKendrick has argued, so too was Strawberry Hill in effect a proclamation of its owner's elevated social position and an index of his leisure-class membership. According to a writer in the *Monthly* in 1798, it was hard to imagine a more economical claim on the attention of the public than Strawberry Hill, 'an *unique* among villas', since Walpole 'could not have obtained fame on so small a scale at a less expence, by any similar draft on public notice'.[27] Yet the diverting potential of Walpolean modern Gothic obviously had to be predicated upon its limited availability, and Walpole felt his position to be compromised whenever his powers of arbitration were threatened. Walpole inevitably faced problems when too many others claimed to be of a similar persuasion, finding his 'little stock of reputation very troublesome, both to maintain and to undergo the consequences', as he told George Montagu in 1758: 'it has dipped me in erudite correspondences – I receive letters every week that compliment my learning'.[28] Despite his efforts to cultivate an olympian position for himself in relation to the field of architecture, therefore, Walpole intermittently betrayed an anxiety about falling off his perch, dreading – as a writer in the *Gentleman's Magazine* put it in 1812 – 'lest barrow-hunters and tombstone-transcribers, should consider themselves of his fraternity'. According to this sympathetic 'Walpolean', he felt:

as would a man of large fortune and exquisite delight in the Arts, who had erected some magnificent Gothic pile under the direction of Wyatt, at the visit of some pert citizen, who having Gothicised his villa by the road-side with the aid of the village carpenter, came to inspect his edifice, as if they were men of congenial taste.[29]

With his claims to a position of arbitration vulnerable to contest, Walpole periodically struck a pose of modesty and humility, and disavowed any claim after public recognition. In his short work of 1784, *A Description of Strawberry Hill*, Walpole made it clear that his own 'folly' could not bear comparison with the (Palladian) mansion of his father, Robert Walpole, and he admitted that it would show 'a total insensibility to the pride of family' for 'an insignificant Man' such as himself to try and rival 'one of the best and wisest Ministers that this country has enjoyed'. Strawberry Hill, Walpole conceded, was nothing more than 'a small capricious house', built simply 'to please my own taste, and in some degree to realise my own visions'.[30]

As I will later emphasize with regard to *Otranto*'s prefaces, Walpole's tendency to deploy the modesty trope must nonetheless be viewed with scepticism, since such an apparently engaging concession remained continuous with the concern about social status that has been described so far. While he was constantly attentive to his position as an arbiter of taste, it was also an imperative for Walpole that he did not have to appear to compete in order to maintain his reputation; rather than deal with commercial publishers, for example, the financially independent Walpole printed most of his works at his private Strawberry Hill press. Even if he occasionally admitted to valuing fame, Walpole also made it clear, as in a letter to Thomas Gray in 1768, that he was 'indifferent to almost anything I have done to acquire it'.[31] The 'je ne sçais quoi' of aristocratic etiquette defined by Chesterfield's *Letters* was a productively grey area, therefore, but the notion of appropriate behaviour that the phrase referred to was unambiguously defined *against* an inclusive construction of 'labour' that incorporated academic or antiquarian enquiry (and particularly the practice of textual revision) alongside more obviously exerting forms of work.[32] Chesterfield advised his son, for example, to 'take care not to understand editions and title-pages too well', since such an interest savoured of 'pedantry, and not always of learning'.[33] In a similar vein, Walpole frequently downplayed the role of research in his works, as in the 'Advertisement' to *A Catalogue of the Royal and Noble Authors of England* (1758), where he made it clear that, despite its length, the work was 'calculated to amuse' rather than instruct; if it were 'taken too seriously', Walpole stated that he would never for his part become 'so serious as to defend it'.[34] The same attitude towards research, as the antagonist of 'taste', also informed the four-volume *Anecdotes of Painting in England* (1762–71). *Anecdotes* exhaustively catalogues information about the nation's artists within a discourse of antiquarian knowledge, but Walpole dissociated himself from the actual process of collecting information, projecting the task entirely onto the assiduous George Vertue. 'The indefatigable pains of Mr Vertue', as the work's preface states, produced 'near forty volumes' of continually updated notes, which were bought by Walpole from Vertue's widow after his death in 1757.[35] By representing himself as the aristocratic patron of 'Mr Vertue', Walpole was able both to build his own contribution to the *Anecdotes* on a firm antiquarian basis and to clear an olympian position for himself in relation to such laborious research, stating that Vertue was 'so little a slave to his own imagination', that he was 'cautious of trusting to that of others'.[36] Walpole licensed for himself a role of casually authoritative commentary so as 'to enliven the dryness of the subject',[37] and was subsequently praised by the *Monthly Review*'s critic for having 'enlivened and embellished the barren collection of the Compiler', 'the many pertinent reflections, and interesting sentiments, occasionally interspersed throughout this work, manifesting equally the critical sagacity and the refined taste of the Writer'.[38]

Walpole did clearly involve himself in detailed research, as in his *Historic Doubts on the Life and Reign of King Richard the Third* (1768), which disputed 'the testimonies of our historians' about Richard's rule by appealing to 'such abstruse stores as records and charters'.[39] Despite this concession to rigour, however, Walpole was also keen to dissociate the *Historic Doubts* from the history-writing of a contemporary such as David Hume, and he stressed in a letter to Gray that both '*Richard*' and 'the *Noble Authors*' had been 'written with people in the room', and were therefore inevitably prone to error.[40] In the specific case of the *Historic Doubts*, Walpole further established that it was the product of leisure in the work's preface, by exaggerating the incompetence of 'the generality of historians' who had preceded him, and by casually stating that he had only been drawn to the subject in the first place out of 'curiosity and speculation'.[41] Taken together with Strawberry Hill, as a result, Walpole's works of the late 1750s and 1760s seem confidently to construct the past as little more than a site of diversion or recreation. Although such works were contemporaneous with the rapid growth of interest in the national cultural heritage in the mid eighteenth century, it is difficult to assimilate Walpole into the origin-seeking enterprise in which many other writers (Richard Hurd, John Pinkerton, the Wartons, and so on) broadly shared; Walpole was always at pains to associate them with the sterile labour of research while implicitly claiming for himself the somewhat more elusive provinces of charm, novelty, and (sometimes) 'taste'. Whereas an antiquarian such as Thomas Pownall, for example, explicitly defined the 'true' study of antiquity against Walpolean fetishism and the 'devotion for relicks',[42] Walpole was clearly uninterested in even trying to authorize his picturesque interest in the past, and simply did without the historical 'customs and manners' frame that literary critics such as Hurd and Thomas Warton used to legitimize their focus on an authentic literary tradition.

In his correspondence especially, Walpole regularly dismissed the dryness of antiquarian toil, and describing a work such as John Pinkerton's *Dissertation on the Origin and Progress of the Scythians or Goths* (1787), in a letter to Pinkerton himself, he stated his refusal to waste time on 'the origin of nations; unless for an opportunity of smiling at the gravity of the author, or at the absurdity of the manners of those ages': 'I confess I do not care a straw about your subjects, with whom I am no more acquainted than with the ancient inhabitants of Otaheite.'[43] Walpole mocked literary primitivism and the poetry of oral tradition, clearly alluding to the Norse imitations of his friend Gray when he asked in 1768, 'who can care through which horrors a Runic savage arrived at all the joys and glories they could conceive, the supreme felicity of boozing ale out of the skull of an enemy in Odin's hall?'[44] Where Gray, for example, sometimes valorized a period in the distant past as a locus of plenitude, viewed alongside which the present 'benighted age' was clearly deficient, Walpole distanced himself from any notion of history as a court of appeal in public debate, seeming to abide by his statement in a letter of 1766 that 'the dead have lost their power of deceiving'.[45] According to Macaulay's famous article of 1833 in the *Edinburgh Review*, Walpole was forever unwilling to forfeit 'his character of *Gentilhomme*', and consequently regarded with impatience 'the imputation of having attended to any thing so unfashionable as the improvement of his mind'.[46] Instead of declaring a historical interest in the past, therefore, Walpole in effect acknowledged what Macaulay later diagnosed as 'the frivolity of his favourite pursuits':

He rejects all but the attractive parts of his subject. He keeps only what is in itself amusing or what can be made so by the artifice of his diction. Coarser morsels of antiquarian learning he abandons to others, and sets out an entertainment worthy of a Roman epicure, an entertainment consisting of nothing but delicacies, the brains of singing birds, the roe of mullets, the sunny halves of peaches.[47]

Given this obsession with charming novelty, it is tempting to position Walpole as a pioneer in the field of 'camp' taste, defined by Susan Sontag as 'the love of the exaggerated, the "off", . . . things being-what-they-are-not', in a manner which sustains a double interpretation.[48] The apparent affinity of Walpole's work with camp extravagance and modern 'queer' subcultures has been seized upon by Timothy Mowl's recent biography, subtitled 'The Great Outsider', which presents Walpole as 'one of the most successful deviant infiltrators that the English establishment has ever produced': 'He was a sexual outsider and because of this he was also an aesthetic outsider.'[49] Yet it is historically inaccurate to elevate Walpole's probable sexual orientation above his social class as a determinant upon his work, and it is important, moreover, to take account of the fictionality of the 'aristocratic' identity which Walpole sought to fashion. From John Pinkerton's *Walpoliana* (1800) onwards, biographers have portrayed Walpole as an archetypally

English eccentric, and underlined the 'ease and carelessness' of his life, by paying a disproportionate amount of attention to the anecdote and the *bon mot*.[50] Despite the superficial attractions of such a generous approach, narratives of extrapolitical diversion tend to ignore the extent to which Walpole's aristocratic identity was a construct, which he had continually to rehearse, and tend to neglect the sometimes precarious nature of the position which Walpole cultivated.

After his death in 1797, many commentators used the perspective of distance in a very different way, so as to examine the meaning of the 'disdain' that informed Walpole's position-taking. It was widely understood in Walpole's lifetime, as Chesterfield explained to his son, that 'no man can make a figure in this country, but by parliament',[51] and Walpole's habitual renunciation of this form of ambition consequently led him to search for other means of distinction. This search was liable to be frustrating, as the *Monthly*'s 1798 review of Walpole's *Works* recognized when it stated that 'Nature gave to Mr. Walpole a tongue to talk virtue, and even heroism, but not a mind or body adapted to act either.'[52] The *Monthly*'s focus on Walpole's physical incapacity to achieve anything genuinely impressive, its veiled reference to his alleged homosexuality, was followed up by Isaac D'Israeli, in his article on 'The Pains of Fastidious Egotism': though 'singularity of opinion, vivacity of ridicule, and polished epigrams in prose, were the means by which Horace Walpole sought distinction', D'Israeli argued, he only ever succeeded in creating 'plants of sickly delicacy, which could never endure the open air, and only lived in the artificial atmosphere of a private collection'.[53] As Hazlitt claimed in the *Edinburgh Review* in 1818, Walpole was reliant throughout his career on achieving recognition via the assumption of exaggeratedly contrary positions, and often resorted to direct abuse of competitors in the fields he entered, 'never [speaking] with respect of any man of genius or talent, and, least of all, of those master spirits who "have got the start of this majestic world"'.[54] Most famously of all, Macaulay also played up Walpole's reputation as an effeminate aesthete by drawing attention to 'the faults of [his] head and heart': 'none but an unhealthy and disorganized mind could have produced [his] literary luxuries'.[55] If these commentators all agreed that Walpole was always an amusing writer, they challenged his self-representation and, in particular, his tendency to disavow ambition or interest.

Despite Walpole's claims about his carefree bypassing of the world of politics, as a result, the works quoted above make the modern reader alert to the existence of an agenda which came into conflict with the 'aristocratic' position that he cultivated. Walpole affected an indifference to 'politics' (along with 'ambition' and 'research', for example), but he remained a player in the political arena. Archibald S. Foord has claimed that Walpole's only political interests concerned the continuance of his sinecure income, the reputation of his father, and the progress of his cousin, Henry Conway.[56] Yet Walpole also expressed strong opinions on most issues of controversy during his lifetime, and though he only rarely spoke in Parliament during his career as a Member (1741–68), he was in fact a behind-the-scenes activist who wrote extensive notes and journals in the role of an observer or spectator of contemporary politics.[57] Walpole was essentially a private critic, in that most of this commentary appeared in letters or in works published only after his death, but he frequently adopted a principled, old Whig, oppositional stance, as in his reading of the situation in America, which he saw as the revenge of Old English political virtue upon modern English corruption. Evident in many of Walpole's later letters, especially, is a palpable sense of disillusionment with the state of the proverbially once proud nation, and at such times Walpole seems to define diversion primarily in terms of retreat or escape, as in his letter to William Mason in April 1775: 'America and feathers and masquerades will drive us into libraries, and there I am well content to live as an humble companion to Gray and you.'[58]

If a project such as Strawberry Hill, begun in the late 1740s, seems to have been initially dependent upon a secure or confident relation to the past, Walpole's journals and letters were also concerned, from the 1770s onwards especially, with larger matters of national politics, unconnected with personal interests such as Court manoeuvres or the reputation of his father. Such evidence serves to caution the modern reader against quoting too selectively and privileging small areas of Walpole's massive correspondence, and it foregrounds the need to reconsider the relationship between frivolity and disaffection in Walpole's work as a whole. At the same time, however, it must be recognized that such position-takings on contemporary affairs are themselves difficult to dissociate from an account of aristocratic diversion, given that Walpole so often represented his interest in the proceedings of the House of Commons in such a detached way. When Walpole predicted the waning popularity of Pitt in a letter to George Montagu in 1766, for example, he claimed to be 'pleased, and much more diverted. I have nothing to do but laugh, a humour you know I am apt to indulge.'[59] Walpole was at no period connected with any oppositional constituency and dealt largely in a language of sloganeering Whiggery delivered from a standpoint of retirement, uniting, as Hazlitt argued, 'Whig professions' with 'an insufferable deal of aristocratical pretension'.[60] While Walpole regularly denounced British foreign policy from a principled position, therefore, he also exaggerated his dedication to principle almost as if he were in competition with his ostensible allies, declaring himself at one time 'the only unadulterated Whig left in England'.[61] Walpole often referred to his practice of hanging 'the Magna Charta and the warrant for King Charles's execution' on either side of his bed at Strawberry Hill, and joyously recorded the Earl of Harcourt's gift of 'the glorious and immortal spurs of King William'.[62] As Macaulay put it, indeed, 'Walpole's Whiggism . . . was of a very harmless kind', which he kept 'as he kept the old spears and helmets at Strawberry Hill, merely for show'; politics, like fine art or literature, was merely one more field where Walpole was 'drawn by some strange attraction from the great to the little, from the useful to the odd'.[63] It is clearly important to complicate and contextualize the aura of aristocratic ease that Walpole cultivated, therefore, but as the quotations from Macaulay imply, it is hard to 'translate' any of his works into an overt intervention in the field of politics, or to claim that the facade can be stripped away to reveal a hidden essence or truth about Walpole and his agenda. Walpole remained, in Macaulay's terms, 'the most eccentric, the most artificial, the most fastidious, the most capricious, of men':

His mind was a bundle of inconsistent whims and affectations. His features were covered by mask within mask. When the outer disguise of obvious affectation was removed, you were still as far as ever from seeing the real man. He played innumerable parts, and over-acted them all. When he talked misanthropy, he out-Timoned Timon. When he talked philanthropy, he left Howard at an immeasurable distance. He scoffed at Courts, and kept a chronicle of their most trifling scandal, at Society, and was blown about by its slightest veerings of opinion, – at Literary fame, and left fair copies of his private letters, with copious notes, to be published after his decease[.][64]

II

The quotation from Macaulay is important not so much for its psychological insight as for the way that it alerts the modern reader to the different layers or registers of Walpole's self-representation. In the light of this focus on the nuances of 'register', the rest of this chapter will

examine Walpole's most famous work, *The Castle of Otranto*, and seek to
complicate the myths of origin that it sponsored. The most common
literary-historical explanation of *Otranto*'s genesis remains the one offered by the work's second preface: Walpole was fearful of being
ridiculed for his presumption, and therefore sought a means by which to
shelter his daring until a time when he could safely claim responsibility
for his audacious experiment. *Otranto* has often been viewed in connection with the influence of Burkean theories of sublimity or with the
emergent Gothic aesthetic defined by contemporaries such as Richard
Hurd, and further regarded both as one of the first works of historically
minded fiction and as a manifestation of a long-confined 'unreason'.
Though *Otranto* has to be acknowledged as a pioneering work, in that it
offered a plot and certain character-types that many later writers exploited, I will nonetheless primarily be concerned in the rest of this
chapter to qualify the claims which have been made about its status as
the origin of a genre. These claims can only be made by ignoring most of
the evidence about *Otranto*'s immediate context of production and, as I
have suggested already, they tend to underwrite a seamless narrative of
a heterogeneous and contested genre. Examining Walpole's prefaces
and his extensive correspondence about *Otranto* along with his other
works in the period, this section will relocate Walpole's emphasis on
'fancy' and 'imagination' in the context of the aristocratic self-
fashioning which has been described so far. I will go on to suggest that
most critics and reviewers in the eighteenth and nineteenth centuries
recognized the status of Walpole's work, for good or bad, as a frivolous
diversion – a work that had as much in common with the tales of the
Arabian Nights as with the romances of other canonical Gothic writers
such as Ann Radcliffe.

   Accounts of Walpole's anxiety about the publication of *Otranto* concentrate primarily on the work's prefaces, and the way that they constructed then dismantled an apparatus of authentication. According to
the common view of Walpole as a cautious innovator, *Otranto*'s first
edition supplied both a means for him to conceal his authorship and a
framework of 'factual fiction' conventions, such as the retrieved manuscript trope, within which polite readers could enjoy fictional novelty.
The antiquarian master-discourse of *Otranto*'s first edition served to
extricate the work from questions about the moral health of its first
readers, and enabled these readers to enjoy the 'miracles, visions,
necromancy, dreams, and other preternatural events' which (the
preface claimed) had all but disappeared from the province of

literature.[65] Despite 'the censure to which romances are but too liable' (5), as a result, the preface sought to circumscribe the role of the supernatural by projecting responsibility onto the popular belief of an earlier period, in a very similar way to Richard Hurd in his *Letters on Chivalry and Romance* (hence the tendency to see Hurd and Walpole as involved in more or less the same enterprise). *Otranto*'s 'air of the miraculous', in the first preface's terms, merely proved the antiquity of the black letter original, and given the supposed age of the work, the preface was able to claim that its recourse to supernatural agency was simply a consequence of the Italian author, 'Onuphrio Muralto', being 'faithful to the manners of the times' – 'the darkest ages of christianity' (4). All that contemporary readers needed was the assurance that popular belief had once accepted the miraculous elements of the tale, an assurance which then allowed both an experience of the supernatural on its own terms, and a feeling of superiority over those people who had (once) really thought such visions to be true.[66]

The evidence available suggests that at least some readers and reviewers of *Otranto*'s first edition accepted the contractual terms of this authenticating framework, even if they also suspected the work to be a recent production. In the *Monthly Review* in February 1765, as a result, it was possible for John Langhorne to claim that *Otranto* contained 'an assemblage of beautiful pictures', since the official character of the work, as the probable production of a Jesuit, made it easy for him 'to excuse the preposterous phenomena, and consider them as sacrifices to a gross and unenlightened age'.[67] Scott further elaborated upon this principle of faithful reading, Coleridge's 'suspension of disbelief', in his biographical account of Walpole for Ballantyne's *Novelist's Library*:

The reader, who is required to admit the belief of supernatural interference, understands precisely what is demanded of him; and, if he be truly a gentle reader, throws his mind into the attitude best adapted to humour the deceit which is presented for his entertainment, and grants, for the time of perusal, the premises on which the fable depends.[68]

Accounts of Walpole's initial unease are usually substantiated in more detail still by reference to *Otranto*'s second preface, in which 'the author', in the third person, modestly acknowledged his responsibility for the work, and apologized for the deceit that he had been forced into: 'diffidence of his own abilities, and the novelty of the attempt, were his sole inducements to assume that disguise', Walpole claimed, and he 'resigned his performance to the impartial judgment of the public;

determined to let it perish in obscurity, if disapproved; nor meaning to avow such a trifle, unless better judges should pronounce that he might own it without a blush' (7). The second preface is renowned in particular for the supposed manifesto of Gothic fiction ('a new species of romance') that it contains, and for Walpole's presentation of his work as 'an attempt to blend the two kinds of romance, the ancient and the modern', a fusion which he claimed would restore 'fancy', 'imagination', and 'invention' to the contemporary novel of 'common life' (7). Walpole pointed to the example of Shakespeare as the 'higher authority' for the 'new route' (8) his work struck out, as is well known, and his subsequent defence of Shakespearean tragi-comedy against the criticism of Voltaire is often held up as further evidence of Walpole's involvement in a larger movement of 'Gothic' reaction against the hegemony of classical or Augustan taste.

Several of Walpole's letters in this period appear to justify such a reading of *Otranto*'s significance, since he regularly lamented the naturalness of modern novels, and praised writers such as his friend Gray for the 'genius' and the superiority to rules that their work displayed. As I argued in the previous section, however, it is inaccurate to associate Walpole and his work too closely with other contemporary writers on the Gothic, such as Hurd, or with theorists of 'original genius', such as William Duff or Edward Young, because Walpole himself was always so zealous about protecting his own 'aristocratic' position within the literary field. Where Hurd's *Letters on Chivalry and Romance* celebrated the inspired work of poets such as Ariosto, Tasso, Spenser, and Milton, who had been 'seduced' or 'charmed by the *Gothic Romances*', Walpole for his part explicitly defined himself against the example of such writers, and in effect aligned himself with those who were condemned by Hurd as sceptical and ridiculing 'philosophic moderns'.[69] Epic poetry, Walpole casually stated to William Mason in 1782, was 'the art of being as long as possible in telling an uninteresting story', and Walpole went so far indeed as to single out all of the heroes of Hurd's canon, with the exception of Shakespeare, for the absurdity of their work: Milton was therefore said to have 'produced a monster' (*Paradise Lost*), just as Ariosto was described as 'a more agreeable *Amadis de Gaul* in a bawdy-house', Spenser was 'John Bunyan in rhyme', and Tasso's work was said to 'weary' the reader with its 'insuperable crime[s] of stanza' and its 'thousand puerilities that are the very opposite of that dull dignity which is demanded for epic'.[70] It is clearly necessary to distinguish Walpole from the various romance revivalists, as a result, since his views on literary heritage differed so much from theirs – and in such a self-conscious and deliberate way. Walpole disdainfully recognized the weight of research in Thomas Warton's massive *History of English Poetry* (1774), for example, but he found nothing that showed any 'parts or learning' in the works that Warton dealt with, nothing to compare with the work of the classic 'Augustan' poet, Pope.[71] It is equally important to distinguish *Otranto* from other nearly contemporary literary forgeries, such as the works of James Macpherson's 'Ossian'. Katie Trumpener has recently described the rise in this period of a 'a new national literary history under the sign of the bard, a figure who represents the resistance of vernacular oral traditions to the historical pressures of English imperialism'.[72] Walpole – unsurprisingly – showed little sympathy towards this literary nationalism and, most importantly, was relentlessly sceptical about the testimonial authenticity of bardic poetry.

This evidence about Walpole's relation to literary tradition and the romance revival means that it is important to reconsider the face-value meaning of the terms, such as 'fancy' and 'imagination', which are deployed in his correspondence and in the prefaces to *Otranto*. A close reading of *Otranto*'s introductory material shows indeed that *both* prefaces sought to confuse or confound their readers. The first preface, for example, makes the precise claim that the 'story' must have been written 'between 1095, the aera of the first crusade, and 1243, the date of the last, or not long afterwards', only to follow up with the contradictory claim that 'the Spanish names of the domestics seem to indicate that this work was not composed until the establishment of the Arragonian kings in Naples had made Spanish appellations familiar in that country' (3) – which would date the tale no earlier than 1442. The first preface subsequently invites the complicit reader, with 'leisure to employ in such researches' (6), to discover the real Italian castle on which Otranto is based, even though Walpole admitted elsewhere that he had founded it on Strawberry Hill and Trinity College, Cambridge.[73] As Elizabeth Napier has shown, there is an obvious tension between the claims which Walpole made for his work and the 'practice' of the tale itself, the 'exaggerated gravity' of Walpole's first preface alerting the reader 'not only to the infirmity of Walpole's theorizing but to problems of tone that permeate the two prefaces, the work itself, and Walpole's attitude towards it'.[74] The first preface's claim that the translated work displays 'no bombast' (4) sits uneasily next to the actual behaviour and speech of Manfred, just as the preface's praise of *Otranto*'s piety collides with the work's self-evident flippancy and frivolity. Despite the clarification which it seems to offer about the provenance of *Otranto*, Walpole's second preface is no more trustworthy than the first, since it defends the tale in terms which are just as unlikely. Though Walpole appealed to the authority of Shakespeare so as to claim that *Otranto*'s 'domestics' amplify the sublime character of its 'princes and heroes' (8), the actual function of the long episode where Diego and Jaquez try to describe the giant limb they have seen (31–3), as Napier argues, is to 'cast ridicule' on Manfred, and to render him 'a victim of his servants' incompetence – laughable and powerless, not tragic'.[75] If Walpole's defence of Shakespeare against Voltaire seems to have been serious, he was surely in control of the fact that his appeal to the rhetoric of genius and sublimity was a spurious one.

It is similarly hard to credit the view that Walpole was particularly anxious about *Otranto*'s initial publication. Walpole did admit to a degree of uncertainty in letters of March and April 1765, it is true, but the modesty trope these letters deployed, like the second preface's claim about its author's 'diffidence' (7), was continuous with the self-conscious disavowal of ambition referred to in the previous section. Instead of being anxious about the opinion of 'better judges', Walpole seems – successfully – to have presented his work so that it should defy classification, as he emphasized to Mme du Deffand in 1767 when he stated that *Otranto* had been written 'in spite of rules, critics and philosophers'.[76] Where the *Monthly Review* acquiesced in the self-presentation of *Otranto*'s first edition, for example, the *Critical*'s brief review of the work in January 1765 was at once hostile and quizzical: 'whether he speaks seriously or ironically, we neither know nor care. The publication of any work, at this time, in England composed of such rotten materials, is a phenomenon we cannot account for';[77] once the *Monthly*'s reviewer had become aware of *Otranto*'s status as 'a modern performance', in addition, he was unable to circumscribe his pleasure any longer, or to comprehend how 'an Author, of a refined and polished genius' could be 'an advocate for re-establishing the barbarous superstitions of Gothic devilism!'[78] Though it is difficult to determine how far Walpole was concerned to make readers of *Otranto*'s first edition accept it as an antiquarian work, therefore, it is fair to say that he ensured from the outset that he had the scope, if necessary, to present *Otranto* as a calculated deceit: in the same letter to Mme du Deffand in 1767, for example, Walpole stated that 'J'ai voulu qu'elle passât pour ancienne: et presque tout le monde en fut la dupe.'[79] What was important for Walpole all along, it seems, was both to downplay the effort that went into writing *Otranto* (he began to write it, he told William Cole, 'without knowing in the least what to say or relate')[80] and to capitalize on the doubts of readers about what they were dealing with – in the same way that he had sought to confuse uninitiated visitors to Strawberry Hill. When William Warburton earnestly praised *Otranto* in Aristotelian terms as 'a Master-piece' which *'purges the passions by pity and terror'*, Walpole mocked such an inappropriate defence of his work, even though he had also invoked the contrast between terror and pity in the first preface: in a letter to Robert Jephson, Walpole claimed instead that he had had no intention 'but to amuse myself – no, not even a plan, till some pages were written'.[81]

A brief reference to Walpole's other activities in this period further serves to underline the pleasure he took in orchestrating and presiding over different forms of deception. In 1764, for example, Walpole published the autobiography of Lord Herbert of Cherbury, a work that Gray and himself had first read 'laughing and screaming', and to which Walpole contributed 'an equivocal preface' to signal – to the right readers – his amusement at what he was presenting before the public:

Hitherto Lord Herbert has been little known but as an Author. I much mistake, if hereafter he is not considered as one of the most extraordinary characters which this country has produced. Men of the proudest blood shall not blush to distinguish themselves in letters as well as arms, when they learn what excellence Lord Herbert attained in both.[82]

A year later, Walpole provoked a heated debate by sending a letter to Rousseau which purported to have been written by Frederick, the King of Prussia (intending, Walpole told William Cole, to 'laugh at his affectations'); in 1766, in addition, Walpole was probably responsible for 'An Account of the Giants lately Discovered', a narrative of Captain Byron's apparent discovery of the Patagonians, in which, as the *Monthly Review* described it, the author's 'main purport' was 'to laugh at the credulity of the gaping public, ever ready to swallow any wonderful tale, or to credit the grossest absurdities'.[83] Though the unpublished *Hieroglyphic Tales*, composed between 1766 and 1772, were too blatantly excessive to stand any chance of duping their readers, the work's preface displayed a similar impulse to mock the credulity of those who were taken in by frameworks of authentication and oral transmission. Echoing the false gravity of *Otranto*'s introductory material, the collection's preface stated that the six short tales

were undoubtedly written before the creation of the world, and have ever since been preserved, by oral tradition, in the mountains of Crampcraggiri, an uninhabited island, not yet discovered. Of these few facts we could have the most authentic attestations of several clergymen, who remember to have heard them repeated by old men long before they, the said clergymen, were born. We do not trouble the reader with these attestations as we are sure every body will believe them as much as if they had seen them. – [W]hether [the author] wrote the Tales six thousand years ago, as we believe, or whether they were written for him within these ten years, they are incontestably the most ancient work in the world.[84]

   Along with all the evidence considered so far about Walpole's relation to antiquarianism and the romance revival, the quotation above provides an especially useful perspective on the meaning of terms such as 'fancy', 'imagination', and 'the Gothic' in Walpole's work. Critics of the Gothic romance still sometimes read *The Castle of Otranto* as a work which signalled the eruption of a hitherto submerged 'unreason', and (with perhaps more justification) continue to appeal to the judgement of Scott in reading *Otranto* as a historically conscious evocation of super-natural incident. Scott elevated Walpole above later Gothic romancers, because he was 'a statesman, a poet, and a man of the world, "who knew the world like a man"',[85] and his brief biographical memoir of Walpole famously dignified the motivation behind *Otranto*:

It is doing injustice to Mr. Walpole's memory to allege that all which he aimed at in *The Castle of Otranto* was 'the art of exciting surprise and horror'; or, in other words, the appeal to that secret and reserved feeling of love for the marvellous and supernatural, which occupies a hidden corner in every one's bosom. Were this all which he had attempted, the means by which he sought to attain his purpose might, with justice, be termed both clumsy and puerile. But Mr. Walpole's purpose was both more difficult of attainment, and more important when attained. It was his object to draw such a picture of domestic life and manners, during the feudal times, as might actually have existed, and to paint it checkered and agitated by the action of supernatural machinery, such as the superstition of the period received as matter of devout credulity.[86]

Despite such powerful claims, it is nonetheless difficult to see much evidence on Walpole's part of a *historical* as opposed to a picturesque interest in the details of the past, since what strikes the modern reader most about Walpole's references to *Otranto* is the way that he privileges amusement and diversion. Walpole did represent *Otranto*'s appeal to Joseph Warton in March 1765, for example, as its 'ambition of copying the manners of an age which you love',[87] but alongside all of his other letters about *Otranto* in the mid 1760s, this one seems like a piece of special pleading in a specific register, calculated to impress an earnest antiquarian. Walpole far more frequently drew attention to the frivolity of his work, introducing it to his regular correspondent William Cole in February 1765, for example, as 'a profane work in the style of former centuries', with a title whose aura was designed primarily to 'tempt' potential readers.[88] In March of the same year, Walpole told the Earl of Hertford that had he been aware at an earlier date of his 'history' of a hyena in the Lower Languedoc 'it would have appeared in *The Castle of Otranto*', since it was 'exactly the enchanted monster of old romances'; to Elie de Beaumont, in the same month, Walpole declared that his work was 'a narrative of the most improbable and absurd adventures'.[89]

Though Walpole framed the wildness of his work by appealing to a Shakespearean precedent, and by claiming that his appeal to 'the great resources of fancy' arose out of a need to supplement the 'strict adherence to common life' (7) of the modern romance, it is clear elsewhere that he continued to denounce his competitors in more characteristically 'aristocratic' terms. This is evident in Walpole's casual dismissal of Richardson's 'deplorably tedious lamentations, *Clarissa* and *Sir Charles Grandison*', 'pictures of high life as conceived by a bookseller', as well as in his attack upon Clara Reeve's *The Old English Baron*, 'a professed imitation of mine, only stripped of the marvellous; and so entirely stripped, except in one awkward attempt at a ghost or two, that it is the most insipid dull thing you ever saw'.[90] The scathing criticism of Reeve's work revealingly betrays the 'literary' criteria that Walpole himself privileged, nowhere more openly than when he complained that 'it certainly does not make one laugh, for what makes one doze seldom makes one merry'.[91] Such abuse in turn points to the fact that Walpole most frequently defined his notion of 'fancy', like his version of the Gothic, in antagonistic terms, as is clear from his negative statement of purpose in the Postscript to the *Hieroglyphic Tales*:

[the tales] deserve at most to be considered as an attempt to vary the stale and beaten class of stories and novels, which, though works of invention, are almost always devoid of imagination. It would scarcely be credited, were it not evident from the Bibliotheque des Romans, which contains the fictitious adventures that have been written in all ages and all countries, that there should have been so little fancy, so little variety, and so little novelty, in writings in which the imagination is fettered by no rules, and by no obligation of speaking truth.[92]

Rather than being a proto-historical novel preoccupied with the accurate description of medieval customs and manners, *Otranto* like Strawberry Hill seems to have been based upon a recourse to the past which was mainly concerned about, on the one hand, subsuming eccentricity for a modern, leisured audience, and, on the other, confounding those readers without the necessary discrimination to accommodate such novelty. *Otranto*, like Strawberry Hill, offered (at least) a 'doubled' meaning, but the nuances of the higher or private perspective were at first available, it seems, only to a fairly select group who were initiated into a knowledge of what Walpole was doing. Thomas Gray, for example, praised *Otranto* in a suitably knowing fashion at the end of 1764, telling Walpole that 'the C: of O:' had engaged all of his colleagues at Pembroke College, Cambridge: 'it . . . makes some of us cry a little, & all in general afraid to go to bed o' nights'.[93] Walpole's concern with amusing novelty is most obviously 'allegorized' by *Otranto*'s narrative in the way that it presents the role of supernatural agency – usually regarded as one of the defining components of 'Gothic' fiction. *Otranto*'s use of the supernatural, as David Punter has argued, is intended less to terrify than 'to interest and amuse by its self-conscious quaintness',[94] as is clear in the episode – a pastiche of *Hamlet* – where the ghost of Manfred's grandfather descends from his portrait 'with a grave and melancholy air', marching 'sedately, but dejected' (24), or when 'the sable plumes on the enchanted helmet' of Alfonso the Good are 'tempestuously agitated, – as if bowed by some invisible wearer' (56). According to Isaac D'Israeli's debunking article cited in the previous section, Walpole 'had recourse to the *marvellous* in imagination on the principle he had adopted the *paradoxical* in history';[95] such a strategy, by its sheer perversity, was calculated by Walpole to attract attention without him having to compete for recognition. *Otranto* is especially renowned for the enormous pseudo-antiquarian relics (the helmet and the sword, the fragments of armour) which in effect litter its plot, and the extravagance of these objects makes them continuous in many ways with the heterogeneous decoration and ornament that Walpole assembled at Strawberry Hill. Stephen Bann has argued that the strategy of the 'historically minded pioneer' in the early nineteenth century was to aim for an internal consistency in the 'rhetoric of evocation' – to 'delimit an area designated as authentic, and to people it with objects which will collectively attest that authenticity'.[96] If *Otranto* delimited a medieval historical setting in its first preface, however, the actual 'period' objects that are foregrounded by Walpole's work ultimately exceed the bounds of this framework and assume a fetishistic status as pantomime props (just like the 'gigantic hand in armour' which Walpole saw in the famous dream that supposedly inspired his work).[97] Despite Walpole's spurious prefatory claim to the effect that 'belief in every kind of prodigy was so established in those dark ages, that an author would not be faithful to the *manners* of the times who should omit all mention of them' (4), the nature of 'the *miraculous*' (4) in *Otranto* remains uncontained by any legitimizing frame – challenging readers to assimilate or comprehend it however they can.

Georg Lukács endorsed this view of *Otranto*'s frivolity in his brief consideration of its status as 'the most famous "historical novel" of the eighteenth century': where Scott's novels derived 'the individuality of characters from the historical peculiarity of their age', Walpole's work by contrast treated history as 'mere costumery', a source of 'curiosities and oddities'.[98] This sense of oddity can further be gauged by looking at the specific ways in which Walpole complicated the tone of his work, and by following up the tension, described earlier, between the tale and its prefaces. Though Walpole drew heavily upon the Shakespearean drama which his second preface celebrated, alluding especially to *Hamlet* and *Macbeth*, the identity and tone of *Otranto* remain ambiguous. The narratorial interjections in *Otranto* continually serve to underline Walpole's detached relation to his materials, and the overall consequence of this authorial distance is that the work constantly hovers on the verge of bathos. The tale abruptly begins with the death of Conrad on his birthday and wedding day, 'dashed to pieces, and almost buried under an enormous helmet, an hundred times more large than any casque ever made for human being, and shaded with a proportionable quantity of black feathers' (17). This episode, cited by the *Critical* in January 1765 as a prime instance of *Otranto*'s absurdity, is said to be 'unprecedented' (18) and, like all of the other bizarre episodes in the work depicting supernatural phenomena, it allows Walpole the chance to describe the efforts of 'the vulgar spectators' (19) to explain what they have seen. Alerted by the 'young peasant' (18), Theodore, that the helmet is missing from the statue of Alfonso the Good,

the mob, who wanted some object within the scope of their capacities on whom they might discharge their bewildered reasonings, caught the words from the mouth of their lord, and re-echoed, Ay, ay, 'tis he, 'tis he: he has stolen the helmet from good Alfonso's tomb, and dashed out the brains of our young prince with it: – never reflecting how enormous the disproportion was between the marble helmet that had been in the church, and that of steel before their eyes; nor how impossible it was for a youth, seemingly not twenty, to wield a piece of armour of so prodigious a weight. (19)

The 'generality' subsequently endorse Manfred's decision to imprison

Theodore beneath the giant casque, 'firmly believ[ing] that by his diabolical skill he could easily supply himself with nutriment' (20). At the same time, Manfred's status as defiant villain or Faustian over-reacher is also subject to repeated qualification. Walpole's prefatory sonnet to Lady Mary Coke, for example, presents *Otranto* as a work that tells 'Of fell ambition scourg'd by fate' (13), and Manfred is intermittently made to cast himself as a forbidding, arbitrary ruler, as when he announces his decision to divorce Hippolita, and marry Conrad's betrothed, Isabella: 'Heaven nor hell shall impede my designs' (23). If Manfred is sometimes presented as a potentially sublime or tragic figure, however, *Otranto* also accentuates – for the knowing reader – the absurdity of his role. Hearing how Theodore had opened the lock of a trap-door in the castle, Manfred is said to be staggered by the 'presence of mind, joined to the frankness of the youth', and even 'felt a disposition towards pardoning one who had been guilty of no crime'; though he is a tyrant, the reader is assured, 'Manfred was not one of those savage tyrants who wanton in cruelty unprovoked' (30).

Instead of allowing the sublime and the pathetic to complement each other in the manner of a tragi-comedy, therefore, *Otranto* collapses the distinction altogether, as is evident in the episode where 'the stranger knight and his train' (61) arrive at Otranto, 'an hundred gentlemen bearing an enormous sword' (62):

Manfred directed the stranger's retinue to be conducted to an adjacent hospital, founded by the princess Hippolita for the reception of pilgrims. As they made the circuit of the court to return towards the gate, the gigantic sword burst from the supporters, and, falling, to the ground opposite to the helmet, remained immoveable. Manfred, almost hardened to preternatural appearances, surmounted the shock of this new prodigy; and returning to the hall, where by this time the feast was ready, he invited his silent guests to take their places. (63)

The actual procession of Frederic's followers is one of the longest descriptive passages in the work, and has been cited by W. S. Lewis as evidence of a calculated move on Walpole's part to provide information for the reader about the costume of the Middle Ages.[99] In typical fashion, though, this lengthy account of harbingers, heralds, knights, and squires is immediately followed by the comical account of Frederic's men maintaining complete silence in the hall of the castle, 'rais[ing] their vizors but sufficiently to feed themselves, and that sparingly' (63); the 'stranger knight', later revealed to be Frederic himself, thereafter communicates with Manfred by nods of the head alone (64–5).

Examples of bathos can easily be multiplied and they caution against a
face-value acceptance of Walpole's prefatory claim about his work's
truth to 'nature' (8), just as the actual supernatural machinery of the
work is liable, as I have described above, to make readers sceptical about
Otranto's supposed status as an imitation of ancient romance: 'what
analogy', John Dunlop asked in 1814, 'have skulls or skeletons – sliding
pannels – damp vaults – trap-doors – and dismal apartments, to the
tented fields of chivalry and its airy enchantments?'[100]

Otranto's self-consciously theatrical dialogue further collides with Walpole's claim about having made all his characters 'think, speak and act,
as it might be supposed mere men and women would do in extraordinary positions' (8), a collision perfectly exemplified by the episode
where Matilda seeks forgiveness from her father after he has fatally
stabbed her: in response to Father Jerome's statement about 'the com-
pletion of woe fulfilled on [Manfred's] impious and devoted head' (105),
Matilda dubs him a 'Cruel man! – to aggravate the woes of a parent!'
Theodore, imitating the reaction of Hamlet to the death of Ophelia,
subsequently expresses his desire to marry Matilda regardless: 'He
printed a thousand kisses on her clay-cold hands, and uttered every
expression that despairing love could dictate' (108). If Walpole's work is
a 'blend' of anything, as a result, it is a blend not of ancient and modern
romance, but of bathos and hyperbole (or perhaps the 'buffoonery and
solemnity' that Walpole identified in his second preface, 9). *Otranto* can
be characterized, and distinguished from nearly all of the Gothic romances which follow it, by the way that it so often reduces its action to
farce. As is the case with Beckford's *Vathek*, the role of bathos in *Otranto* is
so pervasive that it calls into question the work's moral framework and
the tone of its apparently sombre conclusion. Manfred's final confession
is undercut by the way that he proclaims it as 'a warning to future
tyrants!' (109), while the work's catharsis is similarly ambiguous, with the
reader told that Theodore eventually marries Isabella in order better to
commemorate Matilda, and to 'indulge the melancholy that had taken
possession of his soul' (110). In a clear allusion to the work's first preface,
Father Jerome tells Manfred that he has 'an authentic writing' to prove
the claim of Theodore; Manfred replies that 'the horrors of these days,
the vision we have but now seen, all corroborate thy evidence beyond a
thousand parchments' (110).

At this stage it is important to re-emphasize what I claimed at the end
of the first section about the olympian tone that pervades all of Walpole's work: it can at least in part be attributed to his self-conscious

alienation from 'the world', and to his continual efforts to find a role
which would compensate him for the political career that he rejected.
Though *Otranto* was clearly conceived of in frivolous terms, a survey of
Walpole's correspondence in this period shows that disaffection
remained beneath the surface, as he repeatedly declared his tiredness
with 'the world, its politics, its pursuits, and its pleasures':

Visions, you know, have always been my pasture; and so far from growing old
enough to quarrel with their emptiness, I almost think there is no wisdom
comparable to that of exchanging what is called the realities of life for dreams.
Old castles, old pictures, old histories, and the babble of old people make one
live back into centuries that cannot disappoint one.[101]

The year of *Otranto*'s composition, 1764, was in the words of Robert
Mack 'the most stressful and intense period of political activity in
Walpole's career', which saw the dismissal of his cousin and protégé,
Henry Conway, from two prestigious offices, and Walpole implicated in
a scandal about his alleged homosexuality, brought about by his zeal to
uphold the reputation of his friend.[102] One pleasure in writing *Otranto*,
Walpole told William Cole in 1765, was the scope it provided him 'to
think of anything rather than politics', and in this respect the work
arguably resembles in some ways the 'private' poetry of writers such as
Gray and Collins, characterized by John Sitter in terms of its 'flight from
history'.[103]

Alternatively, as several recent critics have argued, *Otranto* can also be
read – at the level of its plot – as a work which finally re-engages with
history. Despite the fact that it is 'a virtuoso performance in novelty and
the exotic', *Otranto* remains 'serious about history' at a mythic level, as
David Punter has claimed, because it stages widespread anxieties about
the coercive force of the past, with its basic narrative exemplifying the
moral drawn in the first preface, that '*the sins of fathers are visited on their
children to the third and fourth generation*' (5).[104] In its presentation of legitimacy overthrowing corruption, moreover, *Otranto* seems to pay tribute
to a powerful contemporary myth of nemesis, since, as Marilyn Butler
has stated, it 'makes a villain out of a corrupt Italian tyrant . . . and a
hero out of a manly freespoken peasant with the significantly Gothic
name of Theodore':[105] Oliver Goldsmith invoked the conquest of Italy
by 'Theodric the Ostrogoth' as part of a polemic against the evil of
'luxury', in a letter to *Lloyd's Evening Post* in 1762, while Gibbon's *The
Decline and Fall of the Roman Empire* (1776–88) similarly celebrated the
martial reputation of Theodore, King of the Goths.[106] If Walpole based

his eclecticism on the premise that 'the dead have exhausted their power of deceiving', therefore, *Otranto* also demonstrates the potentially troublesome ability of the past to haunt and judge the present, and it suggestively credits the 'public' co-ordinates of the Gothic – such as bravery, candour, and political virtue – in the 'noble, handsome and commanding' (52) figure of its hero. The bizarre literalness of the supernatural in *Otranto* consequently derives, according to such a reading, from what Ian Duncan has called 'the epic topos expressing ancestral heroism as superior size and strength': the vulnerable Conrad, as a result, is crushed to death on the morning of his wedding by a gigantic helmet that belongs to the genuinely heroic Father of the royal dynasty.[107] Though the gargantuan fragments of a figure in armour initially seem to be comically inexplicable, they finally reassemble so as to present a spectacle of legitimate nobility, in the form of a vision of the usurped Lord, Alfonso the Good. 'Dilated to an immense magnitude', the shade of Alfonso authoritatively pronounces Theodore's status as the rightful heir of the principality, before ascending to heaven and leaving the rest of the work's characters to contemplate the ruins of Otranto Castle (108).

Otranto certainly helped to establish the vocabulary of the 'Gothic' genre, and the figures of the tyrant (Manfred), the prince disguised as a peasant (Theodore), and the consciously innocent heroine (Matilda and/or Isabella) clearly recur in numerous eighteenth-century romances, from Clara Reeve's *The Old English Baron* onwards. As I will argue in the next chapter, in addition, the resonance of *Otranto*'s plot – its emphasis on the recovery of the past, in particular – was recognized, and refigured, by many works within the Loyalist Gothic tradition. Despite the way that this basic plot privileges the issues of legitimacy and succession, however, there is little evidence of *Otranto* itself actually being read as an allegory of the kind discussed in the paragraph above, or indeed of it being read as anything other than an aristocratic *jeu d'esprit*. (The first preface, for example, playfully distanced itself from *Otranto*'s restoration of Theodore as the rightful heir, claiming that the work would have been more valuable had it displayed 'a more useful moral'.) Any reading of *Otranto* that privileges the restoration plot at the expense of the frivolity described in this section ultimately has to ignore too much of the work's excess and extravagance. Though, as is well known, Clara Reeve proclaimed that *The Old English Baron* was 'the literary offspring of the Castle of Otranto', she presented her work as a sober corrective to the bathos of Walpole's:

A sword so large as to require an hundred men to lift it; a helmet that by its own weight forces a passage through a court-yard into an arched vault, big enough for a man to go through; a picture that walks out of its frame; a skeleton ghost in a hermit's cowl: – When your expectation is wound up to the highest pitch, these circumstances take it down with a witness, destroy the work of imagination, and instead of attention, excite laughter.[108]

A genealogy of the Gothic romance in the eighteenth century needs to account for the way that Walpole was also cited as an inspiration by a work such as the *Modern Anecdote of the Ancient Family of the Kinkvervankotsdarsprakengotchderns: A Tale for Christmas* (1779), which was dedicated to Walpole, and used many of the ingredients of *Otranto*'s plot for comic effect.[109] The work which seems most to resemble *Otranto* in this period, indeed, William Beckford's *Vathek* (published in 1786), is rarely considered to be 'Gothic' at all. Space does not permit an extended focus on *Vathek* here, but it is fair to say that Beckford sought to forge a similarly 'aristocratic' position for himself and his work, effecting a distance from orientalist ethnography in the same way that Walpole disdained antiquarianism. Beckford's work, though it does not deal with the issue of property, depicts the fall of an overreaching tyrant, the Caliph Vathek, tempted by the promise of the Giaour to lead him to the Palace of Subterranean Fire.[110] Like *Otranto*, *Vathek* can be characterized by the nature of its narratorial intrusions and by the consequent instability of its tone; like *Otranto*, moreover, *Vathek* has proved to be resistant to literary-historical classification.

Otranto's initial reputation as a 'diversion' survived well into the nineteenth century and seems, on closer examination, to have been foregrounded by nearly all of the diverse critics and reviewers who discussed the work. John Pinkerton invoked the example of *Otranto* to defend the romance genre as a whole from charges of immorality, claiming that Walpole's work presented only 'a cup of slight and momentary intoxication', just as Anna Barbauld's preface in the *British Novelists* series similarly celebrated *Otranto* as 'the sportive effusion of a man of genius', which continued to stand out from all of the lesser attempts at imitation.[111] For many other critics in the period, meanwhile, the frivolity of *Otranto* was its chief drawback, and the perspective of distance was invoked so as to undermine Walpole's reputation as an arbiter of taste. Anne Grant, the historian of Highland folklore, also viewed Walpole as a pioneer 'in the regions of necromancy', but she condemned him because of his lack of respect for popular superstition, since after *Otranto*, she claimed, 'it became the occupation of the few to *make believe* to be frightful, and of the many to *make believe* to be afraid', a contractual arrangement that showed 'contempt for the honest believers who trembled at ghosts they thought real'.[112] Hazlitt, in his 1819 lecture 'On the English Novelists', similarly seized upon the artificiality of *Otranto*, and contrasted its construction of supernatural agency, described in detail earlier, with the more authentic 'fascination' of Ann Radcliffe's work: 'the great hand and arm, which are thrust into the court-yard, and remain there all day long, are the pasteboard machinery of a pantomime; they shock the senses, and have no purchase upon the imagination. They are a matter-of-fact impossibility; a fixture, and no longer a phantom.'[113] A further comparison of Walpole and Radcliffe, in an article on 'Mrs Radcliffe's Posthumous Romance' in the *New Monthly Magazine* in 1826, set 'the farcical extravagances of the *Castle of Otranto*' against Radcliffe's talent for spreading 'vast, sombre, and consistent pictures before the eye of the fancy'.[114]

Given my interest in suspending the connection between *Otranto* and the 'Gothic tradition', all of these comments on the work's frivolity usefully serve to complicate the modern emphasis on its status as the origin of a literature of terror. *The Castle of Otranto* was the first work of prose fiction to call itself 'Gothic', of course, and a number of critics in the late eighteenth and early nineteenth centuries recognized its influence either as 'the archetype of all that miserable trash which now deluges the press', or as the inspiring 'foundation of all the subsequent romances of any merit published in England'.[115] Despite the descriptive convenience of making Walpole stand as the father of the Gothic romance, though, it is fair to say that *Otranto* was as often affiliated by critics in this period with prior works such as 'the tales of Count Hamilton', as Anna Barbauld claimed,[116] as it was associated with the work of other canonical 'Gothic' writers such as Ann Radcliffe. Considering the impact of Walpole on Radcliffe, for example, a contributor to the *Edinburgh Review* in 1834 stated that 'The *Castle of Otranto* was too obviously a mere caprice of imagination': 'its gigantic helmets, its pictures descending from their frames, its spectral figures dilating themselves in the moonlight to the height of the castle battlements – if they did not border on the ludicrous, no more impressed the mind with a feeling of awe, than the enchantments and talismans, the genii and peris, of the *Arabian Nights*'.[117] Certainly when *Otranto* is examined in detail, and alongside Walpole's other work, it becomes much harder to argue that it was a manifesto for a new species of writing, since *Otranto* ultimately seems to have far more in common with a work such as *Vathek* than it does with the romance which is usually regarded as its first imitator, Clara Reeve's *The Old English Baron*. Though *Otranto* to some extent paved the way for *The Old English Baron* and the romances of the Loyalist Gothic tradition, these works have to be viewed apart from Walpole's since the way that they resorted to the Gothic and the category of romance was so divergent. The next chapter will further consider the imitation of *Otranto*, and it will discuss the specific ways in which Walpole's work was both refigured and repudiated by writers with a very different agenda.

CHAPTER 2

The Loyalist Gothic romance

> Speak then, the hour demands; Is learning fled?
> Spent all her vigour, all her spirit dead?
> Have Gallick arms and unrelenting war
> Borne all her trophies from Britannia far?
> Shall nought but ghosts and trinkets be display'd,
> Since Walpole ply'd the virtuoso's trade,
> Bade sober truth revers'd for fiction pass,
> And mus'd o'er Gothick toys through Gothick glass?
>
> T. J. Mathias, *The Pursuits of Literature: A Satirical Poem*, 1798[1]

In James White's *Earl Strongbow* (1789), a tourist at Chepstow Castle finds a manuscript which tells of a confrontation between a prisoner of Charles II and the ghost of a former Lord of Chepstow, Earl Strongbow, intent on narrating the story of his life. Like *The Castle of Otranto*, *Earl Strongbow* seems to resort to the costume of the distant past for its absurd and amusing 'detail', as its title character relates a series of anecdotes which culminate in an account of him hurling his squire from the castle battlements during a fit of rage. In *The Adventures of John of Gaunt, Duke of Lancaster* and *The Adventures of King Richard Coeur de Lion*, both written in 1791, White similarly catered for a knowing and leisured audience, expressing gratitude (in the latter's preface) to the fashionable readers who were 'gothically given' enough to divert themselves with his chronicles, and resolving to 'explore the remote doings of antiquity, – and evince that our forefathers were as foolish as we are ourselves'.[2] While the Whiggish *Monthly Review* drew attention to White's 'heterogeneous plan of combining History with Romance, Chivalry and burlesque Ridicule', however, very few of the short notices of White's work engaged with its levity, and many emphasized instead what they saw as the fidelity with which he depicted 'the customs of chivalry' or imitated (ancient) 'Gothic romance'.[3] Despite the admission in *Earl Strongbow*, for example, that the 'system of life' in the twelfth century was 'in some degree, objectionable', the pseudo-historical setting of White's work in fact also allowed explicit criticisms of the present by way of an idealizing appeal to the same past realm: 'the reflexions are ingenious and just', as the *Gentleman's Magazine* put it, 'not a few of them deep and severe'.[4] Whereas late-eighteenth-century Chepstow is a 'contemptible' and 'dirty' town for *Earl Strongbow*'s framing narrator, the majestic Chepstow Castle for Strongbow himself stands as 'the abode of virtuous pleasure, and of princely hospitality', and – like *'the sublime institution of chivalry'* which he later invokes – it represents a locus of certainty and value in an otherwise degenerate age.[5] Where Strongbow is made to argue that the 'stately and robust' knights of the twelfth century 'travelled into distant lands to right wrongs and redress grievances', he accuses their eighteenth-century social equivalents, 'an enervated and unmajestic generation', of going abroad only 'to commit wrongs, and cause grievances'.[6] And while the work is overtly critical of rapacious imperialism – White was involved in the impeachment of the East India Company's Warren Hastings – *Earl Strongbow* nonetheless incorporates the twelfth-century invasion of Ireland into its hero's narrative, representing this conquest as a particularly beneficial one for the 'undisciplined barbarians', taught 'the principles of peace' by the English.[7] Accompanying Strongbow's polemic against luxury and corruption is a myth of manifest destiny which promotes Ireland's role as 'an invaluable portion of the British Empire!', just as *John of Gaunt* celebrates the exploits of the Black Prince and the way that he taught 'the Scottish adversary to bend beneath our arms'.[8] This national myth is similarly powerful in *King Richard*, a romance which details the adventures of Richard after his release from captivity in Austria. Once again this work has its share of farcical episodes and Quixotic characters, such as the 'Knight of the Pitcher' who has his head wedged inside a vessel of honey, but again the emphasis on a glorious military heritage is eventually dominant, as White's romance describes some of the 'splendid acts' which 'extended to hostile shores the high fame of English chivalry'.[9] Despite the work's wilful absurdity, White can still claim that 'this and other chronicles, which I have written, may be looked upon as supplements to the history of this nation, and as such, should be valued and applauded by the worthy'.[10]

White's romances display an obvious affinity with the playful excess and frivolity of *The Castle of Otranto*, yet at the same time they *also* accentuate the 'native' associations of the Gothic and of romance, reasserting the dignity of ancestors in the name of a belligerent patriotism. Positioned between Walpolean Gothic and the 'Loyalist Gothic' which is the subject of this chapter, White's romances usefully exemplify the range of possibilities afforded by romance in the final quarter of the eighteenth century. The historical and/or geographical remoteness that characterizes romance was constructed in very different ways by different authors, so that where Walpole, and to some extent White, resorted to a notional past realm in order to provide amusing novelty for a leisured audience, as T. J. Mathias laments in the quotation above, many later writers opted instead for one of Samuel Johnson's definitions of romance, 'a military fable of the middle ages', and appealed to a highly idealized version of the past for its exemplary value.[11] This chapter will continue by looking at two contrasting adaptations of *The Castle of Otranto*, William Godwin's *Imogen* and Clara Reeve's *The Old English Baron*, and it will examine in particular the way in which Reeve's work, the prototype of the Loyalist Gothic, combined elements of *Otranto*'s plot with the existing genre of the historical romance. During the period that encompassed the loss of the American colonies and the protracted conflict with France, the drive to refashion the self-image of Britain led to the 'historical' category of Gothic being purged of its associations with either democracy or frivolity and defined increasingly in terms of a proud military heritage. This development will be traced in a brief discussion of the reputation of Alfred the Great and the meaning of Gothic architecture in the 1790s, and it will be presented as a contextual framework for understanding many of the works which are now accommodated under the Gothic heading. Many romances in the period were informed by a transparently loyalist agenda, and I will go on to argue that the Loyalist Gothic romance displays certain structural properties which serve clearly to differentiate it from other canonical Gothic works, and other varieties of contemporary fiction. A focus on the Loyalist Gothic romance serves further to complicate the map of eighteenth-century and early-nineteenth-century Gothic fiction, and this chapter is consequently offered as a further contribution towards describing the diverse affiliations of the genre.

Before the connections I have posited between the Gothic and loyalist political discourse are outlined, it is necessary first of all to acknowledge that the language of patriotism remained potentially ambiguous in the period under discussion, and carried radical or reformist associations well beyond the Chartist movement in the following century. The label of 'patriot' had been appropriated earlier in the eighteenth century by members of the Tory and old Whig Country party during Robert

Walpole's period of office, and a patriotic stance continued to be cultivated thereafter as a means of legitimizing political opposition. In the 1760s, for example, the London radical John Wilkes played up his patriotism in order to cast himself as a plain and honest citizen, opposed to the corruption of the Crown and its government, while in the 1790s, despite the power of Tom Paine's appeal to abstract rights, many radicals were still unable to relinquish the idea that Britain was an essentially free nation; writers continued to appeal to the ancient – and sometimes Gothic – constitution as an alternative, genuine source of political authority.

Such a residual sense of patriotism informed one of the first adaptations of *The Castle of Otranto*, William Godwin's *Imogen: A Pastoral Romance, From the Ancient British* (1784). Godwin, like Walpole, offered his romance as a work which derived from a manuscript source, but he rewrote *Otranto* by forcing it into a far more obviously resonant political context. The plot of *Imogen*, in brief, concerns the abduction of the title character by the protean aristocratic villain, Roderic, and it depicts her removal from the 'happy equality' of the valley of Clwyd, where 'all was rectitude and guileless truth', to Roderic's luxurious mansion, a castle of 'thoughtless pleasure', where she is tempted by 'supernatural scenes'.[12] Roderic's power is limited, however, by a curse pronounced at his birth, which predicts that he will be overthrown by a 'simple swain', and Imogen's former companion Edwin (the work's Theodore figure) is instructed by a Druid hermit, Madoc, on how to exploit this prophecy in order to break Roderic's spell.[13] Protected by an amulet given him by the Druid, Edwin follows his instructions, and Roderic's castle – like Otranto – is brought crashing to the ground amid thunder and lightning, before Imogen and Edwin are finally reunited and return to their previous state of pastoral contentment. Though this plot clearly synthesizes many elements from the British Protestant romance tradition (particularly from Spenser's *The Faerie Queene*, Milton's *Comus*, and Thomson's *The Castle of Indolence*) the extra detail supplied by Godwin made *Imogen* into what Pamela Clemit has described as a 'proto-revolutionary narrative' for the 1780s.[14] Set in primitive Wales, *Imogen* must be placed in the context of the nationalist literary historiography which constructed an image of pure, uncorrupted society in the mythical past, as a bulwark against the hegemonic forces of English imperialism. Though there are few signs of such an affiliation in Godwin's later work, *Imogen* aligned itself with an ideology of radical primitivism and – in contrast to a work such as Gray's elegy 'The Bard'

– hinted at the reversibility of acts of trespass or usurpation (such as Edward I's conquest of Wales);[15] Godwin staged 'a symbolic confrontation of old and new orders', as Clemit has argued, setting the vices of a decadent and irredeemable aristocracy against the simple virtue of Edwin and Imogen.[16]

A work such as _Imogen_ serves as a useful reminder of the diverse resources provided by the distant past for writers of romance, paying tribute to the long association between theories of the ancient constitution and the popular, anti-aristocratic myth of the freeborn citizen. While an explicitly Gothic model of government had been celebrated by writers of the oppositional Country party such as Bolingbroke, however, it seems that radicals such as Major Cartwright later in the century were much more wary about referring to the historical constitution as 'Gothic'.[17] By the late eighteenth century, indeed, the idea that the constitution had degenerated from its original principles was increasingly being contested, in conservative circles, by a powerful common-law ideology of the customary or the immemorial, expounded most famously by writers such as William Blackstone and Edmund Burke. Radicals also appealed to time beyond memory in defence of certain basic rights, of course, but what was different about the work of Blackstone and Burke, to quote J. G. A. Pocock, was their _denial_ of 'the concept of an antiquity which could be used to discredit or even evaluate the existent'.[18] Rejecting any idea that the Norman invasion had constituted an act of usurpation, Blackstone invoked the Gothic in order to endorse a benign narrative of incremental political progress, and to underwrite the legal sublime of 'ancestor-wisdom', as the utilitarian Jeremy Bentham identified in _A Fragment on Government_ (1776).[19] In Blackstone's terms, the idiosyncratic architecture of 'an old Gothic castle' served as a perfect image for the 'fictions and circuities' of English law, and the constitution, despite acknowledged 'faults', was said to resemble a 'noble pile', since it required only occasional 'repair' and beautification.[20] What the Gothic represented for Blackstone was, if anything, even more vague than what it had represented for the different writers of the 'Commonwealth' tradition earlier in the century – a semi-imaginary division of history; what Blackstone's metaphor clearly served, however, was the idea of an exceptionalist national identity and the notion of a largely unexaminable yet prescriptively authoritative British heritage.

Towards the end of the century, as I suggested at the outset, the category of Gothic was increasingly invoked as part of the urgent project to re-imagine national identity. This process is exemplified in the domain of romance by another rewriting of *The Castle of Otranto*, Clara Reeve's *The Old English Baron: A Gothic Story* (1778). Reeve acknowledged that her work was 'the literary offspring of the Castle of Otranto' and she emphasized in the preface to its second edition that her romance was equally 'distinguished by the appellation of a Gothic story'.[21] Following its dismissal by Walpole as 'the most insipid dull thing you ever saw', and later by Scott as a 'tame and tedious, not to say mean and tiresome work',[22] *The Old English Baron* is perhaps best known today as a timid imitation of *Otranto*. Yet it is important to read Reeve's work on its own terms, since it was not only a rewriting of *Otranto* but also a work with connections to another emergent genre, the historical romance.[23] Thomas Leland's *Longsword, Earl of Salisbury: An Historical Romance* (1762), for example, was widely praised on its appearance as belonging to 'a new and agreeable species of writing, in which the beauties of poetry, and the advantages of history are happily united'.[24] *Longsword* deals with the life and times of the Earl of Salisbury, an illegitimate son of Henry II, and portrays the efforts of the devious Raymond to usurp the title character's castle, and carry off his wife, while he is fighting in France. As is the case in the works which I will discuss later, the villain in *Longsword* finally confesses and commits suicide after his plot is frustrated, and the hero is subsequently reunited with his wife and has his property restored. Along with *Otranto*, Leland's work clearly contributed towards establishing the component features of the Loyalist Gothic romance, most notably by introducing a degree of topical historical reference; written towards the end of the Seven Years War, *Longsword* perhaps above all helped to popularize an English medieval setting, where conflict with the French is taken for granted.

Longsword is praised by the figure of Euphrasia in Reeve's *The Progress of Romance* as 'a Romance – and not a Novel. – A story like those of the middle ages, composed of Chivalry, Love, and Religion'.[25] As the preface to *The Old English Baron* makes clear, Reeve was concerned both to define her work against the bathos and frivolity of *Otranto* and to exploit the affective power and exemplary potential of prose fiction. Reeve avowedly subordinated the role of 'the marvellous' to a larger didactic purpose: 'The business of Romance is, first, to excite the attention; and, secondly, to direct it to some useful, or at least innocent end; Happy the writer who attains both these points, like Richardson! and not unfortunate, or undeserving praise, he who gains only the latter, and furnishes out an entertainment for the reader!' (4). Walpole, of course, had similarly advertised the 'piety' of his own Gothic romance in the ambiguous first preface to *Otranto*, but, as I argued at the end of the previous chapter, there is little evidence to suggest that he was concerned with the 'utility' of romance or with the potential of the Gothic as a counter in political debate. Reeve, by contrast, explicitly proclaimed her desire to eschew the 'melancholy retrospect' of history in order to paint instead 'the amiable side of the picture', and this construction of amiability involved the idealizing recourse to an era of 'Gothic times and manners' (3). Though Gary Kelly has recently described Reeve's romance as a work which projects 'late eighteenth-century middle-class virtues onto the social and political conflicts of late-medieval England, showing their triumph over courtly intrigue and plebeian "superstition"', *The Old English Baron* nonetheless seems to uphold a rigid and hierarchical, if harmonious, system of class relations.[26] When it is still assumed that the work's hero is 'the son of a cottager', for example, the Baron Fitz-Owen claims that Edmund Twyford's 'uncommon merit, and gentleness of manners, distinguishes him from those of his own class' (17). Edmund is distinct from 'his own class' at this time, however, only because his noble birth shines through, as characters such as the servant Joseph continually emphasize: 'I cannot help thinking you were born to a higher station than what you now possess' (25). In obvious contrast to Godwin's later work *Imogen*, therefore, *The Old English Baron* presents an aristocracy which is redeemable *because* it is possessed of merit.

Where *Imogen* sets its action in a semi-mythical Wales, *The Old English Baron* transports the basic plot of *Otranto* into medieval England and, like *Longsword* and the other Loyalist Gothic romances which I will refer to later, underwrites the distinction between good and evil with the aid of reference to familiar portions of English history. Sir Philip Harclay, the close friend of the murdered Lord Lovel, for example, is described as a 'worthy Knight', 'who had served under the glorious King Henry the Fifth' (7), while the virtuous 'peasant', Edmund Twyford, raised upon 'histories of wars, and Knights, and Lords, and great men' (61), is similarly celebrated for his military exploits in France, and presented to the Regent at one point, after a skirmish near Rouen, 'as the man to whom the victory was chiefly owing' (30). Some form of past usurpation has to be acknowledged by *The Old English Baron*, of course, but the supernatural in Reeve's work plays a significantly benign and predictable role in the service of the hero, troubling only those characters with an interest in concealing Edmund's legitimate status as the rightful Lord of Lovel Castle. While still the foster-son of Baron Fitz-Owen, to whom the castle had been sold by the usurping Sir Walter Lovel, Edmund is forced to undergo a trial of courage in the haunted apartment in which his father had been murdered. Edmund's lamp is blown out by the wind, and he then hears 'a hollow rustling noise like that of a person coming through a narow passage', at which point 'all the concurrent circumstances of his situation struck upon his heart, and gave him a new and disagreeable sensation' (42). After this brief concession to an aesthetic of terror, however, Edmund's 'courage' and 'confidence' (43) are said to return, and he endeavours to discover the cause of the mysterious phenomena. Edmund is subsequently visited in a dream by the ghosts of his parents, who inform him that he is the 'sweet hope of a house that is thought past hope!' (45), just as the loyal Father Oswald also tells him, later on, that he is 'designed by heaven to be its instrument in bringing . . . deeds of darkness to light' (54). This interpretation of events is repeatedly confirmed, most emphatically when, after Harclay's defeat of Sir Walter Lovel in armed combat, Edmund finally returns to the castle as its rightful owner and 'every door in the house' (130) spontaneously flies open to receive him. Edmund's marriage to the daughter of Fitz-Owen is celebrated in a festive conclusion, and a moral is offered about 'the over-ruling hand of Providence, and the certainty of RETRIBUTION' (153). Rather than exploit the aesthetic of terror for which the Gothic romance has become renowned, Reeve accentuated the role of legitimacy and property in her plot, so as to purge *Otranto* of its frivolity and provide a reassuring moral and patriotic fable during a period of national crisis.

The basic contrast between the different patriotic traditions informing *The Old English Baron* and *Imogen* can certainly be complicated, since a number of works within the broadly defined 'romance revival' in the second half of the century seem to elude the terms of my schematic account. A diverse group of writers became involved from about 1750 onwards in what Gerald Newman has described as 'a period of extraordinary and unprecedented activity in the collection, study and promotion of everything pertaining to the national cultural heritage'.[27] Such a widespread expansion of research inevitably generated controversy (notably, for example, between writers such as Thomas Percy and Joseph Ritson, who constructed opposing genealogies of the metrical romance and the popular ballad), but what is nonetheless striking is the pervasiveness in this period of an apparently bipartisan obsession with ancestry and origins. A normative Gallophobia certainly pervades a key work such as Richard Hurd's *Letters on Chivalry and Romance* (1762), for example, but it is difficult now to translate its construction of an authentic Gothic cultural heritage into more readable ideological terms, just as it is difficult to interpret the non-frivolous delight and enthusiasm with which Elizabeth Carter styled herself as a 'Goth' and a votary of 'Gothic grandeur' in her correspondence of the 1760s and 1770s.[28] The same ambiguity surrounds several other nearly contemporary works which also praised the Goths in native, ancestral terms: *An Essay on Epic Poetry* (1782) by Blake's patron William Hayley, for example, saluted the Scandinavian Goths as 'Ye brave Progenitors, ye vigorous Source, / Of modern Freedom and of Europe's force', while the antiquarian John Pinkerton's *A Dissertation on the Origin and Progress of the Scythians or Goths* (1787) compared 'the contempt we bear to the Goths' with 'that of a spendthrift heir to a great and prudent father'.[29] Richard Hole's *Arthur; or, The Northern Enchantment. A Poetical Romance* (1789) was still able to read the Gothic in terms of a largely creative or poetic plenitude, in the manner of Hurd's *Letters* or William Duff's *An Essay on Original Genius* ('the old Gothic fables exhibit a peculiarity of manners and situation, which . . . from their being less hackneyed, afford more materials for the writer's imagination'), and the congenial, masculine appeal of Gothic vigour continued to be invoked thereafter as a means of legitimizing the 'wildness' of folk tales: the turn from 'classic brightness' to 'Gothic gloom', according to the 'Introductory Dialogue' of *Tales of Terror* (1801), 'breathes awe and rapture o'er the soul', and wakes 'Imagination's darkest powers!'[30]

Despite the persistence of such an ostensibly universal fascination with cultural origins, however, it is easier to distinguish between different recourses to the distant past *after* the mid 1770s, since the American Revolution, as I suggested earlier, significantly jeopardized the existence of a common rhetoric of patriotism. During and after the American war, it became increasingly difficult to combine reformist ancient constitutionalism with bellicose patriotism because, as John Brewer has argued, the colonists provided many English reformers with 'the key . . . to unlock the fetters imposed by an unreformed representation'.[31] Many radicals in this period adopted a stance of principled internationalism ahead of a patriotism stigmatized by Richard Price in terms of 'the love of domination', and the 'thirst for grandeur and glory'.[32] Focusing on the duration and the aftermath of the American war, therefore, it is arguably much easier to distinguish between what could provisionally be termed 'democratic' and 'militarist' resorts to the past. A work such as Major Cartwright's *Take Your Choice!* (1776), on the one hand, followed the influential *Historical Essay on the English Constitution* (1771) in appealing to the purity of a Saxon democratic tradition in need of restoration, albeit with a residual Gallophobia consistent with 'Norman Yoke' ideology. More belligerently patriotic writers, on the other hand, defined their competing ideas of a unique national identity primarily in terms of a heritage of military victory. The bifurcation of patriotic discourse during and after the American war was accentuated by the French Revolution and the widespread, almost global conflict which followed. While radical patriotism seems to have been largely stifled in this period of near continuous war, the strength of its Protestantism and its Gallophobia was recuperated by the state, as Britain became, in the words of David Cannadine, 'the most successful counter-revolutionary nation in Europe'.[33] 'Official nationalism' developed during the period, in the terms of Benedict Anderson, as 'an anticipatory strategy adopted by dominant groups – threatened with marginalization or exclusion from an emerging nationally-imagined community'.[34] Burke's definition of the nation as a 'moral essence', rather than 'a geographical arrangement, or a denomination of the nomenclator' usefully points to the efforts which were made to encourage a cohesive yet also hierarchical form of loyalist attachment,[35] a familial patriotism that even now exerts a strong hold on British society. Ancestral heroes were increasingly invoked from above to provide reinvigorating stories of nationhood, so that while George III incorporated Benjamin West's paintings of episodes in the life of Edward III into his Audience Chamber at Windsor Castle, popular variants on the same theme were the broadsides which defined the 'ancient name and character' of the British in terms of 'our Edwards and Henries'. In clear contrast to Cartwright's emphasis on 'RESTORING THE THINGS THAT ARE GONE TO DECAY', such appeals to a pantheon of national heroes were usually made in militarist terms, as in a popular handbill such as 'The Old English Lion': 'Our lifestreams unsullied flow down these veins / Which fed fame on Cressy's and Agincourt's plains.'[36]

'National' epics had been written throughout the eighteenth century, of course, but what is interesting in the 1790s especially is the way in which the non-specific rhetoric of Gothic liberty and vigour, most famously associated with the poetic canon of Hurd's *Letters*, was increasingly linked in a variety of works with a celebration of actual, if mythologized, historical figures and/or events. As Christopher Hill's groundbreaking essay on 'The Norman Yoke' has made clear, Alfred the Great was the paradigmatic hero of reformist patriotism in the eighteenth century, an iconically 'English' figure widely credited with the institution of a bicameral national Parliament, as well as trial by jury.[37] Though Alfred retained this status into the 1790s and beyond, however, as in the work of Major Cartwright or in the writings of the Millenarian Spenceans identified by Iain McCalman, Tory historians and poets increasingly contested the myth of Alfred and inflected it in a very different way, in order to purge it of its democratic potential. Seeking to explain what he regards as 'the triumph of the conservative reaction', H. T. Dickinson has stressed that it is crucial to 'take into account the impressive achievements of the loyalists in countering the ideology, the political organizations, and the political activities of the radicals'; many loyalists were strategically astute in 'replying not only in kind, but to greater effect, to every political tactic adopted by the radicals'.[38] Sharon Turner's *The History of the Anglo-Saxons* (1799–1805) usefully exemplifies this thesis, since Turner's massive work initially seems to follow Whig historiography, and stress the resemblance between the Anglo-Saxon Witenagemot and the early-nineteenth-century parliament. Importantly, however, Turner only made this move in order to authorize what he went on to claim was a similarly limited franchise. Where Cartwright, for example, had presented Alfred as a ruler who both 'disdained the title of *monarch*' and penetrated 'the depths of political science', Turner idealized Alfred because of his own interest, in the words of Alice Chandler, 'not so much . . . in liberty as in law, not so much . . . with the antiquity of English freedom as with the glory of her hereditary monarchy'.[39]

Such a reworking of the Alfred myth is perhaps most powerfully evident in the Alfred epics of Joseph Cottle, the dissenting Bristol publisher, and Henry Pye, the poet laureate and prominent anti-Jacobin. Like Hurd's *Letters*, for example, Cottle's *Alfred, an Epic Poem* (1800) acknowledges 'the peculiar scope to the imagination' afforded by 'the wildness of the Gothic superstitions'.[40] Where Hurd's valorization of the Gothic is difficult to 'translate' for the modern reader, however, Cottle's work clearly addressed its immediate audience by aligning itself with 'the cause of religion and virtue'.[41] Cottle invoked the quintessentially native and poetic resources of 'Gods, and Faeries, and Witches', therefore, but at the same time he incorporated this mythology into a transparently resonant tale about the successful resistance of an invasion from the continent, making the character of Alfred predict with confidence, in the final book, that:

> if, in times hereafter, there should rise
> Great foes and many, we may proudly hope,
> Our progeny, thinking of us their Sires,
> Will rise vindictive, and th' Invader's spear
> Trample in dust as we this day have done.[42]

Compared to Cottle's work, Henry Pye's *Alfred; an Epic Poem* (1801) says far more about Alfred's celebrated status as 'the Founder of the Jurisprudence, the Improver of the Constitution, and the Patron of the Literature of my Country'; even so, Pye's poem is organized around Alfred's role as a military hero, and takes for its main action Alfred's successful marshalling of the opposition to a foreign invasion.[43] Pye, in fact, deliberately countered the radical Whig or democratic myth of Alfred with the aid of extensive footnotes designed to discredit the theory of the Norman Yoke (claiming, for example, that William I had a better claim to the throne than Harold).[44] A Druid prophesies in Pye's poem, for example, that Alfred's 'code, arranged by nature's purest plan / Shall guard the freedom and the rights of man', but such a radical Whig commonplace is immediately qualified when it is made clear that these rights are actually established in Britain under the already happy constitution: 'Man's real rights – not folly's maniac dream, / Senseless Equality's pernicious theme'.[45] Pye's *Alfred* all but divested its hero of a critical function, as a result, appealing instead to the myth of a 'parent monarch' and to a military example (the resistance of an invasion, again) in obvious need of emulation.[46] In the same way that loyalist Volunteer associations contested the republican ideal of fraternity, Pye's poem can be seen to counter the democratic rhetoric concerning the restoration of rights, as the figure of the Druid is made to stress during a critical stage in the campaign against the Danes:

> I see, once more, *Britannia's arms restored,*
> Once more the indignant Briton grasp the sword,
> The rural empire hail its rural band,
> And Chatham renovate what Alfred plann'd.[47] (My emphasis.)

In the course of Richard Hurd's dialogue 'On the Age of Queen Elizabeth', the third of his *Moral and Political Dialogues* (1760), the figure of Addison confidently works the spectacle of Kenilworth Castle's ruins into a narrative of progress from barbarism to civility: the ruins are said to awaken 'an indignation against . . . the tyranny of those wretched times', while also fostering 'a generous pleasure in . . . the happiness we enjoy under a juster and more equal government'.[48] By the mid 1790s, in contrast, it seems as though it was no longer possible to project such a distance except in a 'revolutionary' way, and a great range of works as a result sought to assert their intimacy with a military tradition, so as to construct a model of a continuous British heritage of martial vigour, manifest, in Henry Pye's celebratory terms, all the way

> From her scyth'd cars that wide destruction hurl'd
> On the proud master of a subject world,
> To her bold fleets that o'er the azure main,
> Teach Earth's remotest shores to bless her GEORGE's reign.[49]

This trend followed not just from the threat posed by France in the 1790s, but also from the mood of defensive introspection evident in the long-running attempt to put a positive gloss on American Independence and represent it as a purging of 'poisonous' factions: 'Freed from the pest alone Britannia stands / Bulwark and envy of surrounding lands.'[50] It was still possible to construct the distant past and the Gothic as largely 'poetic' resources, of course, but the Gothic in particular was increasingly associated in an explicit way, as countless works show, with an array of semi-mythical military heroes and even heroines. These figures were often as historically distant as Boadicea and Caractacus, represented in poems by George Richards, and they also included rulers such as Alfred the Great, discussed above, and Richard I, the subject of a massive poem by James Burges, as well as the recurrent 'Edwards and Henries'; just as frequently – with little regard for evidence or accuracy – all of these (and more) were combined in a single pantheon. The perceived need to connect with or tap into such a living past often resulted in what now seem like absurd anachronisms, as is the case with Henry Pye's 'Ode for the New Year, 1797', which closes by exhorting its readers 'To arms!':

> your ensigns straight display!
> Now set the battle in array!
> The oracle for war declares,
> Success depends upon our hearts and spears
> Britons, strike home! revenge your country's wrongs
> Fight, and record yourselves in Druid songs![51]

Pye's poem usefully testifies, nonetheless, to some of the ways in which contemporary writers constructed the powerful self-image of a warrior race. Though the Gothic probably never lost its associations with a rhetoric of native liberty and freedom from restraint, literary as well as political, it is fair to say that more and more effort was made to purge the distant past of its democratic potential, and assimilate it instead into an exemplary narrative of military vigour. This effort remained a priority even as 'late' as Robert Southey's epic of 1814, *Roderick, the Last of the Goths*: where Southey's earlier fragment *Harold* (1791) had 'democratized' Richard I by associating him with Robin Hood and his men, *Roderick* focused upon the redemption of the Spanish Wisi-Goth line, via the defeat of the Moors and their allies, and presented the heroic Goths in such a way as to parallel the Spanish patriots in opposition to Napoleon.

Similar attempts to assert the proximity or at least downplay the distance of past glories can be seen in the field of architecture, where the visibility of decay made the subject of ruins a particularly sensitive one in the mid to late 1790s. The changing climate of opinion about ruins and about Gothic architecture can most usefully be followed via the extensive correspondence in the proudly loyalist *Gentleman's Magazine*, a monthly publication that proclaimed its allegiance to 'true Protestantism and true Patriotism'.[52] Ruins in particular supplied a topic for private poetry on the theme of 'mutability' throughout the eighteenth century, and were further represented in the terms of William Gilpin, for example, as an 'animating' focus for the picturesque eye.[53] More and more was at stake as the 1790s progressed, however, to the extent that a contributor in 1798 expressed concern whether 'some readers might conclude that I was actuated by motives not consistent with a "Christian Antiquary" and an Artist'.[54] Whereas in 1765, for example, it had been possible to argue, like Hurd's Addison, that the disrepair of Windsor Castle actually signified the 'happy union between prince and people', castles and abbeys in the 1790s increasingly assumed the status of monuments, and were seen to embody what Wordsworth later referred to in the sonnet 'Lowther' as 'the strength of backward-looking thoughts'.[55] Regardless of their private ownership and their specific histories, the imperatives of the present demanded that castles and abbeys be viewed as symbols of the immemorial, if embattled, authority of Fortress Britain. This view of Gothic architecture had the effect of making certain contributors try even to make a tentative defence of 'the Monastic Institution', and it led to an array of unlikely characters, such as Richard II and the republican poet Milton, being assimilated alongside the more familiar names into a unifying notion of heritage.[56] In 'this age of threatened invasion', as 'An Architect' wrote in March 1799, it was seen to be vital that

our antient remains of art, that every where meet our eyes . . . remind us of the sublime genius of their authors; remind us of the heroic acts of those defenders of their country who brought perfidious France beneath their triumphant swords; remind us of our long race of sovereigns, the admiration and dread of surrounding nations, and remind us of our duty to our Creator, to ourselves, and to mankind.[57]

If castles had offered resonant associations throughout the eighteenth century, it is clear in the late 1790s that these meanings were subject to control or policing, as in Burke's polemical *Letter to a Noble Lord* (1796), which explicitly connects the architectural integrity of Windsor Castle and the future of the monarchy:

as long as the British monarchy, not more limited than fenced by the orders of the State, shall, like the proud Keep of Windsor, rising in the majesty of proportion, and girt with the double belt of its kindred and coeval towers, as long as this awful structure shall oversee and guard the subjected land – so long the mounds and dykes of the low, fat Bedford level will have nothing to fear from the pickaxes of all the levellers of France.[58]

What was important for Burke, as for so many other writers in the period, was not only to remind Britons of what bound them together, but also to stress this unity in a suitably chastening and humbling way. Taken together with his use of Windsor Castle in *Letters on A Regicide Peace*, the quotation from Burke above serves to foreground the prevalent anxiety that Britons should draw the correct inferences from different aspects of the national heritage. 'Only in Great Britain', Linda Colley has argued, 'did it prove possible to float the idea that aristocratic property was in some magical and strictly intangible way *the people's property* also.'[59] Such anxiety was felt, nonetheless, that many contributors to the debate in the late 1790s found it no longer possible even to admit 'Gothic' as a term of praise. In September 1798, for example, the *Gentleman's Magazine* published the first in a long series of articles 'On the Pursuits of Architectural Innovation', aiming to point out for the 'abhorrence' of the reader 'the knowledge of those remains of our country's antient splendour' which may, 'from time to time, give way' to the improver's 'iron hand'.[60] The appeal of a national style of Saxon and Norman architecture was still couched in familiar common-law terms, and contributors unambiguously expressed their opposition to 'innovation *in whatever shape it may appear*',[61] yet 'Gothic' could not be admitted as a term of value, since it had been contaminated both by the reformist or radical emphasis on its connotations of primitive ignorance *and* by the improvers' use of the term to describe their grotesque and implicitly effeminate or foreign 'heterogeneous jumble'.[62]

As I argued at the beginning of my first chapter, the category of Gothic offered a wide range of possible constructions throughout the eighteenth century, nearly all of which had to accommodate or account for the historical distance of the 'Gothic' period – however it was defined – and its residual associations of barbarism and backwardness. While the *Gentleman's Magazine* debates pay tribute to the impact which reformers and radicals had in turning this sense of the Gothic back on their opponents, however, it is nonetheless fair to say that the idea of the Gothic as an exemplary pseudo-historical period became increasingly dominant towards the end of the century. In many ways there was a continuity between the so-called Gothic theory of Richard Hurd, coming out of the 1760s, and the works of a poet such as Henry Pye, written mainly at the turn of the century, since both writers resorted to the Gothic as a locus of value which was seen as antithetical both to the refinement of modernity and to all things French. Where the critical function of Gothic 'wonders' was relatively ambiguous for Hurd, though, since he only gestured beyond talking about poetry, constructions of the Gothic were far more readable by the 1790s, because they generated associations of a military heritage and a unique national identity, as well as of a native poetic tradition. In a poem such as *The Old English Gentleman* (1797), for example, by the prominent anti-Jacobin Richard Polwhele, the nature of the reference to an example of Gothic domestic architecture provides one obvious marker, among many, of the work's loyalist politics. The poem begins by presenting 'Old *Andarton*', in its 'Gothic gloom', as the country seat of the Gentleman in the work's title, Sir Humphrey Andarton, and the reader is told of the timeless occupation of this 'pleasant site' by the Andarton line, 'a race of spotless name / Not trump'd by glory'.[63] The family and the 'hoar-patcht mansion' indeed are closely bound up with the history of the nation ('Ere o'er the land his spear the *Norman* shook, / Those honest gentry held this little nook') and Sir Humphrey in turn is idealized as the avuncular superintendent of a moral economy, and a Justice of the Peace 'of mickle worth'; an enemy of 'the merchant, the borough-monger, or the nabob', but 'still to the good Pretender half a friend'.[64] Polwhele's work is forced to concede that Sir Humphrey's is a character too good to be true, and this spell of benign customary authority is ultimately broken by his death. The poem continually foregrounds the exemplary role of its hero, however, and stresses what is required of 'the rural squire' in the way of emulation: locally and nationally, survival alone in such a time of crisis necessitates the reawakening of 'the faded fire / That, in a HENRY's or an EDWARD's age, / Stream'd o'er the bosom with heroic rage'.[65]

Along with this last recourse to a heritage of 'Edwards and Henries', what all of the works referred to so far seem to have in common is their construction of a living – and sometimes explicitly Gothic – past, with an exemplary meaning for the present. This chapter began by arguing how important it is to discriminate between the different resorts to the distant past that were made by late-eighteenth-century romances, and what needs to be stressed now is the way that the contextual framework established above helps to illuminate so many of the fictions which were published in the period under headings such as 'Legendary Tale', 'Old English Tale', 'Historical Story', or 'Historical Romance'.[66] In a similar way to the poetry of Pye and Cottle or to the articles in the *Gentleman's Magazine*, a great number of romances in the 1790s invoked familiar counters of loyalist discourse, celebrating both a pantheon of national heroes and the symbolism of a proud architectural heritage, and calling for unity in the face of a foreign threat. The rest of this chapter will examine a variety of works, including historical romances which appealed to a Gothic era within a loose fictional framework, romances which explicitly described themselves as 'Gothic' stories or tales, and romances which are now commonly labelled 'Gothic', and that were equally candid about their motivation. Rather than focus on the vexed issue of whether or not some of these works should be called 'Gothic', my emphasis will be on explaining some of the diverse affiliations of the genre, and on describing the way that so many works now accommodated by this label were politically conservative. Where *The Castle of Otranto* offered a pseudo-historical tale for the amusement of the leisured reader, a vast number of works followed instead the example set by Clara Reeve's *The Old English Baron* and the emergent genre of the historical romance, defining themselves (as I suggested at the outset) *against* Walpolean frivolity. Loyalist Gothic romances, I will argue in the rest of this chapter, can be distinguished by the way that – with the aid of selective historical reference – they located their action in a predominantly English medieval setting, and depicted the conflict between patriotism and a variant of misguided ambition in a period of chivalric manners, all the time underlining the lessons that such a conflict presented for readers in the 1790s. Writers of Loyalist Gothic romances modestly disavowed any claim after the recognition that 'risk-takers' such as Walpole and Lewis sought, and, perhaps most significantly, they chose to privilege the exemplary purpose of romance

rather than exploit sensational material or provide narratives of suspense. Though the supernatural in *Otranto* plays an ultimately benign
role, for example, its extravagance was primarily calculated as a claim
upon the attention of the work's readers; in Loyalist Gothic romances,
by contrast, supernatural agency is minimally presented and subordinated to the purpose of purging rogue family members and restoring
legitimate rulers and/or property claims. While the goal of inviting the
reader's anxieties is still commonly projected onto the Gothic genre,
therefore, the contextual framework developed above complicates such
a preconception, and helps to isolate a specific agenda which informed
many of the fictions written in the period, marking them out from more
canonical and more famous Gothic works.

Clara Reeve's *Memoirs of Sir Roger De Clarendon* (1793) cannot be
regarded as a Gothic romance by any modern criteria, but it
nonetheless offers an instructive statement of purpose which serves to
illuminate its choice of an English medieval setting. Like so much of the
poetry discussed above, and like her own work *The Old English Baron*
which I discussed earlier, Reeve's *Sir Roger* is openly concerned with the
issue of example or emulation, stating as its aim the need to address
'young and ingenuous minds', as yet 'uncontaminated by the vile
indolence, effeminacy, and extravagance of modern life and manners'.[67]
Grounded on the assumption that 'great men' inspire in people 'a more
ardent desire to imitate and excel them', Reeve's essentially plotless
work is chiefly made up of Sir Roger's account of the glories of Edward
III's reign (the battle of Crecy, the founding of the Order of the Garter,
the building of St George's Chapel at Windsor and so on) supplemented
by authorial digression and necessary 'inferences to all orders and
degrees of people'.[68] According to Reeve in her preface, it is the 'duty of
every son of Britain' to be 'thoroughly informed in the annals of his
country': 'when we read of our glorious ancestors, their actions ought to
stimulate us to equal them, to support and maintain the honour of our
country: to be ashamed to degenerate from our forefathers'.[69] Like
Cottle and Pye in their Alfred epics, Reeve's preface takes a staple
ingredient of reformist discourse, the notion of *constitutional*
degeneration, and translates it into military or heroic terms. Defining
itself against 'the new philosophy' and its 'levelling principle', *Sir Roger*
focuses on 'the age of King Edward IIId' not only because it was 'one of
the most fruitful of eminent men', but also since it was a time of
symbiotic social ties, when 'a true subordination of ranks and degrees
was observed'.[70] Like *The Old English Baron*, *Sir Roger*'s explicit

idealization of 'our Gothic ancestors' conjures up images both of exemplary military valour and of simple, frugal virtue: 'our ancestors were magnificent in some respects, while in others they were mean and uncomfortable; they were ignorant of the arts of polished manners and of refinements in luxury'.[71] Given such an earnest recourse to a Gothic era, it is important for Reeve to exorcize any hint of the Gothic's residual associations of frivolity – still evident, as was claimed at the outset, in the novels of James White. *Sir Roger*'s celebration of Edward III (and later, more briefly, of Henry V) consequently coexists with the attack upon the succeeding monarch, the effeminate Richard II. The reader is told early on, for example, that 'King Richard was too fond of dress and gewgaws', loving 'every thing that indicated a light, vain, and frivolous mind', and Sir Roger is made to reiterate the point when he laments the differences between Richard and his father and grandfather: 'alas! he is weak, vain, dissipated and extravagant'.[72] These failings are not just personal, however, since they are causally linked with tangible problems in the nation itself. Richard's 'weakness' is presented as the cause of his apparent susceptibility to Lollardy, a weakness driven home by Reeve's incorporation of the Lollards into a genealogy of fanaticism extending via the execution of Charles I all the way to the 1790s. Frivolity, credulity and military incompetence are all interconnected in the case of Richard: written at a time of intense United Irish agitation, Reeve's work informs the reader that the Lollards 'practised the art of insinuation so effectually, on the weak and jealous mind of King Richard, that he abandoned the fair prospect of reducing all Ireland, and returned home immediately'.[73]

Though, as I suggested above, *Sir Roger* itself cannot usefully be called a Gothic romance, it sets up a powerful contrast between the exemplary and the corrupt ruler, as the *Monthly Review*'s brief notice recognized: 'the chaste and amiable pictures of female virtue, [and] the glorious achievements of heroes . . . cannot but sensibly affect the heart, and call forth our noblest affections'.[74] Many of the romances which either described themselves as, or are now regarded as, 'Gothic' were similarly schematic. Despite the currency of the view that the action in Gothic romances usually takes place abroad, depicting Catholic tyranny in a Mediterranean setting, a surprisingly large number of these works in the 1790s are set not only in England, as I claimed above, but also in and around real castles. Most important of all, many of these works display an earnest and distinctly loyalist agenda. If it is difficult to offer conclusive evidence that Walpolean Gothic served as an antagonist in the

1790s, a work such as Richard Warner's *Netley Abbey: A Gothic Story* (1795) nonetheless sought to exorcize the effeminate or frivolous associations of the Gothic in the same way as Clara Reeve's more obviously polemical *Sir Roger De Clarendon*. Unlike the more famous and more exotic productions of writers such as Walpole and Matthew Lewis, *Netley Abbey* employs a real castle, which was very popular with contemporary poets and antiquarians, and refers to some of the real historical figures so commonly invoked by other works in the 1790s. 'Sprung from an ancient *Norman* family' (my emphasis) and 'devoted to the pursuit of military glory', the ex-crusader Baron de Villars is introduced as a loyal servant of the lionized monarch Edward I, and therefore immediately confirmed as a good character; because of his opposition to the influence of Gaveston, however (the 'frivolous favourite' on whom the new King 'lavished all his regards'), he is banished from the court of Edward II.[75] Forced to retire from public life, de Villars proceeds to indulge his melancholy at a castle near to both Netley Abbey and Netley Castle, the estate of Sir Hildebrand Warren (nephew of de Villars's old friend Sir Raymond, who is said to have died with his daughter Agnes two years earlier). Shortly after their arrival, de Villars's son Edward is given a supernatural warning about the sinister events taking place at Netley Abbey, and, 'determined to exert himself in endeavouring to discover what part it pleased providence that he should act', he goes on finally to rescue a captive – Agnes Warren.[76] Sir Hildebrand, meanwhile, has kidnapped de Villars's daughter, Eleanor, with the intention of forcing her to marry him, but she is eventually rescued by a mysterious black knight, the son of de Villars's former friend Sir Raymond, recently returned from the continent (where he had also been given supernatural warning about events at the abbey). It comes to light that the libertine Sir Hildebrand was responsible for starving Sir Raymond to death and imprisoning Agnes, as well as usurping the title to Netley Castle. Justice is done, though, when Hildebrand and the Abbot of Netley – blaming each other for the failure of their plans – kill each other in a fight, before (finally) the families of de Villars and Warren are reunited, and the children marry.

An examination of *Netley Abbey* underlines the problems inherent in describing the Gothic romance as a genre which is solely preoccupied with the aesthetics of terror and the fears and anxieties of the reader. Contextualizing criticism has to acknowledge the role of 'suspense' in the contemporary market for fiction, of course, but any construction of the Gothic romance in such an exclusive way works to efface both the political affiliation of individual works and the contested nature of the genre as a whole. *Netley Abbey* clearly deploys many of the tropes and plot devices which *The Castle of Otranto* helped to establish, notably in its use of supernatural agency to discover tyranny and hasten the restoration of legitimate authority. At the same time, however, it is important to recognize that *Netley Abbey* is a refiguring or rewriting of *Otranto*, since it connects the 'redemption' of Netley Abbey and Netley Castle, via the return of their rightful inhabitants and the resumption of their traditional charitable roles, with the restoration of national integrity. It is plausible to suggest, indeed, that *Netley Abbey* implicitly defined itself against the frivolity of Walpole's work, by deploying a homosexual stereotype as an index of national corruption. Where the 'military glory' achieved during the reign of Edward I is clearly celebrated, as it was in so many other works of the period, Edward II (a rogue member of the pantheon of 'Edwards and Henries') is noted only for his 'absurd partiality' to Gaveston, and he is said to rule with a 'feeble hand', under which 'the laws relapsed into laxity and contempt'; while he is still an advisor to Edward I, for example, de Villars is shown to recognize that 'young Edward's infatuation for Gaveston might hereafter be productive of the greatest discomfort to himself, and injury to the nation'.[77] Though Warner's romance has to recognize the potentially disturbing fact of usurpation, *Netley Abbey* ultimately stages the purging of corruption via the agency of a benign supernatural power which brings to light the crimes of the work's villains. Like the similarly unambiguous *The Old English Baron*, with which it shares many features, and like the Radcliffean romance of the 1790s which will be examined later, *Netley Abbey* closes with a tableau of punishment for the corrupt and irreligious and reward for those with faith in the workings of Providence:

THERE IS NO SITUATION TO WHICH PERSECUTED VIRTUE CAN BE REDUCED, SO LOW, AS TO AUTHORIZE DESPAIR; THERE ARE NO CIRCUMSTANCES TO WHICH HARDENED IMPIETY CAN BE RAISED, SO ELEVATED, AND SECURE, AS TO PRECLUDE THE FEAR OF DOWNFALL AND DISGRACE.[78]

A very similar scenario is presented in the anonymous *Mort Castle. A Gothic Story* (1798), a work dedicated to 'Her Royal Highness the Dutchess of York'. As is the case with *Netley Abbey*, the plot of *Mort Castle* is centred on a real castle, near Ilfracombe in Devon, and deals with revelations about a rogue member of a noble family. The work begins with the wealthy Baron de Courcy having been granted the right by Henry II to occupy Mort Castle, the former property of Sir William de

Tracey (one of the murderers of Thomas Beckett). Shortly after his arrival, de Courcy encounters a dying shipwrecked knight clutching an orphan baby girl, Amanda, and he is warned by the knight that 'part of [his] blood is tainted'.[79] The knight's prophecy begins to come true, after a number of years, as one of de Courcy's sons (Albert) falls in love with Amanda, while the other (Hubert) conspires against his brother – murdering his accomplices after the failure of his first plot. Albert mysteriously disappears on the night before his proposed wedding to Amanda, and – equally mysterious – de Courcy falls seriously ill, having apparently given notice that only Hubert should attend him in his chamber. De Courcy's reported death leaves Hubert as both the sole heir of Mort Castle and the guardian of Amanda. Doubts about Hubert's conduct are rife, though, with the faithful domestic, Maurice, for example, unable to 'resist a prepossession that indicated he had played foully for his estate and title'.[80] Suspicions about Hubert's conduct are heightened when another domestic, Launcelot, reports a sighting of the spirit of the 'old master' (a further instance of the benign supernatural), and relays a message from de Courcy to the effect that he is at rest, '*save when the permitted hour of retribution calls my departed likeness back to earth for reasons thou shalt learn hereafter*'.[81] Hubert, meanwhile, is plagued by troubled visions about his conduct, and his introspection allows Amanda to escape from the castle with yet another faithful domestic, Blanche (who had been saved from a future of slavery in the West Indies, the reader is told, when the mate of a ship, 'a British seaman, more humane than the rest', had intervened to frustrate the plans of her libertine French husband).[82] Matters are eventually resolved when Albert is sighted by Maurice, and proceeds to give an account of the adventures that befell him after he had been kidnapped by Hubert's men. Unable to live with the stirrings of his conscience, Hubert kills himself, leaving behind a full description of the murder of his father. Albert then reveals his identity, goes on to marry Amanda (who turns out to be the daughter of one of the nuns at the Priory to which she fled) and outlines for the benefit of the reader the way in which the death of Hubert furnishes 'a lesson to posterity, of the over-ruling hand of Providence, and the certainty of retribution'.[83] Like so many other romances in the period, *Mort Castle* finally closes with a description of the hero's domestic idyll and his revival of a harmonious moral economy:

Albert, in the arms of love and friendship, enjoyed the blessings that surrounded him, with a heart overflowing with benevolence to his fellow-creatures, and gratitude to his Maker. His lady and himself were examples of conjugal happiness and affection, and Maurice, with good old Launcelot, were the happy sharers of their felicity.[84]

Few full-length romances followed _Netley Abbey_ or _Mort Castle_ in calling themselves 'Gothic', but a great number set their action around English castles, and used a strikingly similar one-dimensional plot which dealt with the exorcism of 'corruption' and the restoration of property to legitimate heirs. This kind of plot is structurally bound to present the corruption which has to be exorcized, of course, and both _Netley Abbey_ and _Mort Castle_ provide scenarios of the type which have come to be regarded as typically Gothic: _Netley Abbey_ describes the imprisonment of Agnes Warren and her father in 'subterraneous abodes' beneath the abbey (a taper later expires on Edward de Villars as he explores their cell), while _Mort Castle_ presents the orphaned Amanda in a situation where she is 'at the mercy' of the villainous Hubert, 'a wretch, void of honor or humanity'.[85] Despite such episodes, and despite the suggestive resonance of the 'abbey' or 'castle' title, it is nonetheless fair to say that these works do relatively little to exploit either the plot device of the persecuted heroine or the 'terrific' potential of supernatural agency, placing their emphasis instead almost entirely on reversing an act of usurpation which has already taken place, and on restoring the status quo. Though the Gothic castle has provided a powerful metaphor for psychoanalytic literary criticism in recent decades, it is important to recognize the more literal role which the castle played in the political discourse and in the fiction of the late eighteenth and early nineteenth centuries. Castles are always redeemed in the course of Loyalist Gothic romances, and they reassume the monumental status discussed above in the short section on Gothic architecture, in contrast to the self-destructing Castle of Otranto or the abandoned Castle of Udolpho.[86] Many little-known works such as John Bird's _The Castle of Hardayne, A Romance_ (1795) and T. J. Horsley Curties's _Ethelwina, or The House of Fitz-Auburne. A Romance of Former Times_ (1799), along with shorter tales such as 'Kilverstone Castle, or The Heir Restored, A Gothic Story' (1799), for example, resolve their plots by returning the castle to a benign role as a fount of charity within the local moral economy. Elizabeth Bonhote actually owned the land on which the action of her _Bungay Castle: A Novel_ (1796) is set, and in the introduction to her work she framed the potentially 'terrific' associations of 'wonderful castles' by aligning herself with a notion of innocent entertainment rather than literary ambition: 'In times like these, every book that serves to amuse the mind, and withdraw the attention from scenes of real distress, without inflaming the passions, or corrupting the heart, must surely be as acceptable to the reader as it may have been found pleasant to the writer, and should exempt the latter from the severity of criticism.'[87] Despite the concessionary title, Stephen Cullen's *The Castle of Inchvally: A Tale – Alas! Too True* (1796) also qualified the sensational role of its castle, beginning with a preface about the recent history of a structure 'built, or at least supposed to be built, as far back as the reign of Henry the Second'.[88] The Castle of Inchvally, like Blackstone's Gothic castle of a constitution, had 'with occasional repairs . . . descended to the eighteenth century in a state of almost unimpaired preservation'. At one time, Cullen's preface claims, 'a fine lady of quality, who had received her education in France' came by marriage into possession of 'the gothic beauties of Inchvally', and ordered it to be 'pulled down, for the purpose of building a mansion in the modern taste on the site'; 'the cement and stone' of the castle were found 'so indurated by the hand of time', however, 'that the architect employed for that purpose declared it immovable, unless at an expence far greater than that of building a new one'. 'Thus', the reader is told. 'the venerable mansion, which for ages had been the resort of beneficence, virtue, valour, and hospitality, was rescued by its age from the sacrilegious hand of Taste, and left to be commemorated in the following pages.'[89]

Regardless of the persisting associations of the Gothic romance and 'terror-fiction', it is fair to say that many romances in this period carefully framed their presentation of sensational incident, and appeared to subordinate their interest in Gothic castles and supernatural phenomena to the larger 'exemplary' purpose I have identified. The only romance by Ann Radcliffe *not* to explain away the supernatural, for example, was also by far the most conspicuously conservative or loyalist of all the works that she wrote. *Gaston de Blondeville; Or, The Court of Henry III Keeping Festival in Ardenne: A Romance*, unpublished until 1826 but probably written in 1802, is markedly different from Radcliffe's other work, since not only does it credit the supernatural, but it is set in England, and is far more historically specific as a result (to the extent that it is the only one of Radcliffe's works to be annotated). The lengthy opening of *Gaston de Blondeville* introduces two tourists at Kenilworth Castle, a popular site for poets and antiquarians in the period. While surveying the castle, Willoughton and Simpson are accosted by a local man who claims to have seen an armed knight by the tiltyard, and given a 'black letter' manuscript, the 'Trew Chronique' of an episode that took place there in the reign of Henry III. A long discussion follows in which the travellers debate the authenticity of the manuscript, but while this frame makes *Gaston* far more self-reflexive than the works dealt with above,[90] the narrative offered by the 'Trew Chronique' is itself an unambiguous one. Set in 1256, the narrative begins by describing how Gaston de Blondeville, 'a young Provencal' who had 'risen to favour' under the King, has been publicly accused by Hugh Woodreeve, a Bristol merchant, of being the murderer of his kinsman, one Sir Reginald de Folville.[91] Woodreeve is imprisoned as a result of his scandalous charge, and de Blondeville's reputation remains largely unspoiled until his marriage feast, when a minstrel alludes in a ballad to his shady past, and the murder of which he is accused is recreated in a dumb show. (Once again, *Hamlet* provides a model for depicting how the past returns to haunt the present.) As in the romances mentioned above, the supernatural plays an ultimately benign role in the work, with de Blondeville being hounded by an armed knight, a likeness of his murder victim, who mysteriously sheds three drops of blood – like the statue of Alfonso the Good in *Otranto* – onto the Baron's robe. De Blondeville is further incriminated when he later handles a medallion that had belonged to the murdered knight, at which point the three drops of blood spread all over his clothing. Though de Blondeville's allies manage to convict Woodreeve of sorcery, matters are finally resolved when de Blondeville is challenged to combat by the same knight, and meets his death. The stranger appears before the King, exhorting him to 'Release the innocent' and equilibrium is restored, as it is made clear that the villains of the peace were all of French origin: the Prior who had attempted to incriminate Woodreeve, for example, 'was conjectured to have come with [de Blondeville] from Gascony; for, he spoke that tongue, and had all the craft and soaring vanity of that people'.[92] Though *Gaston* makes no use of the property restoration plot discussed above, it is fair to say nonetheless that, like *The Old English Baron* and *Netley Abbey*, it uses a loosely 'historical' setting in order to make specific connections with the present. If Radcliffe's work identifies the 'weakness' of Henry III and the future 'treachery' of Simon de Montfort, it also celebrates the then 'Prince Edward' (one of the first to credit Woodreeve's story) in very familiar terms, as the embodiment of 'the virtues which were hereafter to restore the kingdom': he is the 'queller of rebellion, the corrector of abuses, the restorer of general order, the enactor of wise laws, the administrator of justice, the mighty ruler, who, by his wisdom and vigorous perseverance, bound up the wounds of his country, strengthened its sinews, and pruned away its exuberant vices'.[93]

The main argument of this chapter is that the works above must be seen alongside the better known – and rhetorically richer – instances of 'Gothic' fiction, such as *The Mysteries of Udolpho* or *The Monk*, whenever the genre as a whole is under consideration. The few avowedly Gothic works such as *Netley Abbey* or *Mort Castle* are politically unambiguous, as this chapter has argued, but rather than claim that such works are more genuinely 'Gothic' than others, my aim has been to suspend a holistic notion of the Gothic, and to underline instead the currency of the appeal to an exemplary (usually medieval) era in the romances of this period. The meaning of this appeal to English medieval history is illuminated by the contrasting example set by the liberal or reformist writers who employed certain Gothic plot devices, yet located the action of their novels in the present so as to confront the reader with 'things as they are' or, as in Charlotte Smith's *The Old Manor House* (1793), with contemporary debates on the American Revolution or the slave trade.[94] Where Loyalist Gothic romances glossed over the impact of the Norman Conquest, and often indicated that their heroes were of Norman descent, a later work such as Charles Maturin's *Melmoth the Wanderer* (1820) stressed the persistence of past conflicts in the present, displaying a preoccupation with the crimes of the Anglo-Irish ruling class (of which Melmoth's family are members).[95] Despite the subversive or transgressive reputation that is often projected back onto the Gothic genre as a result of remarkable works such as *Melmoth*, however, it is important to acknowledge that most writers in this period were highly conscious of the propriety and 'tendency' of their work, and concerned to 'seize for their shield innocence of intention', as the preface to the anonymous *Days of Chivalry: A Romance* (1797) put it, so that their brand of fiction be 'raised to a rank even more respectable than that it now possesses'.[96] If anything, the romances I have grouped together above were far more likely to be criticized for a lack of literary 'quality' than for a suspect moral tendency. Even the staunchly loyalist *British Critic* had to stress in the case of Clara Reeve's *Sir Roger de Clarendon*, for example, that 'Morality alone . . . cannot support a novel', while for the writer of the *Critical*'s notice, *Sir Roger* was simply 'for history too trivial, and for romance too dull'.[97] From a critical perspective, what redeemed these works was the way that they sought to associate themselves with higher literary genres such as the epic. The preface to John Ogilvie's *Britannia: A National Epic Poem* (1801), for example, celebrated the epic for its fitness to describe 'the deeds of heroism' and provide evidence for modern

readers of the way that 'men, before they were emasculated in great
cities by the enfeebling refinements of luxury, possessed powers of body,
as well as an energy of mind by which they undertook and accomplished
the most perilous atchievements'.[98] While they were inevitably bound
up with the workings of an increasingly commercialized novel market,
the works described above likewise defined themselves against the
feminized space of romance production and the false refinement of
romance readers.

As I have argued so far, it is important to complicate any seamless
narrative of the Gothic romance, and important to do justice to the
variety of the works that the 'Gothic' label is made to accommodate.
Many of the works which are now regarded as Gothic, and nearly all of
those which explicitly invoked the term, were unambiguously loyalist in
the way that they framed supernatural incident, and in the way that they
appealed instead to an exemplary medieval era, and to real historical
figures and events. Many of these romances sought to give the native,
Protestant aesthetic defended by Richard Hurd (as well as by Walpole's
second preface to *Otranto*) a military inflection or emphasis, defining a
distinctively English 'genius' against French, and – later – German
excess. The transgressive reputation which the Gothic romance still has,
I will argue in the next chapter, results primarily from certain atypical
yet renowned works such as *The Monk*, along with a few of the other
works in the period that were also translated or imitated 'from the
German'. According to an obituary in 1818, Lewis 'was a leader in this
northern invasion' – the invasion of German literature – who triumphed
'in the common degradation of the English genius'.[99] This identification
of Lewis's literary affiliations and his malign influence is an important
one for my purposes, since though the terminology is by no means
precise or consistent, it is fair to say that critics and reviewers in the 1790s
were far more likely to stigmatize a work as 'German' rather than
'Gothic'. The term 'German' undoubtedly retained a certain cachet,
into the early nineteenth century at least, as a marker of horror or
mystery, hence the desire of so many writers and publishers to claim
German descent for their novels and tales. Certainly after the Illuminati
controversy of the late 1790s, though, a mythical Germany became
associated with a deluded revolutionary idealism, almost to the same
extent as France, and 'German' fiction became almost universally
associated with a potentially dangerous excess. The need to dissociate
'the English' (or, as in the work of many of the writers discussed above,
the 'Old English') from 'the German' was heightened by what David

Simpson has termed the 'imperfect ideological differentiation' between the two countries, since it was an eighteenth-century commonplace to claim that English liberty 'came to this country from the woods of Germany'.[100] Where T. J. Mathias praised Ann Radcliffe for her journeying into the 'shrines of Gothick superstition', he also made it clear that 'No German nonsense sways my English heart, / Unus'd at ghosts and rattling bones to start.'[101] Similarly, Nathan Drake in his *Literary Hours* (1798) expressed the desire to hold onto 'the sublime, the terrible, and the fanciful' elements in English literature (since 'romantic legends' were seen to be part of 'our national poetry') but also recorded his concern about how supernatural machinery could 'lead to dangerous credulity'.[102] Though it was still possible to praise 'the Germans' for the exuberance and vigour of their writing, a brief survey of contemporary literary criticism shows not only that 'German' was a far more current term than 'Gothic', but also that it referred to a corpus of writing perceived to require strict legislation. The next chapter will develop this investigation of the relations between 'Gothic' and 'German' literature, and it will try and account more specifically for both the hostile reception that many romances met with in the 1790s and early 1800s and the aura of subversion that still surrounds these works in the present.

CHAPTER 3

Gothic 'subversion': German literature, the Minerva Press, Matthew Lewis

> Grim-visaged heroes, class'd in martial hosts,
> And walking skeletons, and sheeted ghosts,
> Here hold their court, from German fetters free,
> And doom poor common sense to slavery.
> Here fleeting phantoms of the heated brain
> Swarm forth like locusts from the press of LANE
>
> 'Modern Literature', *Aberdeen Magazine*, 1798[1]

> There is no book perhaps of modern production that has excited
> a greater share of curiosity, or been more the subject of public
> opinion, and public conversation, than the Romance of the
> 'Monk'
>
> 'Impartial Strictures on the Poem Called "The Pursuits of
> Literature": and Particularly a Vindication of the Romance of
> "The Monk"', 1798[2]

I

While Loyalist Gothic romances followed an uncomplicated pattern, as I argued in the previous chapter, questions nonetheless remain about what precisely contributed to the notoriety of so many other Gothic works in their moment of production. In the first half of this chapter, I want to work towards historicizing this reputation by discussing the connections between the Gothic romance and German literature, and by examining the Gothic romance in relation to the growing market for escapist fiction in general. As a term of self-description for novels and romances, 'German' was much more current than 'Gothic' in the 1790s, but it increasingly carried a series of revolutionary associations which, by the end of the decade, led to the abuse of virtually every work claiming such a descent. By the 1790s, as I will further argue, commercial presses such as William Lane's Minerva were publishing a rapidly increasing number of new novels and romances in response to a growing public demand, a development which served to amplify long-standing anxieties about the spread of literacy and the growth of an undisciplined reading public. In the context of this focus on the perceived effects of prose fiction, the second half of this chapter will go on to look much more closely at the most scandalous of the eighteenth-century 'Gothic' romances, Matthew Lewis's *The Monk*, published by Joseph Bell in 1796, in order to see what was responsible for the controversy that it generated. Lewis, according to Walter Scott, was the writer 'who first attempted to introduce something like the German taste into English fictitious, dramatic and poetical composition', and *The Monk*, as Coleridge claimed, was a work which sought to 'shock the imagination and mangle the feelings'.[3] Yet criticism of *The Monk* only got underway once Lewis's authorship and the extent of his readership were recognized, and Lewis's resort to German source material was ultimately far less important for critics than the fact that *The Monk*, like the romances published by William Lane, provided a focus for anxiety about 'unlicensed' reading. Despite its reputation as 'the most Gothic of eighteenth-century Gothic romances',[4] I will go on to argue that the 'content' and method of *The Monk* were untypical of works in the period, at least in the 1790s, and that the subversive aura of the Gothic romance – which partly depends upon the fame of Lewis's work – needs to be reassessed as a result. Though, as I will claim towards the end, several works written in the early nineteenth century were clearly affiliated to *The Monk*, it is hard to argue that Lewis's work was representative of any larger genre. Instead, when read alongside works such as *The Castle Spectre* (1797) and *The Bravo of Venice* (1805), *The Monk* seems to position Lewis as a writer who was primarily concerned, in a similar way to Walpole, to distinguish his own position within the field of literary production; whereas Walpole took great care to fashion an 'aristocratic' authorial identity, however, Lewis's quest for reputation was far more indiscriminate, and resulted in works which were consequently even more extravagant.

Any treatment of the impact of German writing in Britain in this period must begin by acknowledging the extent of its popularity, at least after the first translation in 1779 of Goethe's *The Sorrows of Young Werther* (written in 1774). As commentators such as Walter Scott and Margaret Baron-Wilson later recognized, this popularity owed much to the perceived stagnation of English literature after the heyday of the mid eighteenth century. Even in the mid 1780s, it is true that objections were made about imported German fictions, implicitly in William Blake's derogatory reference to the readership of 'Werter' in his early satire 'An Island in the Moon' (1784–5) and, much more explicitly, in Clara Reeve's *The Progress of Romance* of 1785, in which the trustworthy Euphrasia refers to her desire to collect together and burn *all* German stories and translations.[5] In general, though, works in the German language were enthusiastically seized upon by readers in search of a 'newly discovered spring of literature', as Scott wrote in his 'Essay on Imitations of the Ancient Ballad' (1830), an enthusiasm which was at least in part the result of the language being seen to be 'cognate with the English, and possessed of the same manly force of expression'.[6] Certainly after Henry Mackenzie's celebrated address on German Drama to the Royal Society of Edinburgh in 1788, the key moment in Scott's retrospective account, 'a new species of literature began to be introduced into this country', and curiosity became much more widespread about the supposedly untutored genius of writers such as Schiller.[7] When William Beckford (anonymously) published his loosely translated *Popular Tales of the Germans* in 1791, as a result, he did so with a knowledge of the cachet of things 'German', and he played up the wildness of their origin, making the figure of the Publisher in the Introductory Dialogue speculate, for example, that the original author 'for ought I know or care, may be freezing in Saturn or frying in Mercury'.[8]

The influx of German romances began in 1794, with the translation of Carl Kramer's *Herman of Unna*, succeeded most famously by translations of Schiller's unfinished work *The Ghost-Seer* and Cajetan Tschink's *The Victim of Magical Delusions* in 1795, and two versions of Carl Grosse's *The Genius* in 1796.[9] These works, dealing with outlaws or social outcasts and the conspiracies of secret societies, helped to provide an entirely new fictional register for British writers and readers. *Horrid Mysteries*, for example, one of the translations of Grosse's *The Genius*, depicts the continually frustrated efforts of its protagonist, Don Carlos, to escape the clutches of the subversive brotherhood into which he has fallen, and – despite the relish with which it describes the details of Don Carlos's seduction and temptation – the work offers itself as a topical cautionary tale, warning against the influence of freethinkers and illuminati. Along with translations of German *Schaurromane* (but with a much greater degree of critical approval), German ballads were similarly credited with revitalizing the field of literature, as one of the many translators of Bürger, William Taylor ('of Norwich'), claimed in the *Monthly Magazine* in 1796:

Bürger is every where distinguished for manly sentiment and force of style. His extraordinary powers of language are founded on a rejection of the conventional phraseology of regular poetry, in favour of popular forms of expression, caught by the listening artist from the voice of agitated nature.[10]

During the same period, many German plays also assumed, as Scott wrote in 1830, 'a new, interesting, and highly impressive character, to which it became impossible for strangers to shut their eyes'.[11] Alexander Tytler's preface to his 1792 translation of Schiller's influential drama *The Robbers*, for example, appealed to a paradigm of original genius in opposition to 'Aristotelian rules', and rehearsed the terms of praise which were recurrent in contemporary criticism: Schiller's work displayed 'a certain wildness of fancy', the nature of its language was 'bold and energetic', and the character of its hero, Karl Moor, displayed a 'strong stamp of originality'.[12]

As Tytler's preface to *The Robbers* illustrates, the popularity of German literature in the early years of the 1790s owed not only to the fact that it was new or original, and yet still congenial to readers of English, but also to the way in which it was so widely credited with a certain intensity or vitality, a quality foregrounded by the German label *Sturm und Drang*. Loyalist Gothic romances also defined themselves against the feminized space of romance production, as I argued at the end of the previous chapter, but whereas they humbly appealed to episodes of English history as a bulwark against 'refinement', German works more ambitiously appropriated the rhetoric of energy and vigour. Peter Teuthold's *The Necromancer: Or The Tale of the Black Forest* (1794), 'Translated from the German of Lawrence Flammenberg' and published by the Minerva Press, serves as a good example here because of the way that it defined itself against 'tiresome Love Intrigues', basing its claims to 'Novelty' on the depiction of 'mysterious Events' founded on authentic 'Facts': 'To those who are pleased with tales that "freeze the blood", and harrow up the soul', the *Analytical*'s reviewer wrote in 1794, 'the *Necromancer* will afford a delightful treat.'[13] A parallel claim was made for 'german works of fancy' in the *Analytical Review*'s notice of *Albert de Nordenshild: or the Modern Alcibiades* in October 1796, which stated that the translation's 'interesting warmth of imagination, and truth of passion' were especially welcome 'at the very period when the romantic rants of false refinement, in the majority of the modern novels of France and England, only excite a restless curiosity, which fatigues the head, without touching the heart'.[14] Probably the most famous association of German literature and 'genius' appeared in Coleridge's letter to

Southey describing his first reading of *The Robbers*. Schiller appears in this letter as a 'Convulser of the Heart' who must have written his work 'amid the yelling of Fiends', and he is said to supersede even an iconic representative of English poetic genius: 'Why have we ever called Milton sublime?'[15]

Coleridge was impressed enough by Schiller to go on to adapt *The Ghost-Seer* (as *Osorio*) and translate *Wallenstein*, as well as to dedicate a poem 'To The Author of "The Robbers"', in a footnote which he further referred to the thrilling experience of reading *The Robbers* for the first time ('a drama, the very name of which I had never before heard of: – A winter midnight – the wind high . . . !').[16] A brief examination of the critical reception of Coleridge's work in the later 1790s, however, usefully illustrates the way in which 'German' translations and imitations were seen to be increasingly suspect as the decade progressed. Some German works were already being savaged for their absurdity in the mid 1790s, especially in the Tory press, but by the end of the decade, this abuse became far more indiscriminate, as in many of the early reviews of the *Lyrical Ballads*. For the *Analytical*'s reviewer in 1798, Coleridge's 'Rime of the ancyent Marinere', for example, had 'more of the extravagance of a mad german poet, than of the simplicity of our ancient ballad writers', while for Robert Southey in the *Critical Review* in the same year, the 'Rime' was 'a Dutch attempt at German sublimity'.[17] Significantly, Charles Lamb (in a letter to Southey) was only able to defend Coleridge's 'Rime' by claiming it to be a 'native' rather than a foreign work ('a right English attempt, and a successful one, to dethrone German sublimity'), just as Francis Jeffrey sought to emphasize in a letter of 1799 that the poem – in terms of 'true poetical horror' and 'new images' – actually superseded 'all the German ballads and tragedies'.[18]

The first reviews of the 'Rime' in the late 1790s point to a much more general phenomenon, as a result, whereby translations or imitations of 'German' works (except perhaps ballads grounded in oral tradition) were increasingly associated with a regressive immaturity or, more seriously, an energy beyond containment. According to F. W. Stokoe, both the *Monthly Review* and – to a lesser extent – the *Analytical Review* continued their discriminating coverage of German literature until at least 1800, under the influence of the Norwich dissenting circle of William Taylor and Henry Crabb Robinson, an associate of Words-worth and Coleridge.[19] Writers such as Taylor and Robinson became increasingly marginalized towards the end of the decade, however, and even Taylor predicted the impending 'sunset of German literature', claiming, in a letter to Southey in December 1798, that Germany would assume a role as 'the Alexandria which is to re-barbarize the intellect of French Rome, and, through it, all of Europe'.[20] By the late 1790s, it is fair to say that the reputation for boldness had all but given way to a virtual consensus about the pernicious effects of German literature and its imitators, testimony in part at least to the impact of the *Anti-Jacobin Review*, founded in 1797 by George Canning. Lockhart's *Memoirs of the Life of Sir Walter Scott* (1837–8), for example, claimed that Scott's 1798 translation of Goethe's *Götz von Berlichingen* had been 'condemned to oblivion, through the unsparing ridicule showered on whatever bore the name of German play, by the inimitable caricature of *The Rovers*'.[21] While it would be inaccurate to ascribe too much impact to a single source, the parodies published by the *Anti-Jacobin* (and particularly *The Rovers; or, The Double Arrangement*, which appeared in June 1798) very powerfully equated German literature with an excess both of sentiment and rationality, at the same time as they wilfully ignored the cultural context and the nationalist agenda of the *Sturm und Drang* movement.[22] The association of formal freedoms and political 'licence' is evident in the Prologue to *The Rovers*, for example, when it describes the methods of the author, 'Mr. Higgins':

> To-night our Bard, who scorns pedantic rules,
> His plot has borrow'd from the German schools;
> – The German schools – where no dull maxims bind
> The bold expansion of the electric mind.
> Fix'd to no period, circled by no space,
> He leaps the flaming bounds of time and place.[23]

On one level, *The Rovers* stood as a travesty of a particular play widely seen to have a democratic tendency (Schiller's *The Robbers*), and its author(s) predictably sought to amplify the famous story about the 'copycat' incident at Fribourg, claiming that 'the whole of a German University went upon the highway' because of the play. In addition to this attack on Schiller, though, the author(s) of the play managed to cast doubts on 'The German Theatre' as a whole, implying that all German plays (and imitations) desired, in the words of Mr Higgins, 'to substitute in lieu of a sober contentment, and regular discharge of the duties incident to each man's particular situation, a wild desire of indefinable latitude and extravagance'.[24]

Towards the end of the 1790s German works became guilty by association, not just with the democratic reputation of Schiller and the licentious one of the more prominent Kotzebue, but also with the sinister workings of Illuminism. Allied to the influence of the *Anti-Jacobin*, another major factor contributing to the attacks on German literature was the popularization of conspiracy theories about the role of Freemasons and rationalists in attempting to bring down established governments. As David Simpson has pointed out, Burke had written as early as 1791, in his 'Thoughts on French Affairs', about the dangerous workings of 'Illuminatenorden and Freemasons' in Saxony, and their connections with the Revolution in France.[25] Though the Illuminati, a small group of freethinkers with masonic affiliations, remained together for only ten years before they were banned by the Bavarian authorities, they had by the late 1790s been demonized in several prominent works for their sinister role in the generation of Jacobinism, and for their suspected influence in other European countries. The most famous of these works, the Abbé Barruel's *Memoirs Illustrating the History of Jacobinism* (1797), was followed in the same year by John Robison's *Proofs of a Conspiracy against All the Religions and Governments of Europe, Carried on in the Secret Meetings of Free Masons, Illuminati and Reading Societies*. Robison's 'special contribution', according to Simpson again, 'was to play up the rhetoric of sexual revolution', and it is fair to say that his work together with Barruel's (and the numerous reprints and abridgements which they spawned) made readers newly sensitive to the dangers of things German, and aware of more and more forms of immorality and covert revolutionary 'propaganda'.[26]

In reviews of German literature in the late 1790s, as a result, a new, almost hysterical, tone was consistently apparent for the first time, particularly in criticism of German drama and the prolific Kotzebue. In the preface to her 1798 adaptation of Kotzebue's *Child of Love*, commonly known as *Lovers' Vows* (and famous for its role in Jane Austen's *Mansfield Park*), Elizabeth Inchbald was scrupulously careful to explain that because of her 'profound respect for the judgment of a British audience', the manners of the characters in the play were 'adapted to the English rather than to the German taste'.[27] Despite this extreme caution, however, the play was still seized upon by the *Anti-Jacobin*'s reviewer in June 1799 as a contagion, and as 'part of a system adopted by the new philosophy, . . . assiduously cultivated in every possible way, so as to loosen those bonds which have hitherto successfully held society together'. The article went on in a tone of heightened invective to denounce the way that 'Shakespeare, Otway, Rowe, and all those ornaments of my native country' were being 'thrust aside', in order 'to make way for the filthy effusions of this German dunce!', and the reviewer finished by issuing the kind of imperative familiar from the previous chapter on Loyalist Gothic: 'Forbid it Britons! – forbid it common sense!'[28]

A comparable opposition between national literary traditions was set up by Jane West in the preface to her *Poems and Plays*, also published in 1799: though many 'products of our native stage' were said to be 'ridiculous', their impact was still negligible in relation to the influence of 'the imported merchandize' from Germany, with its blasphemous and levelling tendencies.[29] The satirical poem 'The Shade of Alexander Pope on the Banks of the Thames' (1799), probably written by T. J. Mathias, similarly described the degeneration of English literature at the hands of an army of translators representing (even if they did not know it) the 'German school'.[30] What is particularly important about this kind of commentary is the way in which it set out to contradict the congenial reputation of English and German literature that had been current in the 1780s and early 1790s – and that was to be popular again, especially among conservatives, some ten to fifteen years after the hysteria about German influence-as-infection had died down. The obvious anxiety of many of the attacks on German literature was surely amplified by this perceived need to dissociate what was 'English' (or, as in the work of the Loyalist Gothic writers, 'Old English') from what was 'German'. Where Wordsworth and Coleridge were both to admit twenty years later that the most renowned German writers had first been inspired by English examples,[31] it is difficult to find anyone willing to countenance such interconnection in the last years of the 1790s or the early 1800s. 'Mauritius Moonshine' in 'More Wonders! An Heroic Epistle to M. G. Lewis. Esq. M.P.' (1801), for example, stated the matter clearly in declaring his concern to defend 'the violated decency of national taste' against 'arbitrary invasion', and in representing Lewis's recourse to 'the frenzy of a foreign race' as a move which contaminated the purity of the 'ancient Song', dependent upon oral tradition, that Thomas Percy had assembled in his 'pious *Reliques*'.[32] Many writers similarly repeated the terms of Lamb's defence of Coleridge, quoted earlier, and echoed the insistence of T. J. Mathias in *The Pursuits of Literature*: 'No German nonsense sways my English heart, / Unus'd at ghosts and rattling bones to start.'[33]

The evident interconnection of England (rather than Britain) and Germany was certainly less controversial in the fields of national and constitutional history, and as Samuel Kliger's *The Goths in England* has demonstrated, it was an eighteenth-century ideological commonplace to claim that English Freedom had its roots 'in the forests of Germany'. Despite the fact that such myths of descent were increasingly being appropriated for the cause of loyalism, as I argued in the previous chapter, some conservative critics of German literature were also ready for strategic reasons to deny *any* ideas of a connection between the English experience and a Gothic or German heritage.

This denial was particularly clear in William Preston's 'Reflections on the Peculiarities of Style and Manner in the late German Writers' (1801), a polemic which encapsulated all of the different objections made about German literature in this period. Though Preston's work shared the defensiveness of the loyalist call to arms familiar from the last chapter, it eschewed the recourse to an empowering Gothic or German heritage, and instead cast the German works which threatened 'the republic of letters' as revolutionary *Gothic* barbarians, arriving in 'invading swarms from the northern hive'.[34] The basis of this frenzied attack was Preston's objection both to the 'absurdity' of German works, and to their perceived immorality (though Preston made little reference to actual works, and more candid than most writers in this period, admitted that he could not read German). Like nearly all of the anti-German polemics from the late 1790s onwards, Preston's indiscriminately attacked 'writers of the German school' – nearly always dramatists – both for their pandering to the 'prevailing malady of the times', sentiment, and for their childishly excessive appeal to 'horror', long since outgrown by the English writers, notably Shakespeare, whose original but dated models they were said to have copied.[35] In common with the *Anti-Jacobin*'s various parodies, Preston's work also claimed that all German plays, in particular, tended 'to make men dissatisfied with the existing order of things, the restraints of law, the coercion of civil governments, the distinction of ranks in society, the unequal distribution of property, and with the dispensations of Providence itself'.[36] Just as German works were said to draw upon illusory ideas of liberty, so too were they guilty by association with the false ideas of 'genius' defined by a jacobinized ('deluded' and 'pretentious') natural philosophy – hence the emphasis placed on Germany being the home of the first alchemists, as well as of the Illuminati.[37]

Perhaps the problem given most weight by Preston, however, was simply the great popularity of German literature: at least 27 translations or adaptations of Kotzebue's works appeared in 1799 alone.[38] While it was an article of faith for Preston that 'literature cannot make a more valuable present to the world, than views of life and manners drawn with a faithful and correct hand', he all but admitted that he was fighting a losing battle when he lamented 'the small disposition towards the encouragement of works of poetical genius and imagination, which is now but too observable'.[39] Where works such as *The Robbers* had been praised for their energy and vigour only a decade previously, German works were characterized by Preston in antithetical terms, and deemed to be corrosive of national virtue. What seemed to animate Preston most was the apparent fact that German writers pandered to false taste by responding to the demands of the marketplace. 'A Fair, or open market, for the sale of books', in fact, was 'a phenomenon peculiar to *Germany*' and writers were consequently seen to be more anxious 'to produce the fruits, which the present call of the market requires, than those, which are the free and natural growth of their talents'. This open market, Preston argued, occasioned 'a disgraceful catching at unworthy and improper subjects, merely because they are the topics of fashionable tattle, and popular rumour', and it led to 'a greater solicitude, to swell the quantity, than to improve the quality of literary productions'.[40] The 'excess' which deformed the productions of 'the German school' was ultimately traced back by Preston, as a result, to the market for literature and the demands it made for 'Novelty – Novelty – Surprise – Surprise', which in turn encouraged 'a straining at something superlative, an attempt to surpass nature, that produces only contorsion and grimace'.[41] Like Wordsworth's famous attack on 'sickly and stupid German tragedies' and 'frantic novels' in the preface to the *Lyrical Ballads*, therefore, Preston's near-hysteria was in part at least a symptom of anxiety about the commercialization of literature and its reduction to a debased form of stimulus, beyond discipline or legislation.[42]

A footnote to the satirical poem *The Age* (1810) further connected Germany with a market economy of literature in referring to the famous book fair at Frankfurt, 'during the continuance of which six thousand new volumes, mostly from the pens of continental novelists, are exposed for sale', just as Sharon Turner's *Prolusions on the Present Greatness of Britain* (1819) followed Preston's 'Reflections' in tracing back the prominence of 'German Endriagos' to 'Our rage for novelty':

> Montorios, Bertrams, Christabels delight:
> Ambrosios, sorcerers, bravos, fiends affright
> As if a bedlam were the general school,
> Or Bacchus' orgies gave the poet rule.[43]

In a number of commentaries, as a result, it is very difficult now to separate the problem that critics had with the content of particular plays and romances from the widespread concern about the spread of literacy, the growth of an undisciplined reading public, and the functioning of the book trade as a whole. Returning to the question posed at the outset about the subversive aura of the Gothic romance, then, it is fair to say that while many works were attacked for their formulaic depiction of supernatural agency, as in the first quotation at the head of this chapter, such criticism was always informed by larger concerns about the production and reception of escapist fiction in general. This claim can be illustrated by looking at reactions to some of the works published by William Lane's Minerva Press, the most famous of the commercial publishers of prose fiction in the period. 'So closely identified with cheap fiction was the famous publishing house in Leadenhall Street', Dorothy Blakey wrote in 1939, 'that to nineteenth-century critics the name Minerva meant little more than a convenient epithet of contempt.'[44] Lane presented himself as a patriot and paraded the fact, as in his advertisement 'A Tale Addressed to the Novel Readers of the Present Times' (1795), that the works he published all served the cause of '*Wisdom, Virtue, and Honour*'.[45] Lane was far better known, however, as an entrepreneur, and specifically as a dealer in circulating-library franchises, and it was this fact which undoubtedly contributed to the ill-repute of his press. Rather than being attacked individually for their immorality ('apart from *Horrid Mysteries*', Coral Ann Howells has stated, 'the few "fleshly" novels produced in this period were not published by Lane'),[46] the works published by the Minerva Press provided a focus for concern about perceived changes in the social composition of the reading public. Even though the novels published by Lane were themselves unremarkable and, with very few exceptions, politically conservative, what was seen to be problematic about so many of them was their relationship with, and acknowledgement of, popular demand. Collectively characterized in terms of uncontrollable 'deluges' or 'swarms', Minerva novels were widely 'relegated to the servile sphere of trade and commerce', as Ina Ferris has put it, assuming 'a discursive promiscuity and fertility that threatened to overwhelm the literary sphere'.[47]

All publishers and most authors were obviously concerned to sell books at this time, but the novels published by a press such as Lane's – whether marketed by their authors or by Lane himself – displayed a particularly acute form of commercial awareness. *The Castle of Wolfen-*

bach (1793) and *The Mysterious Warning* (1796) by Eliza Parsons, for example, both subtitled themselves as 'A German Story' in order to exploit the cachet of the label, and they did this even though they had no apparent connection with any German source. Minerva titles exploited other resonant terms ('Castle', 'Abbey', 'Ghost', 'Spectre'), in addition, and all Minerva works carried the name of the press (at least) in Gothic script on their title pages: the edition of *Horrid Mysteries* went much further and depicted, as Blakey describes, 'a head with hair erect and staring eyes, above an ornament in which a crown, a dagger, a pair of fetters, and what seems to be a flaming torch may be distinguished'.[48] Lane was involved in both legitimate and corrupt forms of promotion, using available space in the fly-leaves of novels to advertise other works available from the press, as well as supplying old works with different title-pages so that they could be passed off as new (a practice condemned by the name of 'bookmaking'). Despite their sameness for the modern reader, therefore, many 'Gothic' (and 'German') novels and romances were obviously written and marketed in order to supply a demand for fictional novelty. The prolific Francis Lathom, for example, subtitled his work *The Midnight Bell* (1798) as 'A German Story', but by the time of *The Impenetrable Secret, Find it Out!* (1805), he played a different card and lamented the evil caused by 'the translations which have been made from the works of some of our corrupt neighbours'.[49] Lathom's preface to *Mystery* (1800) stated that 'nothing is allowed to please generally which does not excite surprise or horror', and consequently appealed to 'those powerful assistants – novelty and mystery'; in the preface to his *Human Beings* (1807), however, Lathom declared that since 'an equal proportion' of novel readers still retained 'a relish for what is natural and consistent', he was ready to oblige them in 'quitting the gloomy and terrific tracks of a Radcliffe for the more lively walks of a Burney or Robinson'.[50] Such acknowledgement of popular demand was precisely the reason why so many fictions in the period were condemned so unreservedly. Terror-fiction was often the subject of recipe-satires which gave the formula for modern romance-writing, and this kind of criticism was frequently couched in terms of a genial reproach to writers and their readers: 'Are the duties of life so changed, that all the instruction necessary is for a young person to walk at night upon the battlements of an old castle, to creep hands and feet along a narrow passage, and meet the devil at the end of it?' At the same time, though, such criticism nearly always betrayed the agenda that informed its ostensibly affectionate satire, so often rehearsing a reactionary polemic against the reading of fiction by women or the lower classes: 'Can our young ladies be taught nothing more necessary in life, than to sleep in a dungeon with venomous reptiles, walk through a ward with assassins, and carry bloody daggers in their pockets, instead of pin-cushions and needle-books[?]'[51]

Where 'German' works were seen to be immoral by association in the late 1790s, the 'Gothic' romances published by a press such as William Lane's generated anxiety primarily because of their quantity, their self-proclaimed commodity status, and – ultimately – their popularity. The popularity of Minerva fictions, in turn, led to widespread concern about the times and places in which these works were read: whereas 'high-cultural production' in this period 'invites the language of "reception"', the symbolic giving and receiving of texts between great writers and singular, sensitive readers', as Jon Klancher has argued, 'mass-cultural production yields up the harsher vocabulary of "consumption", supply and demand among innumerable writers and vast, faceless audiences'.[52] It is difficult to find any suggestion that Minerva novels themselves were morally suspect, apart from perhaps a few of the German translations such as *Horrid Mysteries*, but they were implicitly connected with a destabilizing form of modernity which provided the conditions in which social upheaval might occur (just as the Waverley novels were later connected by Thomas Carlyle with a state of 'DEMOCRACY', in which printing had become as promiscuous as 'talk').[53] Thomas Trotter's *A View of the Nervous Temperament* (1807), for example, examined reading within a quasi-medical discourse of addiction: the widespread reading of 'love-sick trash' and the popularity of 'loose German plays', he claimed, were palpable 'causes of nervous diseases', especially among women, and these diseases were themselves symptomatic of a dangerous state of 'riches and high living', steadily widening its circle until the time when 'polished society may be said to bring on its own *dotage,* and to dig its own *grave!*'[54] As Wordsworth famously complained, in a similarly apocalyptic vein, the canon of English literature was being superseded and its place taken by works designed to meet the 'degrading thirst after outrageous stimulation' of desensitized city dwellers – the rhetoric of genius was becoming debased, and members of a discriminating cultural elite were being threatened by the workings of mere fashion.[55] Too many works of fiction were being published for them all to be safely vetted by the critical establishment: 'our shelves are groaning with the weight of novels which demand a hearing', as the *British Critic* wrote in 1797, but 'before we can disengage ourselves from the perusal of more important matter, in order to deliberate upon their respective merits, half the number have done their duty at the Circulating Libraries'.[56]

Even though a genuine mass market for the novel still did not exist in the early nineteenth century, critics such as 'The Projector' in the *Gentleman's Magazine* in October 1808, for example, emphasized the contrast between the demand for novels at the time of writing, and the demand 'thirty or forty years ago'.[57] Thirty or forty years previously, the Projector claimed, 'about a dozen Novels was the quantity usually published per *annum*' and 'such was the state of our boarding-schools and our circulating libraries, that it was found adequate to the consumption of the country'. Novelists at that time wrote because of an 'inclination', without looking to make a name or make money, and consequently 'there could be no pretence for crudities, or errors of taste; nor did it appear that any person's materials were exhausted by overworking'. This comfortable economy was contrasted by the Projector with the state of affairs resulting from 'an increased demand'. A 'degeneration' in quality accompanied the apparent commercialization of novel-writing in this period, because 'slight or clumsy imitations' flooded the market as writers and publishers made a bid for quick profits. This new competitiveness among writers arose in conjunction with the emergence in the same period of the general public's 'love of variety', and 'the demand for Novels increased so much, that in the space of fifty years above three thousand of them passed from the booksellers' to the trunkmakers' shops with astonishing rapidity'.[58] Despite their numbers, though, these novels were in fact characterized by their sameness and the imprint of large-scale manufacturing which they bore. Not only did the Projector bemoan the proximity of 'Novel-Factors' and traders in other businesses, then, ('as many tricks have been played with title-pages in one market as with samples in another'), but he concluded that the 'multiplication' of novels had all but bankrupted the form.[59] Some consolation for all 'arbiters of merit' was the prospect of readers becoming bored with 'the miseries of multiplication' and turning their attention elsewhere, and such a note of optimism clearly distinguishes 'The Projector' from William Preston.[60] What characterized the work of both of them, nonetheless, was their profound anxiety about the stability of literature as an economy or system, an anxiety which was clearly informed by much larger concerns about (for example) the growth in literacy and the policing of readers, especially women. Though the licentious 'content' of certain works did provoke critical reaction, as I will argue was the case with *The Monk*, it is always hard to separate the condemnation of immorality from the unease about who precisely was doing the reading, and under what circumstances. The reception of Lewis's work indeed – as I will go on to claim in the second half of this chapter – underlines the importance of reconnecting any explanatory account of the Gothic romance with the history of the novel and the romance in the eighteenth century, since what was largely at stake in the negative reviews of *The Monk*, especially, was the regulation of cultural production itself.

II

After the focus of previous chapters on aristocratic diversion and loyalist political discourse, the preceding discussion of the impact of German literature and the reception of escapist fiction in the 1790s provides another useful point of departure for examining the diverse affiliations of the so-called Gothic romance. In the rest of this chapter, I want to use this contextual framework firstly in order to consider how a key work such as *The Monk* differed from almost anything written by other canonical 'Gothic' writers, and then to explain why Lewis's romance generated the controversy that it did. *The Monk*, according to André Parreaux, was the work which brought English readers 'nearer to the school of the *Sturm und Drang* than any previous book had done',[61] and a discussion of its use of mainly German sources further illuminates the contested status of romance in the 1790s and early 1800s (along with the ambiguous role of German literature itself, as both creative inspiration and contagious disease). Lewis accentuated the sensationalism of his source materials, and supplied a cynical commentary of his own, thereby making *The Monk* a licentious yet also innovative work by the standards of contemporary criticism. What was primarily responsible for the scandal that surrounded *The Monk*, however, was not simply its content alone but also its 'context' of production, since it was ultimately condemned – like so many of the novels and romances published by the Minerva Press – as a result of the way that it circulated so promiscuously among a large and diverse readership. Though the reception of *The Monk* provides a case study of the reasons why some Gothic romances were held to be so dangerous, I will go on to emphasize that it was nonetheless an atypical work which found few imitators. Lewis arguably recognized the politically sensitive nature of literary popularity in the 1790s, and in later works such as *The Castle Spectre* (1797), as I will argue, he went on to maintain the upstart reputation he had gained with *The Monk*, baiting critics and reviewers by knowingly appealing to popular

demand. Briefly referring to early-nineteenth-century works by Charlotte Dacre, P. B. Shelley, and Charles Maturin, this chapter will close
by considering the grounds for the subversive reputation which the
genre still holds.

Like William Beckford in his *Popular Tales of the Germans*, referred to in
the previous section, Lewis consistently rejected the rigorous presentation of source material within an antiquarian framework or a folklorist
narrative of oral descent, favouring instead, in all of his work, the appeal
to an aura of novelty and wildness. Though German ballads were
perhaps more admissible to critics than German plays or romances in
the late 1790s and early 1800s, Lewis made it clear that his own
contributions to the anthology *Tales of Wonder* (1801) were substantially
invented by himself, and he made no concession either to the
purification of the ballad form with which Wordsworth was concerned,
or to the historically minded annotation associated with Scott. In reply
to Scott's offer to provide for the anthology tales 'which a long
Residence in the wildest part of the South of Scotland enabled me to
collect from Tradition', for example, Lewis merely stipulated that 'a
Ghost or a Witch' was 'a sine-qua-non ingredient in all the dishes, of
which I mean to compose my hobgoblin repast'.[62] *The Monk*, in common
with Lewis's later romances, *The Bravo of Venice* (1805) and *Feudal Tyrants*
(1806), similarly drew attention to the liberties it took with its diverse
sources, and its prefatory advertisement referred to further inevitable
'plagiarisms' of which the author was 'at present totally unconscious'.[63]
In her study of the influence of German literature on Lewis and
Maturin, Syndy Conger has demonstrated that *The Monk* made use of a
series of German works, besides the ones listed, which Lewis probably
came across for the first time during his residence at Weimar in the early
1790s. Conger credits Lewis as being the first writer to move away from
the property plot and combine 'Gothic fiction and the Faust legend',
and she further detects the impact of Herder's folk songs, Bürger's
ballads, and Schiller's *The Ghost-Seer*, as well as a range of less famous
works, sections of which were incorporated almost 'word for word'.[64]
Where 'Der Wassermann' clearly served a 'nativist' agenda in the
context of Herder's collection of 1778–9, for example, Lewis's loose
translation of the ballad (as 'The Water-King', appearing in *The Monk*
and, later, the *Tales of Wonder*) along with his adaptation of Bürger's
'Lenore' (as 'Alonzo the Brave, and Fair Imogine', also appearing in *The
Monk*) served to 'reduce the folk songs to the level of bizarre sexual
fantasies'.[65] 'Alonzo', for example, depicts the Fair Imogine being

hounded at her marriage feast, and eventually carried off, by the suitor she has betrayed – an armed knight who lifts his vizor to reveal a 'Skeleton's head':

> All present then uttered a terrified shout;
>   All turned with disgust from the scene.
> The worms, They crept in, and the worms, They crept out,
> And sported his eyes and his temples about,
>   While the Spectre addressed Imogine. (315)

If Lewis dealt in German materials because of the regard for boldness or daring which he shared with the translators and imitators described in the previous section, he also had recourse to German sources, it seems, as a means of 'supplementing' the contemporary romance and making a name for himself by his defiance of the legitimizing conventions, described above, which were observed by writers such as Wordsworth and Scott. Lewis's method was assimilative and wilfully heterogeneous, making *The Monk* in consequence a very difficult work to classify – its content, in the words of Elizabeth Napier, 'a sort of "mixed grill" of prose, poetry, and miscellaneous incident'.[66] *The Monk* opens with a long scene in the Church of the Capuchins reminiscent of a satire or comedy of manners, and the Ambrosio/Matilda plot, for which the work is most famous, is interwoven with a more familiar romance plot concerning the frustrated courtship of Agnes and Raymond, itself punctuated by the embedded 'History of Don Raymond', containing the episode at the wood-cutter's cottage in the forest of Lindenberg where Raymond escapes from a band of robbers. *The Monk* depicts the 'terrific' figures of the Bleeding Nun, the Wandering Jew, and Satan, for example, but it treats supernatural agency in an equivocal fashion, as I will argue in more detail later, since it also allows characters such as Agnes and Don Lorenzo to reflect on 'the influence of superstition and the weakness of human reason' (153). Lewis's work lacks a reliable or trustworthy narratorial discourse to frame this heterogeneity for the reader, and *The Monk* is marked throughout, instead, by tonal ambiguity. While most contemporary 'Gothic' romances (and the majority of the works published by the Minerva Press) generally dealt with issues of legitimacy and property, as I argued in the previous chapter, *The Monk* eschewed the Loyalist Gothic formula, and followed instead the example of works such as *The Castle of Otranto* and *Vathek* in depicting the temptation faced by an overreaching protagonist.[67]

The heterogeneity of *The Monk* was informed by Lewis's desire both to define his work against current romance paradigms and to establish his own profile, as a new writer, within the literary field. Like William Beckford, author of contemptuous satires such as *Modern Novel Writing* (1796) and *Azemia* (1797), Lewis sought to distance himself from the 'feminine' novel of sentiment, beginning his writing career with the fragment, 'The Effusions of Sensibility: or Letters from Lady Honorina Harrow-heart to Miss Sophonisba Simper – a Pathetic Novel in the Modern Taste. Being the First Literary Attempt of a Young Lady of Tender Feelings' (1791). An antagonistic relation with the language of feeling went on to inform almost everything Lewis wrote since, as Jacqueline Howard has recently argued, 'the positive, visionary, and creative aspects of aesthetic sensibility' stressed by Radcliffe had to be exorcized before Lewis could aspire to a properly masculine ideal of authorship: 'an ideal of the author as unconventional, eccentric, extreme – a risk-taker prepared to shock the complacency of respectable elders in order to gain a reputation for genius'.[68] Written mostly during Lewis's time at the British Embassy in The Hague, where he repeatedly complained of boredom and ennui, *The Monk* can perhaps best be characterized as a work of 'rebellious adolescence'.[69] Lewis sought 'to give the impression of youth, boldness, unconventionality, and extraordinary energy' (claiming in a letter to have written *The Monk* in only ten weeks) *and* he tried to distance himself and his work from the language of sentiment and the 'structural' demands of romance closure: the marriage of Raymond and Agnes therefore takes place in the penultimate, rather than the final, chapter.[70] Though the romance occupied only a minor position in the unofficial hierarchy of genres – 'the praise which a romance can claim', according to Coleridge's review of *The Monk*, 'is simply that of having given pleasure during its perusal' – Lewis sought to complicate its status as a form of escapist fiction, via the extravagance of his appeals to the supernatural (as I will argue later), and via his cynical presentation of the persecuted heroine.[71]

Numerous examples could be given of the way that Lewis rewrote Radcliffean romance: where, for example, *Udolpho* simply hints at the apparently dubious past of Emily's father, St Aubert, *The Monk* – in the words of Ian Duncan – 'zealously literaliz[es] the family-plot that Radcliffe's narrative so delicately and elaborately invokes, suspends and conjures away'.[72] It is particularly instructive to contrast *The Monk's* knowing narratorial tone, and its misogynistic commentary on characters like Antonia and Leonella, with the presentation of the heroine in Radcliffean romance. The narrator of *The Monk*, like Fielding in *Shamela*, for example, continually implies that he has access to 'common sense', or to the reality beyond manifest appearances, and it is this knowledge which he uses to dignify the interjections which appear throughout the work: 'Do not encourage the idea', the reader is warned in the opening paragraph, 'that the Crowd [at the Church of the Capuchins] was assembled either from motives of piety or thirst of information' – 'The Women came to show themselves, the Men to see the Women' (7). Leonella, Antonia's aunt, is presented as a grotesque, and made to seem so deluded as to expect to be 'surrounded by Admirers' (34): after the cavalier Don Christoval has grudgingly kissed her 'leathern paw', he complains that he 'shall smell of garlick for this month to come' and 'be taken for a walking Omelet, or some large Onion running to seed!' (24). Antonia, by contrast, is said to be 'wise enough to hold her tongue', but this concession is followed up by a predictable disclaimer: 'as this is the only instance known of a woman's ever having done so, it was judged worthy to be recorded here' (34).

The innocence of Antonia is repeatedly ironized, indeed, as when it is implied that she is fatally attracted to the man who eventually rapes her: at the Church, for example, 'no other of the Spectators felt such violent sensations as did the young Antonia', and 'the sound of his voice seemed to penetrate into her very soul' (18). Imagining herself on 'the bed of death', after having been drugged by Ambrosio, Antonia tells the Monk that 'We shall one day meet in heaven' (341). Shortly afterwards, however, in a scene which parodies *Romeo and Juliet*, 'the sleeping beauty' is transported to the 'Sepulchre' beneath the Abbey ('Love's bower', as Ambrosio styles it, p. 381) where she is raped. The reader, meanwhile, is allowed the role of voyeur, since – in the words of Elizabeth Napier – Lewis 'cunningly infuses Ambrosio's vocabulary into the description of Antonia', most notably in the pornographic description of Ambrosio watching Antonia undress in the mirror provided by Matilda.[73] Antonia intermittently comes across as a Radcliffean heroine in the way that she recites poetry and is said to enjoy the 'calm repose' of an easy conscience:

> Good Angels, take my thanks, that still
> The snares of vice I view with scorn;
> Thanks, that to-night as free from ill
> I sleep, as when I woke at morn. (253)

Her subsequent fate, however, emphasizes all the more the way that she is toyed with by Lewis's work. Where Radcliffe arguably made temporary concessions to a Burkean aesthetic of beauty in distress, Lewis accentuated the passivity of his heroine in depicting the commission of what Ambrosio refers to as 'a crime, blacker than yet the world ever witnessed!' (243). Taking 'the positive associations of freedom which Radcliffe had developed for sublime landscapes and the mountainous or wooded setting of the ancestral Gothic home', Jacqueline Howard has stated, Lewis 'concentrate[d] on their inversion in the claustrophobic terrors of sublime ecclesiastical architecture'.[74] Lewis took the persecution of his innocent heroine to an extreme, telling the reader that 'Antonia was born under an unlucky star' (310), before describing her eventual rape and murder amid the 'rotting bones' and 'putrid half-corrupted Bodies' of the Abbey's dungeons (379).

Given its recourse to a series of common-sense myths and stereotypes, along the lines of the statement that 'possession, which cloys Man, only increases the affection of Woman' (235), or that 'Men have died, and worms have eat them, but not for Love!' (399), *The Monk* can usefully be read as a 'homosocial' work, written for a leisured male audience; it is because of this quality, surely, that John Thorpe is made such a fan of the book in *Northanger Abbey*. Most obviously, perhaps, *The Monk* exceeded other contemporary fictions – and simultaneously appealed to educated, leisured readers – in its extravagant treatment of the supernatural. On the one hand, *The Monk* regularly parodies popular credulity, as when Agnes, disguised as the Bleeding Nun, attempts to return to the Castle of Lindenberg after the failure of her elopement with Raymond, and Don Gaston (Agnes's father) contends that 'for a ghost to knock for admittance was a proceeding till then unwitnessed' (164). On the other hand, however, *The Monk* literalizes the figure of Satan (in addition to its presentation of the Bleeding Nun and the Wandering Jew), and consequently severs the connection foregrounded by *The Castle of Otranto* and the Loyalist Gothic romance between supernatural phenomena and the workings of providence or justice. In an age when, as the Marquis de Sade famously claimed, 'everything seem[ed] already to have been written', and the realities of the French Revolution appeared to exceed anything that contemporary fiction could offer, it became necessary, in order 'to compose works of interest', to 'call upon the aid of hell itself' – and this was of course what Lewis literally did, making *The Monk*, in de Sade's terms, 'superior in all respects to the strange flights of Mrs. Radcliffe's brilliant imagination'.[75] Rather than offer the reader a (Radcliffean) narrative of suspense, Lewis's work provided what Coleridge referred to as a series of '*physical* wonders', culminating in the scene in the final chapter where Ambrosio signs the 'fatal contract' and meets his death. Instead of offering the reader the tantalizing suggestion of 'terror', as Radcliffe was praised for doing, Lewis provided scenes of 'naked horror'.[76]

Despite the well-known outrage which *The Monk* inspired, a surprisingly large number of critics and reviewers concurred with de Sade and defended the boldness of Lewis's enterprise. Although Radcliffe was not mentioned in the *Analytical*'s coverage of *The Monk* in October 1796, her example was implicitly downgraded in the review's praise of *The Monk* for 'not attempting to account for supernatural appearances in a natural way'. What is particularly interesting about this defence of *The Monk* is the way that its author so obviously relished the temptation of Ambrosio. Overlooking the homosexual connotation of the cross-dressing motif by which Matilda is disguised as Rosario, the *Analytical*'s review openly assumed *The Monk*'s implied reader to be male: 'the gradual discovery of Matilda's sex and person . . . is very finely conceived and truly picturesque; indeed the whole temptation is so artfully contrived, that a man, it should seem, were he made as other men are, would deserve to be d--ned who could resist even devilish spells, conducted with such address and assuming such a heavenly form'.[77] Ambrosio was seen by many readers to be a character who inspired sympathy, indeed, since his reaction to temptation was depicted as only natural for someone 'in the full vigour of manhood', and since he was presented as a product of his 'monastic fetters' (90): his 'spirit' had been broken in his youth and his mind 'terrified' by 'the horrors [of] Superstition', the reader is told, whereas 'had his Youth been passed in the world, He would have shown himself possessed of many brilliant and manly qualities' (236). While the treacherous Matilda (like the wicked Prioress) was demonized by the work's reviewers simply as a representative of evil or original sin, therefore, *The Monk* nonetheless provides Ambrosio with a context which partly explains his actions – and many critics were, in any case, ready to defend him as the almost helpless victim of feminine wiles.

Defences of *The Monk* appealed both to paradigms of boldness and genius and to mystifyingly 'realistic' versions of human nature. The author of 'An Apology for the Monk' in the *Monthly Mirror* of April 1797, for example, signed himself as 'A Friend to Genius', just as Thomas Dutton's poem 'The Literary Census' (1798) considered *The Monk* to be a work bearing 'the stamp and incontrovertible evidence of transcendent genius', standing apart from the 'wild and revolting extravagances' of

the 'innumerable horde of romance scribblers', imitators of Ann Radcliffe.[78] Striking a more cynical tone, the anonymous 'Epistle in Rhyme,
to M. G. Lewis, Esq' written in 1798 invoked the argument used
elsewhere by de Sade, in underlining the supposed fidelity to nature of
The Monk's libertinism:

Mr L. should have recollected that we live in an age which is extremely nice in
the choice of words at least; and for *that* which he has most unwarrantably stiled
lust (to the great offence of all well-disposed persons) every circulating library
would have afforded him a thousand gentle expressions, such as *amiable weakness, exquisite sensibility*, &c. &c. This, with a due regard to the maxim of the
courtly preacher, 'who never mentions hell to ears polite', would have ensured
his book an avowed reception with readers of the most scrupulous delicacy, and
an ostensible station even in the boudoir of devotees.[79]

This defence of *The Monk* usefully represents the way in which a certain
group of readers endorsed Lewis's self-definition against a feminized
notion of romance, and affiliated his work with a largely French
tradition of 'philosophical' pornography (as well as with the German
'wildness' described earlier on).[80] Though it is almost impossible to
determine to what extent such writers were attempting to rationalize a
sense of illicit pleasure, what clearly united all of the supporters of Lewis
was their construction of *The Monk* as a distinctly daring, masculine
work.

The Monk must be situated in the context of the competition which
developed among certain male writers to be recognized as the foremost
innovator or risk-taker, unconstrained by critical fiat. Thomas Love
Peacock's 'An Essay on Fashionable Literature' cited *The Monk* as an
example of a work which 'will sometimes attract notice for a little space'
simply by its force of 'originality', *and* as a reminder of the ultimate
transience of such literary fame.[81] According to the *Literary Memoirs of
Living Authors of Great Britain* (1798), *The Monk* possessed 'LITERARY
MERIT', and displayed 'considerable marks of genius', but also lacked
any 'MORAL MERIT', and constituted 'an outrage against decency and
propriety'.[82] Just as Beckford later emphasized that Byron's 'Corsairs &
Don Juans' were 'milk and water Puritans compared with Barkiarokh' (a
character in the unpublished *Episodes of Vathek*),[83] so too was Lewis
obviously motivated by the desire to exceed any boundary or convention. 'To take ghosts and devils from Mr Lewis's tales is to endanger
their very existence', as the *Critical* argued in 1807, and Lewis's late
romance *Feudal Tyrants* was indeed dismissed because it failed to live up
to expectations, being 'neither larger nor finer than [anything] issued

from the pen of many a teeming maiden in the sanctuaries of the Minerva press' ('Mr Lewis's imagination has certainly been in a languishing way').[84] If Lewis's later works disappointed many readers, however, the reputation of *The Monk* for striking originality continued to be endorsed into the nineteenth century, most notably by writers such as Maturin and Scott. During the preparation of *Melmoth the Wanderer*, Maturin wrote to Scott in 1813 that he was composing what he hoped would 'out-Herod all the Herods of the German school, & get possession of the Magic lamp with all its Slaves from the Conjuror *Lewis* himself'.[85] Scott paid a similar tribute to *The Monk*'s example later on when he praised the work – 'the indelicacy of particular passages' notwithstanding – for its 'courageous' management of the 'ponderous strength' of 'supernatural machinery'.[86] Yet although a politically diverse range of critics and reviewers were attracted by *The Monk*'s boldness, it *also* inspired some of the most famous condemnation and invective in the history of literary reviewing. While the majority of reviews issued disclaimers about 'particular passages', what is particularly noticeable about the reception of *The Monk*, I will argue, is that criticism became much more zealous *after* Lewis's authorship was recognized, and when the dangers of the work's circulation were most apparent.

Several critics have claimed that *The Monk* was in part inspired by French melodramas of the early 1790s which depicted 'the Revolution as an opening up of and liberation from the claustral':[87] contemplating the abuses at the Priory of St Clare, for example, Don Lorenzo is said to have 'long observed with disapprobation and contempt the superstition, which governed Madrid's inhabitants', and 'only wished for an opportunity to free them of their monkish fetters' (345). The *European Magazine*'s review in 1797 seized upon *The Monk* as a Jacobin work because of its '*oblique attack* upon *venerable establishments*', in the same way that many other reviews in the late 1790s interpreted any satirical treatment of Catholicism as an attempt 'to render religion odious'.[88] Given the extent of the controversy about *The Monk*, however, there was surprisingly little criticism of it as an explicitly 'revolutionary' work. According to Ronald Paulson's convincing account, for example, *The Monk* offers a politically ambiguous (not to say pornographic) description of 'mob' behaviour, which provides some kind of justification for violence at the same time as it emphasizes the ease with which revenge can become uncontrollably excessive: 'Blinded by resentment, the Mob . . . sacrificed every Nun who fell into their hands' (394–5).[89] The storming of the Convent of St Clare – an account of mass action with few parallels in contemporary fiction – seems to solicit an allegorical reading, therefore, but it is nonetheless difficult to produce a consistent one, just as it is difficult to 'translate' *The Monk*'s casual anticlericalism into anything more specific than a Whiggish contempt for foreign superstition. Objections were also made about Lewis's recourse to German materials in *The Monk* and in his collection *Tales of Wonder*, yet considering the way in which nearly all 'German' translations or imitations were guilty by association in the late 1790s, few reviews made anything of *The Monk*'s use of German sources and, as I have argued, a range of critics continued to praise it as a bold or daring romance.

If most reviewers of *The Monk* acknowledged that there was something excessive about its treatment of 'venerable establishments', or its lewdness, what really amplified the condemnation of the work was the simple fact of its popularity, allied to the high profile of the author. As André Parreaux has argued, adverse criticism of *The Monk* did not really get underway until the appearance in July 1796 of the work's second edition, in which Lewis's name and rank appeared on the title-page for the first time.[90] Before Lewis's authorship was acknowledged, it was still possible for the *Monthly Mirror*, in June 1796, to refer (in just one paragraph) to *The Monk*'s skilful management of 'a German tradition', that reflected 'the highest credit on the judgment and imagination of the writer'.[91] Once the work's authorship was determined, however, it became the central focus of nearly all reviews. In the Advertisement to Part IV of *The Pursuits of Literature* in 1797, therefore, T. J. Mathias progressed from complaining about how 'our peasantry now read the *Rights of Man*' to trying to account for the phenomenon of a work with which 'nothing . . . may be compared':

A legislator in our own parliament, a member of the House of Commons of Great Britain, an elected guardian and defender of the laws, the religion, and the good manners of the country, has neither scrupled nor blushed to depict and to publish to the world the arts of lewd and systematic seduction, and to thrust upon the nation the most open and unqualified blasphemy against the very code and volume of our religion. And all this, with his name, style, and title, prefixed to the novel or romance called 'The Monk'.[92]

A very similar emphasis was evident in Coleridge's article for the *Critical Review* in 1797. Identifying *The Monk*'s recourse to German examples of 'the horrible and the preternatural', Coleridge began indeed by praising the work as 'the offspring of no common genius', and cited the 'truly terrific' figures of the Bleeding Nun, the Wandering Jew and

Ambrosio's seducer, Matilda, as evidence of 'a great vigour of fancy', and 'an imagination rich, powerful, and fervid'.[93] The review went on, though, to attack the 'libidinous minuteness' of Ambrosio's temptation and to censure the 'impiety' pervading the work, and Coleridge indicated that these defects warranted 'particular attention' because of 'the unusual success which [*The Monk*] has experienced', before closing with the disbelieving exclamation: 'Yes! the author of the Monk signs himself a legislator!'[94]

Like the very different romances published by the Minerva Press, *The Monk* ultimately provided a focus for anxieties about unlicensed reading, since as the *Monthly Review* put it in 1797, the work's 'vein of obscenity' made it 'totally unfit for general circulation' (even though it was still said to display 'the essential process of the imagination' in combining the 'beauties' from 'tributary models').[95] A contributor to the *British Critic* in 1798 found it necessary to apologize for the brevity and restraint of its first review of *The Monk*: 'had we written upon it at a later period, when its circulation was unhappily established, we should have sought the strongest words we could collect to express our disapprobation and abhorrence'.[96] An article 'On Novels and Romances' in the *Scots Magazine* in 1802 also concerned itself with the problem of undisciplined reading in imagining a scenario, akin to the one depicted by Gillray's famous satirical print, 'Tales of Wonder!', where women readers illicitly conferred in the act of reading *The Monk*:

What then would be our surprise, were we to understand that this work has been read by a young and beautiful female, on whose every feature sit modesty and virtue? We could not easily believe that the lips which seemed destined only to give utterance to the dictates of a heart, pure as the pious vestal's, would enquire of others, if they had read the Monk?

While many readers clearly found it possible to enjoy *The Monk*'s 'content', as I have argued above, the popularity or renown of the work ironically led the *Scots* reviewer to condemn *The Monk* by connecting it with the symbols of mass-produced uniformity that Lewis so clearly defined his work against: 'It is surely to be regretted, that youth should be exposed to the baneful influence of such works – works which these valuable repositories, circulating libraries, disseminate with unceasing industry.'[97]

As is well known, Lewis himself censored the fourth edition of *The Monk* in 1798, probably in response to some of the threats of legal action which followed the attacks of Mathias and Coleridge. This edition found synonyms for words like 'lust' and 'desire', as the 'Epistle in Rhyme' complained, and it also deleted passages such as those which dealt with Ambrosio's supposed ignorance of the difference between man and woman, his sexual awakening and seduction by Matilda, and his glimpses of Antonia in the magic mirror. Despite this apparent compliance on Lewis's part, though, his private pleas of innocence remained distinctly tongue-in-cheek, like so many of the letters Walpole wrote about *The Castle of Otranto*. In a letter to his father in February 1798, for example, Lewis sought refuge behind one of his sources, Addison's brief oriental tale, 'The story of the Santon Barsisa': 'Un-luckily, in working it up, I thought that the stronger my colours, the more effect would my picture produce; and it never struck me, that the exhibition of vice, in her temporary triumph, might possibly do as much harm as her final exposure and punishment would do good.'[98] Rather than being chastened by the experience of the scandal, Lewis arguably recognized the sensitivity of *The Monk*'s popularity, and became even more indiscriminate in his efforts to maintain a pose of youthful rebel-lion. After the first wave of controversy, Lewis continued to announce his authorship of *The Monk*: 'One thing, which surprises and offends us', a reviewer of Lewis's play *The Minister* wrote in the *British Critic*, 'is that after the severe and most just reprehension he has met with for his pernicious novel, he should choose to make himself known specifically by that book as a previous title to notice.'[99] Towards the end of this chapter, I want briefly to look at the rest of Lewis's work in order to assess the way in which he addressed both critics and a wider audience. Even though Lewis's melodramas, for example, are as difficult as *The Monk* to 'translate' into a language of overt political intervention, it seems as though Lewis continued to provoke his predominantly loyalist critics, by appealing to German sources and, even more importantly, by pandering to popular demand.

Lewis's knowing relation to the literary marketplace is illustrated by one of his earliest plays, *The Castle Spectre*, first performed at Drury Lane in December 1797, and published the following year. Though the play's prologue begins by appealing to 'a fair enchantress . . . Romance her name' in potentially idealizing terms, such a conventional recourse is rapidly undercut by the rest of the prologue, which alludes to some of the scandalous episodes of *The Monk* (Romance is said to rove 'Near graves new-open'd, or midst dungeons damp') and goes on to sexualize this personification of 'the lovely maniac': 'High heav'd her breasts, which struggling passions rent, / As prest to give some fear-fraught mystery vent.'[100] As contemporary reviewers recognized, the plot of *The Castle Spectre* shadows the basic plot of the Loyalist Gothic romance: set in Conway Castle (often referred to in the architectural correspondence of the *Gentleman's Magazine*), the action of the play deals with the supernaturally assisted overthrow of a villainous usurper and the restoration of a rightful heir. As most reviewers also recognized, however, Lewis used his familiarity with the romances of the 1790s in order to twist this common plot: 'What the public have been reading for the last five years, in the novels and fictions which have issued from our circulating libraries', according to the *Monthly Mirror*'s reviewer in 1797, 'is here put into dramatic form, by a gentleman who well understands the nature of the materials he has adopted.'[101] *The Castle Spectre* introduces the clown, Motley, as a privileged commentator-figure, for example, and – like *The Monk* – it both ridicules and credits supernatural agency, thereby allowing Lewis to present an avowed sceptic such as Father Philip running around the stage in retreat from the play's ghost. The published edition of the play accentuated this tone of frivolity all the more, with a series of mock footnotes parodying the way in which many contemporaries sought to legitimize sensational incident. When the hero Percy throws himself from a window in order to escape the retainers of the villain Osmond, for example, Lewis defends his play against accusations of improbability with the spurious claim that 'this incident was furnished me by the German History', in which, we are told, 'a certain Landgrave of Thuringia, being condemned to death, made his escape by taking so desperate a leap from the window of his prison, that he was afterwards known throughout Germany by the name of "Ludwig the Springer"'.[102] The play also uses a footnote to acknowledge a borrowing from Radcliffe's *Udolpho*, when the domestic Alice claims to have seen 'the Devil', but only in order to amplify its divergence from her example, since 'in the Romance it brings forward a terrific scene. In the Play it is intended to produce an effect entirely ludicrous.'[103]

    The Castle Spectre clearly differs from more innocently comic melodramas, nonetheless, in the way that it alludes to sensitive political debates. While *The Monk* suggestively allegorizes revolutionary violence, *The Castle Spectre* even more overtly refers to the topical issue of slavery, giving the 'misanthropic *Negro*' Hassan, in particular, a series of speeches in which to explain the causal link between his treatment in the past and his behaviour in the present: 'Yes, thou art sweet, Vengeance! – Oh! how it joys me when the white man suffers! – Yet weak are his pangs, compared to those I felt when torn from thy shores, O native Africa.'[104]

While *The Castle Spectre* was viewed by some critics simply as an improbable, knockabout drama, it was also seen to qualify or undermine its own simplicity and complicate its status as a comic play, as 'Anser Pen-Drag-On, Esq' put it in the satirical poem *Scribbleomania*: '*Monk Lewis*, of trick most consummate projector, / Bamboozled John Bull with his *Castle and Spectre*.'[105] Alert to the politicization of the 'Gothic' romance plot, and 'pretty attentive to the conduct of the CASTLE-SPECTRE', the *Monthly Visitor* in December 1797 asked three questions of the play's author:

Whether by the introduction of *Father Philip*, he meant to revive old hatreds against the clergy? Whether by the sentiments of his negroes, he wished to countenance the 'sacred right of insurrection!' as practised lately in the West Indies? And whether, in the person of Earl Osmond, by pourtraying a black instance of feudal tyranny, it was supposed to attach to the very existence of nobility?[106]

In response to the *Monthly Visitor*'s review, Lewis openly disavowed any 'democratic' intention in an address to the reader appended to the first published edition of the play. Referring to his 'Africans', for example, Lewis claimed that their inclusion in the play was motivated solely by the desire to 'give a pleasing variety to the characters and dresses', before going on to state that if he could have 'produced the same effect by making my heroine blue, blue I should have made her'.[107] While this address can plausibly be read as a strategy to resist censorship, it also seems to underline the claim made earlier that Lewis's concern to bait critics, and maintain his reputation, ultimately superseded any concern with political intervention. As was the case with Walpole, Lewis's overriding concern seems to have been with his own authorial position or profile. Whereas Walpole appealed to a select group of readers, and worked in a fairly subtle and nuanced way to forge an 'aristocratic' identity, however, Lewis seems to have been far less concerned about what he did to make a name for himself, or about the specific nature of this fame. One obvious way to provoke reviewers was to appeal to the judgement of audiences ahead of critics, as Lewis did in *The Castle Spectre*'s address to the reader, when he stated that audiences were 'not greatly offended' at the anachronism of the slaves, or at the inclusion of a 'real' spectre, which was 'as well treated before the curtain as she had been ill-used behind it'.[108] *The Castle Spectre* was clearly composed as a means of capitalizing upon the new popularity of melodrama and pantomime, concurrent with the enlargement of Drury Lane and Covent Garden theatres in the 1780s and 1790s, and as the *Critical Review* complained in 1798, though it defied 'the approbation of the critic', it secured 'what Mr Lewis perhaps values more, the applause of the multitude'.[109] Wordsworth complained, in a similar vein, that the play 'fitted the taste of the audience like a glove' just as Coleridge attacked the play's 'Lewis-izing' of Schiller, the criticisms of both perhaps amplified by their own failure to get plays (*The Borderers* and *Osorio* respectively) accepted by Covent Garden.[110] Lewis's pride in the popularity and financial success of *The Castle Spectre* was well known, and famously recorded by the *Biographia Dramatica* in its transcription of an apparent dispute between Lewis and Sheridan, to settle which Lewis offered to bet 'all the money which the Castle Spectre had brought' and Sheridan only all that the play was *worth*.[111] Numerous commentators sought to divorce success from merit in this way, and there were clear parallels in this period between the attacks on the growth of an 'illegitimate' melodrama and the attacks on the commodification of prose fiction, since both developments were seen to compromise the true taste of a minority.

Lewis continued to pander to the popular taste for the spectacular, but at the same time he also did enough to foreground the fact that his appeal to the market was a knowing one, and undertaken largely to prove his ability to write whatever he wanted. Responding to the charge of anachronism in *The Castle Spectre* again, for example, Lewis stated that 'to prove of how little consequence [he] esteemed such errors', he would 'write a play upon the Gunpowder Plot, and make Guy Faux in love with the Emperor Charlemagne's daughter!'[112] In the preface to *Adelmorn, The Outlaw; A Romantic Drama* (1801), similarly, Lewis disavowed any claim after critical approval or even acceptance: 'if I do not think my play a good one, why do I publish it? Because it can produce no worse consequences than the making me be thought a stupid fellow, which, in my opinion, is no great misfortune.'[113] In the postscript to the same play, Lewis further drew attention to the 'nonsense' of his 'Novels and Plays', stating that he still had it in his power 'to deluge the town with such an inundation of Ghosts and Magicians, as would satisfy the thirst of the most insatiable swallower of wonders', but also that nothing tempted him to publish or to stage 'more than the splenetic and ludicrous indignation, so ill suited to a subject so trifling, which my productions have excited in certain persons'.[114] Lewis's *Adelgitha; Or, The Fruits of a Single Error. A Tragedy in Five Acts* (1806) further advertised its author's desire to irritate critics and reviewers, by drawing attention in its preface to the play's 'frequent violations of historical veracity' (the *dramatis personae* includes, for example, an Emperor of Byzantium, a Prince of Apulia, Norman Knights and Grecian Noblemen):

Considered . . . in an historical view, nothing can be more defective than this Tragedy; but on the other hand, nothing was further from my intention in writing it, than to compose an historical play . . . If in other respects this Tragedy should be thought to have merit, the lovers of the Drama will probably excuse the want of historical accuracy without much reluctance; on the contrary, if the piece is totally worthless, I am glad that I did not waste my time in removing a defect which to myself appears immaterial, since I should still have left behind so many others of importance.[115]

Lewis went on to produce plays to order, or even in response to 'dares': *Timour the Tartar* was performed in 1811, for example, 'to oblige Mr Harris [a member of the Covent Garden management], who prest me very earnestly to give him a *Spectacle*, in which Horses might be introduced'.[116] If it is difficult to be sure about how far the appeal to the popular can be equated *with* a specific political position, then, Lewis was clearly concerned to define himself *against* a monolithic idea of 'critical opinion' which his prefaces and postscripts helped to construct.

During this period, Lewis also wrote *Rolla; or, The Peruvian Hero* (1799), a part translation of Kotzebue's anti-imperialist *Die Spanier in Peru*, produced some unambiguously Whig poetry, such as the 'Lines Written on returning from the Funeral of the Right Hon. C. J. Fox' (1806), and published another romance 'taken from the German', with the provocative title of *Feudal Tyrants* (1806). Given such evidence, André Parreaux has suggested that Lewis's Whig affiliations were the real cause of the controversy surrounding *The Monk*, and that the critic T. J. Mathias sought 'the end of Lewis's *political* career'.[117] Even if Parreaux were correct, though, it is hard to claim that Lewis was consistently an oppositional writer, since his desire to maintain his profile as a literary *enfant terrible* ultimately overrode any concern with more direct political intervention. Lewis seems to have been most interested, as he wrote in the epilogue to *Adelmorn the Outlaw*, to disprove 'This maxim – "There's nothing new under the sun!"', and to produce instead 'something singular, novel, and strange'.[118] Rather than express shock or take offence, however, many reviewers simply expressed their tiredness with Lewis's tactics, and his continual recourse to the 'old expedient of a ghost': 'his ghosts are become to the public, what he seems to consider them himself, rather ludicrous than terrible'.[119] Later commentators attributed the excess and the 'difference' of his work to a languorous immaturity or a perpetual adolescence, so that according to Scott, Lewis was 'a spoiled child' – albeit of 'high imagination' – who never grew out of a juvenile taste for 'ghost-stories and German romances'; Lewis's work, for Leigh Hunt, betrayed most of all a 'morbid want of excitement' in his life.[120]

Returning to the issue of genre raised at the outset in relation to *The Monk*, the evidence considered above serves to complicate any idea about Lewis's status as a writer of 'Gothic'. Though *The Bravo of Venice*, for example, announced itself in conventional form as another 'Romance: Translated From the German', the work – like *The Castle Spectre* – similarly twisted common plot devices, serving as a vehicle for a bizarre parody of the disguised hero motif and of the 'outcast' theme popularized by *The Robbers* and by German romances of the 1790s. A banished Neapolitan Prince, Count Rosalvo, adopts the disguise of a Venetian Bravo, Abellino, in order to eliminate the Doge's enemies and so regain his own status, and this plot is characteristically 'worked up' by Lewis, as the reader is told about the nature of the disguise that the hero assumes:

if the reader is curious to know what this same fellow Abellino was like, he must picture to himself a young, stout fellow, whose limbs perhaps might have been thought not ill-formed, had not the most horrible countenance, that ever was invented by a caricaturist, or that Milton could have adapted to the ugliest of his fallen angels, entirely marred the advantages of his person . . . His mouth was so wide, that his gums and discoloured teeth were visible, and a kind of convulsive twist which scarcely ever was at rest, had formed its expression into an eternal grin . . . His eye (for he had but one) was sunk deep in his head, and little more than the white of it was visible: and even that little was over-shadowed by the protrusion of his dark and bushy eye-brows . . . In the union of his features were found collected in one hideous assemblage all the most coarse and uncouth traits, which had ever been exhibited singly in wooden cuts; and the observer was left in doubt, whether this repulsive physiognomy exprest stupidity of intellect, or maliciousness of heart, or whether it implied them both together.[121]

Though *The Monk* in particular continues to be celebrated as a quintessentially Gothic work, owing to its 'exploration of the dark irrational hinterland of the human mind',[122] such a brief reference to *The Bravo of Venice* should further call into question the idea that either Lewis or his most famous work is in some way representative of a larger genre. *The Monk* was clearly condemned in a similar fashion to many of the romances published by the Minerva Press, as I have argued in this chapter, but a closer examination of its content and its method shows that Lewis was primarily concerned to define his work *against* current romance paradigms.

Though *The Monk* was quickly followed by several romances which exploited the resonance of Lewis's title,[123] few fictions in the 1790s either defined themselves so consistently against the canons of morality and propriety or concluded on the same dystopian note as Lewis's work. Charlotte Dacre's *Confessions of The Nun of St Omer. A Tale* (1805) was dedicated to the 'very various and brilliant talents' of Lewis,[124] and her *Zofloya; or, The Moor. A Romance of the Fifteenth Century* (1806), like *The Monk*, depicts a protagonist (albeit a woman) who falls victim to the wiles of Satan: Dacre's handling of the virtuous heroine, Lilla, for example, closely parallels Lewis's treatment of Antonia, and *Zofloya*'s anti-heroine, Victoria, meets her death in the same way as Ambrosio, hurled into an abyss. P. B. Shelley's *Zastrozzi: A Romance* (1810) drew heavily upon Dacre's work, in turn, and with *St Irvyne; or, The Rosicrucian: A Romance* (1811) he similarly eschewed the plenitude of romance closure. A decade later, Charles Maturin amplified the anti-Catholicism and the Faustian motifs of *The Monk* in his influential work *Melmoth the Wanderer* (1820). Compared to the mainly eighteenth-century romances which I have discussed so far, many Gothic works written in the early nineteenth century were rhetorically richer and more complex, displaying a much greater interest in formal innovation, a fascination with criminality or transgression, and a desire to complicate the romance schema of punishment and reward. Despite the deserved attention which works by writers such as Dacre, Hogg, Maturin, and the Shelleys are now attracting, however, it is historically inaccurate to project the qualities of their works onto the Gothic romance as a whole, and it is consequently necessary to qualify the aura of subversion which still surrounds the genre. In my next chapter, I will look at the work of another canonical Gothic writer of the 1790s, Ann Radcliffe, in order to show how her romances were not only accommodated, but celebrated, by conservative critics and reviewers.

CHAPTER 4

The first poetess of romantic fiction: Ann Radcliffe

> Long however as our eyes have been now turned on scenes of
> turbulence and anarchy, long as we have listened with horror to the
> storm which has swept over Europe with such ungovernable fury, it
> must, I should imagine, prove highly soothing to the wearied mind,
> to occasionally repose on such topics as literature and imagination
> are willing to afford
>
> Nathan Drake, *Literary Hours: Sketches Critical and Narrative* (1798)[1]

> When the reader travels with a Mrs Radcliffe, he goes on in the
> society of a lady who has made Romance her darling study, and
> who now uninterruptedly executes it with confidence, and real
> pleasure to herself
>
> Joseph Fox, *Santa-Maria; or, The Mysterious Pregnancy. A Romance*
> (1797)[2]

Though there was far less impropriety in the late-eighteenth-century
'Gothic' romance than is commonly assumed, as I argued in the
previous chapter, many ostensibly unremarkable works were still condemned because of their association either with German literature or,
more often, with the perceived commodification of prose fiction in
general. One particular writer was consistently singled out and absolved
from any such criticism, however, 'the mighty magician of UDOLPHO',
Ann Radcliffe.[3] Following Walter Scott's claim that Radcliffe deserved a
'place among the very few, who have been distinguished as the founders
of a class, or school', this chapter will examine the specific ways in which
Radcliffean romance was seen to differ from the other forms of Gothic
fiction which have been considered so far. 'If she derived any hint from
the farcical extravagances of the *Castle of Otranto*, or the insipidity of the
Old English Baron', as the *New Monthly Magazine* stated in 1826, Radcliffe's
achievement was 'rather heightened than reduced' by the fact that 'on
such cold suggestions she could devise solemn and decorous terrors, and
spread out vast, sombre, and consistent pictures before the eye of the

fancy'.[4] Though it is difficult to make specific claims about the 'position-taking' of Radcliffe on the basis of what she wrote, I will argue in this chapter that critics and reviewers allocated Radcliffe a particular niche in the field of romance, and determined a framework within which her distinctive brand of fiction could be enjoyed. Recent criticism has tended to focus on the subtext of Radcliffe's work, and its feminist potential, rather than on the congeniality of Radcliffean romance for conservative critics in the 1790s and early 1800s. After a brief discussion of Radcliffe's ambiguous relation to the so-called female Gothic, this chapter will address the nature of her work's initial popularity, and focus in detail on the way that it was read by critics and reviewers seeking (like Nathan Drake, quoted above) a legitimate form of withdrawal from the troubles of the present. For all the acclaim that Radcliffe's work received, however, I will conclude by describing the way in which many male critics conspicuously qualified their praise, and emphasized that she was only successful in a manifestly low or inferior genre. Regardless of the exemplary morality and propriety of Radcliffe's work, therefore, its claim to 'literary' status remained subject to debate, and was increasingly called into question with the ascendancy of the Waverley novels, and a very different construction of romance.

Radcliffe's first work, *The Castles of Athlin and Dunbayne: A Highland Story* (1789), clearly followed the example of the earliest Loyalist Gothic romances described in the second chapter, such as *The Old English Baron*, both in its use of the property restoration plot and in the telescoped quality of its narrative. Even though the work revolves around the Baron of Dunbayne's imprisonment of his widowed sister-in-law, *The Castles* is tentative in its resort to the aesthetic of terror which is usually held to characterize Radcliffe's work, and does little either to exploit the dramatic potential of its heroines' confinement or to foreground the character of the villain. Like the rightful Baroness and her daughter, presented in the subordinate role of passive victims, Baron Malcolm is an undeveloped figure, who gives a full deathbed confession after his defeat by the Earl of Athlin's forces, at which point the usurped property is redeemed and restored to its lawful owner. After this derivative and virtually unnoticed experiment, Radcliffe's next work, *A Sicilian Romance* (1790), significantly modified the inheritance plot. Instead of resorting again to the example provided by Clara Reeve, *A Sicilian Romance* reveals a debt to Sophia Lee's *The Recess; or, A Tale of Other Times* (1783–5), a work which sought to supplement 'official' history in its focus on the secret lives of the daughters of Mary, Queen of Scots, by a clandestine marriage to the Duke of Norfolk.[5] *The Recess* subverted the loyalist recourse to an idealized pseudo-historical realm by examining some of the *literal* embodiments of Gothic space, and by focusing on two women who begin life in a subterranean apartment in 'St Vincent's Abbey', a ruin of 'Gothic magnificence'.[6] Lee's work deals with the anonymous, underground lives led by her heroines Ellinor and Matilda, and Radcliffe's *A Sicilian Romance* is concerned, in turn, both with the confinement of a pair of sisters, who begin the work having 'never passed the boundaries of their father's domains', and with the imprisonment of their mother in a 'recess of horror' within the family residence, the Castle of Mazzini.[7] If works such as *The Castle of Otranto*, *Vathek*, and *The Monk* are preoccupied with the male figure of the overreaching tyrant, *A Sicilian Romance* offers a contrasting focus on the victims who suffer at his hands, exemplified by the long narrative delivered by the mother of Emilia and Julia after her release from captivity; Radcliffe's work presents the castle as a locus of tyranny, which is eventually abandoned, rather than as a site of ultimately restored legitimacy.

In *A Sicilian Romance* (1790), *The Romance of the Forest* (1791), and *The Mysteries of Udolpho* (1794), Radcliffe's heroines, despite their popular reputation for shrinking passivity, are made to stand up to the impositions of male tyrants and, in particular, to resist arranged marriages. It is easy to see why Radcliffe has become such an important writer for feminist literary critics, therefore, since her works repeatedly focus on the fate of the young, propertied woman negotiating, without protection, the pitfalls of the marriage market. Not only do Radcliffe's works allow their heroines to exercise initiative, but they also isolate the heroine's consciousness, intermittently valorizing a form of subjective insight.

Though I will emphasize later that Radcliffe's romances displayed a series of regulatory mechanisms or strategies which were applauded by conservative readers, it is nonetheless fair to say that her works from *A Sicilian Romance* onwards also paid tribute to a positive form of enthusiasm, manifesting itself both in the heroines' appropriation of sublime experience, and in their heightened perception of dangers and threats.[8] In all of these works, Radcliffe's heroines indulge in the natural sublimity of mountain landscapes as a temporarily empowering release from actuality, and this form of elevated individualism remains potentially at odds with the organic and family-oriented community that is celebrated by moralizing closure. Similarly, Radcliffe can be seen to privilege the intuitive power of her heroines during their periods of confinement by offering a grounding for their apparent paranoia. This is most obviously evident during Emily's period of captivity in *Udolpho*, where it is made clear that her mind only succumbs to 'imaginary terrors' because of a surfeit of real ones, and because 'long-suffering had made her spirits peculiarly sensible'.[9] Instead of presenting her as a female Quixote, therefore, Radcliffe in effect authorizes Emily's experience of 'nameless terrors' (240) at the Castle of Udolpho, via the sensitive description of situations in which, as Marilyn Butler has claimed, 'rage, inadequacy, and threatened identity become felt as sufficiently real to blot out external reality'.[10] By describing, for example, the situation of Emily's chamber at Udolpho as being 'liable to intrusion', and lockable only from the outside, Radcliffe allows the reader to appreciate how the various threats hanging over Emily were 'justly terrible to her imagination' (203): when Count Morano (the one-time ally of Montoni) enters this chamber with a view to carrying Emily off, 'terror' is said to deprive her of 'the power of discrimination' (261).

Though it is true that 'the narrator's moralistic commentaries return the reader to "everyday legality" and so constitute a critique of the obsessiveness and hysteria which sensibility via "sublime" fear and superstition can admit', as Jacqueline Howard has argued, 'this critique is in turn interrogated by those long and suspenseful passages which bring us closer to Emily's consciousness'.[11] What is notable about the 'figural patterning' of *Udolpho*, indeed, is that 'Emily's hunches, intuitions, and intense imaginings so often could have been right that they bolster faith in the irrational and threaten to unravel the whole fabric'. According to Howard's Bakhtinian account, Radcliffean romance stages a 'conflict of voices', whereby – in *Udolpho*, especially – the narratorial warnings against Emily's 'starts of imagination' are set against the extended description of precisely such excess.[12] Whatever the conservatism of her conclusions, Radcliffe's works arguably embody a dialogic principle, and contain some kind of core in which heroines do resist, and in which their intuitive fears are credited and made plausible.

The newness of Radcliffean romance, its difference from the other forms of Gothic romance considered in previous chapters, consists of its alliance of the conventions of *Otranto* or *The Old English Baron* both with the *Bildungsroman* tradition, represented by a contemporary such as Fanny Burney, and with the more subjectively heroine-centred focus of a work like *The Recess*. As is well known, Radcliffe's works from *A Sicilian Romance* onwards are outwardly concerned with the education of their heroines (and readers), and with the proper management of sensibility. Julia in *A Sicilian Romance*, therefore, is said early on to be the more 'susceptible' of the two sisters, with a dangerous ignorance of 'the weakness of humanity', just as the reader is told that Adeline in *The Romance of the Forest* enjoys a delusive 'confidence in the sincerity and goodness of others'; Emily, in *The Mysteries of Udolpho*, is possessed of 'a degree of susceptibility too exquisite to admit of lasting peace' (and is lectured by her dying father about the danger of 'first impressions' and 'the duty of self-command', 5), while Ellena, in *The Italian*, is also initially described as a character 'with much beauty and little knowledge of the world'.[13] In the course of these works, Radcliffe's heroines are all disabused of their illusions about 'the world', and as far as they are able, they resist the arbitrary power of surrogate fathers (the Marquis of Mazzini, La Motte and the Marquis de Montalt, Montoni, and Schedoni, respectively) before a form of providential intervention rewards them with marriage to a feminized hero.

If Radcliffe's works are rhetorically governed by the need to curb the excesses of imagination and sentiment, however, it is nonetheless hard to claim that they finally depict the entrance of their heroines into a larger, public reality. Radcliffe's works ultimately eschew the 'anti-romance' formula of Charlotte Lennox's *The Female Quixote*, or, later, Jane Austen's *Northanger Abbey*, since they acknowledge that the ambiguous yet real threats faced by their heroines can only be overcome by imposing an idealized romance settlement.[14] In the process of being disabused about the outside world, indeed, Radcliffe's heroines often succumb to a general disillusionment, and end up lamenting an almost all-pervasive sense of 'corruption'. After being informed of her guardian's plans to use her as an economic token and marry her off to the libertine aristocrat, the Marquis de Montalt, Adeline (in *The Romance of the Forest*) is made to protest about the depravity of 'human nature' ('Am I doomed to find everybody deceitful?'), just as Ellena in *The Italian* takes an anecdote of Vivaldi's about the Emperor Claudius's use of slave labour as evidence that 'we scarcely dare to trust the truth of history, in some of its traits of human nature'.[15] During her confinement at San Stefano, Ellena goes so far as specifically to attribute all of her sufferings to 'man', deemed to be 'the giant who now held her in captivity', even though Ellena's actual captor at this time is a woman who works at the bidding of Vivaldi's mother.[16] These complaints, though unfocused, testify to an apparently general opposition to 'the transactions and the sufferings of this world',[17] and this outlook is shared by the other transparently good characters in Radcliffe's work. The refuge eventually provided by Radcliffe for her virtuous couples and their extended families needs to be read as a compromised retreat from social criticism, therefore, since as David S. Durant has observed in an article on 'the Conservative Gothic', 'the conclusions make no attempt to disprove the iniquity of the underworld, but prove that a good person neither can nor should deal with the world'.[18] Yet at the same time, Radcliffean romantic closure also represents the only 'realistic' (or, in other words, plausible) means of arriving at a happy ending. If Radcliffe defines history, as Ian Duncan has claimed, solely as 'a synchronic domain of patriarchal coercion' or 'an alien dimension of power or terror', the only available form of transcendence is that provided by an avowedly romantic evasion of history's determinations.[19] Instead of replacing 'the alarms of romance' with 'the anxieties of common life' as in *Northanger Abbey*, Radcliffe's works finally opt to deliver their heroines simply 'from one stage of romance to another'.[20]

Robert Miles has recently drawn attention to the way that Radcliffe's romances stage the triumph of 'the bourgeois values of individualism and "companionate marriage"' over 'the prejudices and vices of a passing aristocratic, patriarchal regime'.[21] Radcliffean closure has a highly ambivalent political charge, however, since if it supposes the necessity of displacing a regressive, patriarchal order, it allocates only a minimal role to human agency. According to Mary Poovey, for example, Radcliffe 'uncovers the root cause of the late-eighteenth-century ideological turmoil, the economic aggressiveness currently victimizing defenceless women of sensibility', but 'rather than proposing an alternative to paternalistic society and its values, she merely reasserts an idealized – and insulated – paternalism and relegates the issues she cannot solve to the background of her narrative'.[22] If on the one hand this mode of closure represents a form of wish-fulfilment, it can also be read more sceptically as a disabling palliative rather than an empowering fantasy. The temptation to read Radcliffe as a proto-feminist writer of 'female Gothic' should perhaps be qualified accordingly since, as I will go on to argue, many conservative readers did find her work to be eminently 'legitimate' and readable, and in addition many other Gothic novels and romances by contemporary women writers were far more searching in their social criticism.

Though Radcliffe's *A Sicilian Romance* clearly owes a debt to a work such as Sophia Lee's *The Recess*, therefore, it is important to recognize that Lee's work eschews any form of utopian closure, and consequently calls into question the appeal to romance itself with 'its attendant fantasy of female power'.[23] While all of Radcliffe's heroines are eventually rewarded with marriage and property, *The Recess* refuses the providential closure characteristic of so many contemporary works, and the 'fortunate orphan' tradition in general, and instead depicts its heroines being steadily overtaken by a series of disasters. The *Monthly*'s reviewer complained in 1786, for example, that *The Recess* failed to provide any 'breathing from calamity and ill fortune', leaving readers troubled by the lack of any 'cheerful and enlivening objects to recover from the stretch of sympathetic anguish'.[24] Ellinor goes insane and dies after her mother and her lover, Essex, are beheaded, while Matilda suffers shipwreck and four years of captivity in a Spanish colony, as well as the loss of her husband, before she is left at the conclusion to complete her memoirs in solitude, unrecognized by her brother, King James. The twins are shown to learn about 'a terrible large place called the World, where a few haughty individuals command . . . miserable millions' just as Radcliffe's Ellena is made to 'learn' a degree of disillusionment and suspicion as she begins to understand what has happened to her.[25] The obvious difference between *The Recess* and a work such as *The Italian*, however, is that Lee allows her heroines no refuge from the nightmare of history, save the recess of the title: 'society, that first of blessings', Matilda is made to claim, 'brings with it evils only death can cure'.[26]

Rosetta Ballin's rarely discussed work, *The Statue Room; An Historical Tale* (1790), provides a similarly dystopian conclusion. Beginning with the statement that 'the unfortunate Queen', Catharine of Aragon, 'was with-child when the King, her husband, put her away', Ballin's romance also contests genealogies of royalty and makes the figure of Queen Elizabeth its main villain.[27] Elizabeth is suspicious of Catharine's daughter, Adelfrida, because of her claim to the throne, and this suspicion is exacerbated when she secretly marries the Duke of Alençon, a one-time suitor of the Queen. Adelfrida is eventually poisoned on Elizabeth's orders, and the focus of the work switches to her daughter, Romelia, who is also persecuted by the Queen, having her husband, Henry Seymour, imprisoned as a traitor. Romelia goes on to give an account of a vision that urges her to avenge her mother's death, and after the death of Henry, Romelia stalks Elizabeth at a masquerade and tries to shoot her, only to miss, and then shoot herself with a second pistol. When Radcliffe is read alongside other contemporary women writers, such as Lee and Ballin, the challenges posed by her work can be located much more accurately, since it becomes apparent that a large number of novels or romances sought to represent the captivity of women in more immediate and recognizable terms than were provided by *The Mysteries of Udolpho* or *The Italian*. Where Lee and Ballin set out to challenge their reader by colliding romance and history, as so many reviewers complained, other works in the 1790s provocatively described the confinement of their heroines in the present, as well as in England. Eliza Fenwick's epistolary novel *Secresy; or, The Ruin on the Rock* (1795) depicts a heroine, Sibella Valmont, who is secluded by her uncle within the 'menacing grandeur' of Valmont Castle for the purpose of ensuring her submission to his will; Sibella dies at the close of the work, following the death of her child. Mary Wollstonecraft's *The Wrongs of Woman; or, Maria* (1798) also forces the loaded symbol of the castle into a contemporary context, with the 'mansion of despair' in which Maria sits being presented as a real asylum, where she has been confined by the orders of her husband, Venables, asserting his legal rights over her person and her wealth.[28] Referring in her preface to 'the partial laws and customs of society', Wollstonecraft's work universalizes the experience of Maria: 'the history ought rather to be considered, as of woman, than of an individual'.[29] In clear contrast to anything written by Radcliffe, then, such works acknowledge female sexual desire, refuse romantic transcendence, and relentlessly literalize the confinement of their central characters. 'Female affliction originates and is rooted in the social, institutional, and secular world' in these works, as Eleanor Ty has recently argued, and 'the Gothic castle which in Radcliffe's *Udolpho* merely suggested patriarchal tyranny, now becomes an explicit thematization of female imprisonment'.[30]

This is not to claim that Radcliffe's romances are monologically conservative since, as I argued above, they negotiated with contemporary constructions of femininity. 'In the hermetically sealed castle or nunnery, often under the protective tyranny of a man', as Mary Poovey has written, 'women like . . . Emily St Aubert are able to exercise ingenuity and express curiosity that would be improper in the outside world.'[31] Writing for Radcliffe herself, moreover, was a way of earning attention without overtly seeking it, so that even though *Udolpho* closes with the author's attempt to justify the labour of her 'weak hand' (672), it should also be recognized that the work actually earned Radcliffe a *public* profile as a writer, as well as an unprecedented fee from her publisher. What the contrast between Radcliffe and some of her contemporaries does underline, however, is the difficulty of speaking about a monolithic category of 'female Gothic' without falling back upon an essentialist notion of women's writing which ignores the potential plurality of context. Jacqueline Howard's Bakhtinian study has put the matter very clearly in stating that the work of North American critics such as Ellen Moers or Sandra Gilbert and Susan Gubar 'ensures that women and their writing remain trapped in the personal, the private, the subjective, body and nature as against the political, the public, the objective, mind and culture'; such criticism, she argues, tends to ignore 'the larger tension-filled discursive environments in which the Gothic and other texts emerge and are later reproduced'.[32] Radcliffe's work certainly provides a great deal of potential for modern feminist criticism, but from a historicizing perspective it is important to recognize that many critics and reviewers were far less interested in the subjective experiences of Radcliffe's heroines than in the larger romance framework within which these insights are contained. There is, unfortunately, little evidence available about the responses of women readers to Radcliffe's work in the 1790s but, as I will argue in the rest of this chapter, conservative critics and reviewers generally found Radcliffe to be a highly readable author, who stood out from her contemporaries in terms of both the skill and the morality that her work displayed. A focus on the immediate reception of Radcliffe's work shows that her romances were widely seen to provide what Scott described as 'a solace from the toils of ordinary existence', a benign and comforting form of 'transport' which derived from 'an excursion into the regions of imagination'.[33]

The extent to which Radcliffe actively sought to frame or legitimize the more sensational aspects of her work remains open to debate. Elizabeth Napier, for example, has argued that Radcliffean romance epitomizes 'the failure of the Gothic' precisely because it is unable to reconcile a 'moral conviction about the rectitude of endurance', on the part of its heroines, with an 'aesthetic attraction to situations that break down such qualities'.[34] In a reading of the 'conflict of voices' in *Udolpho* and *The Italian* rather different from Howard's cited earlier, Napier argues that Radcliffe was both 'interested in the affective powers of the supernatural' and concerned to deny its very existence.[35] Napier's analysis of 'the disjunction of the affective and the moral' in the works of Radcliffe (and in the Gothic romance generally) is a powerful one, which certainly seems to explain the way that Radcliffe allows the suggestion of infidelity on the part of Emily's father to persist right until the end of *Udolpho*. This analysis of a tension between dramatic and moral imperatives remains essentially unhistorical, however, and it ignores the variety of the strategies of closure which conservative critics found so congenial in Radcliffe's work. The narratorial commentary about the need to regulate passion and sensibility which runs alongside the presentation of Emily's enthusiasm in *Udolpho*, for example, in fact constitutes only one of a number of regulatory mechanisms internal to Radcliffean romance. Just as Radcliffe foregrounded the efforts of her central characters to maintain a rational sense of perspective throughout their various trials, so too did her works address the contemporary concern about the 'disciplining' of readers. Radcliffe's romances were often seen to be as 'sensational' as the Gothic works published by the Minerva Press: according to Scott, their readers were liable to be 'aroused, or rather fascinated' by the way that Radcliffe 'called out the feelings of mystery and of awe, while chapter after chapter, and incident after incident, maintained the thrilling attraction of awakened curiosity and suspended interest'.[36] At the same time, however, Radcliffe's works sought to acknowledge prevailing anxieties about the private absorption of the romance reader, not least in the way that they circumscribed both sublime scenery and terrific incident. While a plausible case has been made by Patricia Meyer Spacks for the feminist potential of Radcliffe's undermining of the human sublime, represented by villain-heroes such as Montoni or Schedoni, her framing of a potentially authoritarian natural sublimity also closely paralleled the emergence, in the middle of the 1790s, of what Theresa Kelley has identified as Wordsworth's 'quasi-Burkean' aesthetic of containment.[37] Particularly in *Udolpho* and *The Italian*, Radcliffe's heroines are finally rewarded with a distinctly *beautiful* refuge from corruption (explicitly presented in the latter work as 'a scene of fairy-land')[38] and with marriage to feminized heroes, *Val*an-court and Vi*val*di, whose names themselves embody the triumph of benign tranquillity over arbitrary power.

Radcliffe's larger concern with the question of 'stimulation' was not confined to her conclusions, however, since her works consistently sought to arrest the attention of those readers who were exclusively occupied with the plot or with the unfolding of 'the mysteries'. Along with writers such as Jane Austen and Walter Scott, who helped to legitimize the novel in the early nineteenth century, Radcliffe provided what Gary Kelly has referred to as a 'surplus beyond story'.[39] Where Scott, for example, invoked the authority of the factual discourses of antiquarianism and history, as the next chapter will claim, Radcliffe resorted to the equally prestigious discourse of aesthetics, and sought to define her work, in the words of Chloe Chard, as 'the product of an informed sensibility, capable of recognizing and expounding the complex and paradoxical forms of aesthetic pleasure offered by the sub-lime'.[40] Radcliffe's romances were widely celebrated for their mastery of the techniques of delay and suspense, most famously perhaps in *Northanger Abbey*: Henry Tilney, for example, is made to claim that he finished *Udolpho* 'in two days – my hair standing on end the whole time', while Isabella Tilney and Catherine Morland compare notes about the 'delightful' episode of the black veil.[41] Though Radcliffe's works gratified what the Aikins described as the 'Pleasures Derived from Objects of Terror', they nonetheless authorized this presentation of sensational incident by theorizing it in the terminology of Burke's influential *Philosophical Enquiry* of 1757.[42] When, in *Udolpho*, Emily goes to re-examine the 'veiled picture' in one of the castle's chambers, for example, Radcliffe's narrator interjects in order to describe the compound of fear and pleasure, repulsion and attraction, that her heroine experiences: 'a terror of this nature, as it occupies and expands the mind, and elevates it to high expectation, is purely sublime, and leads us, by a kind of fascination, to seek even the object, from which we appear to shrink' (248).

In a similar fashion, Radcliffe appealed for the attention of discriminating readers by incorporating long passages of natural description that acknowledged the current theories and conventions of the picturesque being formulated by writers such as William Gilpin. Radcliffe attempted to form her readers, and shape the way that they read her work, by enhancing descriptive passages with references to the landscapes of artists like Claude Lorrain and Salvator Rosa, most familiar to the leisured elite able to position themselves as aesthetic observers and undertake picturesque tourism on the Continent: a rugged 'scene of barrenness' presented in the early French episodes of *Udolpho*, for example, 'was such a scene as *Salvator* would have chosen, had he then existed, for his canvas' (30). The name-recognition thus invited clearly enabled readers to separate themselves from an undisciplined majority, just as the recurrent and schematic episodes depicting the different reactions to nature of Radcliffe's characters also provided an index by which readers could measure their cultivation: at Chateau-le-Blanc in *Udolpho*, for example, the Countess de Villefort seeks to avoid a prospect of 'the *horrid* Pyrenees' and her companion reads aloud 'a sentimental novel, on some fashionable system of philosophy', at the same time as Lady Blanche, Emily's kindred spirit, is said to experience 'somewhat of that exquisite delight which awakens the fancy' (476). In theory, as St Aubert tells his daughter, 'sublime spectacles, so infinitely superior to all artificial luxuries! are open for the enjoyment of the poor, as well as of the rich' (60); in practice, though, only a few virtuous characters in Radcliffe's work have the ability to appreciate such spectacles in a legitimate way.

For the critic Hugh Murray, Radcliffe's romances were 'to be considered chiefly as poetry, and in many parts, as the very finest of poetry', in the same way that for Scott, Radcliffe was the 'first poetess of romantic fiction', the first writer 'to introduce into her prose fictions a beautiful and fanciful tone of natural description and impressive narrative, which had hitherto been exclusively applied to poetry'.[43] As I have argued above, this kind of praise was not simply garnered by the quality of Radcliffe's 'grand and comprehensive views' of scenery, but also by the way that these views were seen to amplify both the exemplary morality and the literary status of her work. Though they were seen to be intrinsically valuable in themselves, and were regularly excerpted in reviews, the long, digressive passages of scene-setting in Radcliffe's work arguably served to disrupt the immediate absorption of the reader in the plot – without, at the same time, detracting at all from his or her interest in what was going to happen next. The action in Radcliffean romance is continually punctuated by this detailed natural description, as is the case on the many occasions, in *Udolpho* especially, when Radcliffe refers to the trained observations of a disembodied 'eye' ('the steeps below, over which the eye passed abruptly to the valley, were fringed with thickets of alpine shrubs', p. 53). Radcliffe's heroines also set this process of digression in motion, and while such description sometimes complements the portrayal of character, it just as frequently seems to supersede the unfolding of the plot altogether. In *Udolpho*, for example, just after she has been helped to escape from Montoni's custody by Ludovico and Du Pont, Emily is given time to survey 'the vale of Arno' and is said to behold 'all the charms of sylvan and pastoral landscape united'. At a critical moment in the action of the work, Emily is all but transported from a romance to a travel narrative:

How vivid the shrubs, that embowered the slopes, with the woods, that stretched amphitheatrically along the mountains! and, above all, how elegant the outline of these waving Apennines, now softening from the wildness, which their interior regions exhibited! At a distance, in the east, Emily discovered Florence, with its towers rising on the brilliant horizon, and its luxuriant plain, spreading to the feet of the Apennines, speckled with gardens and magnificent villas, or coloured with groves of orange and lemon, with vines, corn, and plantations of olive and mulberry; while to the west, the vale opened to the waters of the Mediterranean, so distant, that they were known only by a blueish line, that appeared upon the horizon, and by the light marine vapour, which just stained the aether above. (455–6)

Radcliffe's name became a byword for this kind of innocent descriptive surplus, and it was often invoked as a reproach to more ambitious novelists, as in the anti-Jacobin satire *St Godwin* (1800), where the author 'Count Reginald de St Leon' is made to plead for her inspiring guidance: 'I know this is the place for description, but I cannot get on.'[44] The obtrusive role of poetry in Radcliffean romance similarly served to hedge or supplement terrific incident. Radcliffe both allowed her heroines to display their affinity for poetic composition and recital, and provided 'an outside border for the narrative' as a whole, as Gary Kelly has argued, by using literary epigraphs that paid tribute to an English heritage of writers such as Shakespeare, Milton, Thomson, Collins, and Gray.[45] Despite Coleridge's claim that most readers skipped the poetry in Radcliffe's work because it interfered with the unfolding of the plot ('the love of poetry is a taste; curiosity is a kind of appetite, and hurries headlong on, impatient for its complete gratification'), it is fair to say that most reviewers acknowledged and endorsed Radcliffe's concern to elevate her construction of romance within the unofficial hierarchy of genres.[46] What is important for my purposes, above all, is that Radcliffe's different strategies for managing the sublime and the terrific were seized upon, and unambiguously politicized, by conservative critics. Nathan Drake in his *Literary Hours*, therefore, gave 'Mrs Radcliffe' the title of 'the Shakspeare of Romance Writers', because of the way that she offset the 'wild' or sublime virtues of Salvator Rosa with 'the softer graces of a Claude'. Though her works were said to contain 'many scenes truly terrific in their conception', these scenes were 'softened down, and the mind . . . much relieved, by the intermixture of beautiful description, or pathetic incident'; 'the impression of the whole never becomes too strong, never degenerates into horror, but pleasurable emotion is ever the predominating result'.[47]

Radcliffean romance in many ways pre-empted the terms of the polemic in Wordsworth's famous preface to the *Lyrical Ballads*. In response to the mass reading public's 'degrading thirst after outrageous stimulation' and the consequent popularity of 'frantic novels, sickly and stupid German tragedies and deluges of idle and extravagant stories in verse', Wordsworth proclaimed that his own poems would describe 'characters of which the elements are very simple', appealing to nature instead of 'extraordinary incident'. Despite stating that poetry ought to

be the result of a 'spontaneous overflow of powerful feelings', Wordsworth qualified any elevation of the subjective or irrational by emphasizing that good, or genuine, poetry could only be produced by a
man who had acquired the ability to think 'long and deeply', and
recollect 'in tranquillity'.[48] Radcliffe's own concern to provide a comparable perspective on 'extraordinary incident' is particularly evident in
the way that she sought to rationalize the supernatural. Though heroes
and heroines are not immune from superstition in her work, of course,
Radcliffe frequently projected credulity onto domestics and servants, a
class of people – it is repeatedly made clear – who are prone to receive
'any species of the marvellous . . . with avidity'.[49] As is well known, in
addition, every suggestion of a supernatural, or generally 'mysterious',
phenomenon in the work of Radcliffe (before *Gaston de Blondeville*, at
least) is finally closed off by a conclusive explanation: 'in short', as John
Dunlop claimed, 'we may say not only of Mrs Radcliffe's castles, but of
her works in general, that they abound "in passages that lead to
nothing"'.[50] The venting of such frustration was especially concerted
after *The Italian*, Radcliffe's fourth resort to the same formula of
resolution, and complaints were repeatedly voiced by those male
readers and critics who preferred the supernatural to be 'boldly'
avowed, as it is in works like *The Castle of Otranto* or *The Monk*: most
notably, perhaps, Scott complained in 1824 that Radcliffe's method
engendered feelings of 'disappointment and displeasure' in the recreational reader, 'angry with his senses for having been cheated, and
with his reason for having acquiesced in the deception'.[51] Yet despite
such commentary, rationalizing explanation was also frequently
credited as being the means by which Radcliffe and her readers could
enjoy such a degree of fictional licence in the first place, hence the claim
of the *Monthly*'s review of *Udolpho*:

without introducing into her narrative anything really supernatural, Mrs Radcliffe has contrived to produce so powerful an effect as if the invisible world had
been obedient to her magic spell; and the reader experiences in perfection the
strange luxury of artificial terror without being obliged for a moment to
hoodwink his reason, or to yield to the weakness of superstitious credulity.[52]

'Explanation' was often seen to be a structural component of Radcliffean romance which ultimately served as a chastening reminder to
readers about the dangers of becoming consumed with the unfolding of
the plot, of surrendering rational control of themselves and submitting
to an external force. If most readers are initially absorbed by Radcliffean

romance, as Anna Barbauld claimed, they ultimately feel nothing but a 'sort of disappointment and shame at having felt so much, from appearances which had nothing in them beyond this "visible diurnal sphere"'.[53] Even those critics who felt disappointed by the explanation of the supernatural nearly always praised the 'control' of Radcliffe and her ability, as Coleridge put it, to escape 'the guesses of the reader'; 'in this contest of curiosity on one side, and invention on the other, Mrs Radcliffe has certainly the advantage'.[54] Conservative critics, in particular, praised this technique, drawing attention to the parallel between credulity or superstition and revolutionary idealism, and implicitly equating rationalizing explanation with a recovery of the rule of law. In one of the many digressions in his novel *Henry* (1795), for example, Richard Cumberland made much of the fact that although he was technically capable of producing 'beings out of nature, that no sober author ever dreamt of, and forc[ing] beings into nature, that no well-bred reader ever met with', he responsibly chose instead to abstain and to steer clear of any such excess: 'I have lived long enough to see wonderful revolutions effected by an intemperate abuse of power, and shall be cautious how I risk privileges so precious upon experiments so trivial.'[55] Nathan Drake, writing 'On the Government of the Imagination; on the Frenzy of Tasso and Collins', in *Literary Hours*, also drew the implicit parallel between 'the fervour of an imagination too prone to admit the praeternatural and strange' and a youthful or immature brand of politics, and Radcliffe was one of the few writers he found it possible to endorse, as someone who could safely 'arrest attention, and keep an ardent curiosity alive' without ever inducing a 'dangerous credulity'.[56]

The *Anti-Jacobin* contributor Robert Bisset even more explicitly singled out Radcliffe as a writer of legitimate fiction, two years later, in his preface to *Douglas, or, The Highlander* (1800). Lamenting that novels like *Tom Jones* were 'out of fashion', because so 'many readers of our days are much more delighted with stories about raw heads and bloody bones', Bisset exaggeratedly promised 'no ghosts, for I know nothing about them myself', pledging instead – like Austen's narrator in *Northanger Abbey* – to confine himself to 'BRITISH SOCIETY' and to 'human nature, as it is found in these countries'. Despite his general censure of terror-fiction, Bisset was still able to celebrate Radcliffe as the exception to the corrupt rule. The 'lady' who 'has been the means of reviving the ghost-system, by those who did not comprehend the object of her works' could still be read with pleasure, since '*Mrs. Radcliffe has not introduced ghosts*, but the effects of the belief of ghosts on the human imagination': 'she has shewn herself thoroughly acquainted with the workings of the passions, and peculiarly skilled in communicating terrific impressions from imaginary causes; but I must confess I am still more pleased with her power of exhibiting the workings of the understanding and heart, in natural and probable situations'.[57] What writers such as Drake and Bisset found so congenial about Radcliffe, as a result, was the way that her works could be seen, like Austen's, to address the contemporary anxiety about 'first impressions'. If Radcliffe's work intermittently validated a potentially problematic 'enthusiasm', and to some extent dealt in the sensational, as I have already claimed, her romances nonetheless provided enough textual markers for conservative critics and reviewers to be able to enlist her on their side.

As I have argued so far, then, conservative praise of Radcliffe usually went hand in hand with the condemnation of other writers of escapist fiction, and tended to present Radcliffe's work either as an exception to the rule, or as the 'romance' analogue of the so-called proper novel, the domain of writers such as Mary Brunton and Jane West; Radcliffe was in fact included alongside Brunton, West, and Elizabeth Hamilton in an 'honor roll' of women writers that appeared in the *Antijacobin Review* in 1814.[58] From a Whig or liberal political position, William Beckford's satire on the modern romance, *Azemia* (1797), also implicitly represented Radcliffe as a writer of innocent (and therefore innocuous) fiction, making his female narrator plead to be allowed: 'a few extraordinaries – a little rambling in the woods, my dear Sir! – a castle or two, or an abbey – a few ghosts, provided I make out afterwards that they were not ghosts, but wax-work and pasteboard, and just to excite a small emotion of terror!'[59]

The most tangible signal that Radcliffe gave about the 'corruption' of her contemporaries' work is provided by *The Italian* (1797). Where *The Monk*'s narrative of Ambrosio's secret life amplified what *Udolpho* had only teasingly suggested about the past of Emily's father, *The Italian* was clearly offered by Radcliffe, in turn, as a rejoinder to Lewis's work. Coleridge's review of *The Monk* claimed that Lewis exceeded 'the nice boundaries, beyond which terror and sympathy are deserted by the pleasurable emotions', and Radcliffe in response arguably sought to defend and reassert the role of these boundaries.[60] Radcliffe's 'counter-fiction' is by no means monologic, since it goes further than anything else she wrote, as Claudia Johnson has claimed, to probe 'the tension between private affections and public obligations': Vivaldi, for example,

makes the explicit contrast between 'justice' and 'power' when pleading
Ellena's case at the Convent of San Stefano.[61] Yet although Radcliffe's
work suggestively questions family and church authority, *The Italian*
clearly sought to moderate Lewis's work in several identifiable ways.
The opening of *The Italian* obviously parallels *The Monk* in its presentation of Ellena and her guardian Signora Bianchi (counterparts of
Antonia and Leonella) at the church of San Lorenzo, and the work
similarly exploits the mythology of Catholicism, in its portrayal of the
figure of Schedoni. In contrast to Lewis, however, Radcliffe eschewed
the cynical narratorial position described in the previous chapter, and
set out instead to restore the centrality of the courtship plot, as well as to
reinstate some of the innocent and potentially comic properties of the
romance genre – witness, for example, Vivaldi's serenading of Ellena
early in the work, and the concluding scenes which depict Paulo's
devotion to his master, Vivaldi.

Radcliffe was concerned to offer a qualified reclamation of 'sensibility' in general, it seems, as is shown by the way that *The Italian*
assumes the readability of the superficial, and reasserts the transparency
of good and evil. Where *The Monk* gleefully hints at the ambiguity of
'face value' in its presentation of the gulf between Ambrosio's public and
private personae, *The Italian* provides the reader all that there is to know
about its characters simply by describing their 'countenance' or
physiognomy: for Ellena, therefore, the nun who eventually proves to be
her mother is immediately endeared to her by 'a most touching countenance; frank, noble, full of sensibility', just as Olivia herself is said to be
'unwilling to withdraw her eyes from Ellena'; Spalatro (the one-time
cohort of Schedoni), by contrast, is later presented as 'a man who had
"villain" engraved in every line of his face'.[62] Radcliffe further defined
her work against the pornographic excess of *The Monk* in her rewriting of
its incest plot. The tense episode in which Schedoni hovers above the
sleeping figure of Ellena serves to recall Ambrosio's stalking of Antonia,
but whereas Ambrosio does rape and murder his sister in Lewis's work,
Schedoni retreats from killing his supposed daughter, and it finally
transpires anyway (after Radcliffe has exploited the possibility) that he is
not her true father; Ellena is nobly born. Whereas Ambrosio's actions
are to a large extent contextualized as the result of his repressed 'natural'
desires, Schedoni – though he is by far the most complex of Radcliffe's
villains – is ultimately condemned as an 'unnatural' criminal, and his
trial all but redeems the Inquisition as a legal tribunal. Radcliffe's
qualified defence of the Inquisition, along with her presentation of the

familial society at the Convent of Santa della Pieta, arguably constituted *The Italian*'s most overt response to the liberal, and suspiciously 'jacobin', politics of *The Monk*'s anti-Catholicism. Any hint of direct engagement with political controversy is finally dispelled, though, by the 'general gaiety' of the festive romance ending, which allows the servant, Paulo, to state that virtue will always meet its reward: 'you see how people get through their misfortunes, if they have but a heart to bear up against them, and do nothing that can lie on their conscience afterwards; and how suddenly one comes to be happy, just when one is beginning to think one never is to be happy again!'[63]

Contemporary critics for their part also distinguished Radcliffean romance from the malign example of Lewis in their demonization of a monolithic 'German' literature, widely seen as I argued in the previous chapter to be a formative influence on *The Monk*. The elevation of Radcliffe is exemplified by Robert Bisset's satirical novel, *Modern Literature* (1804), which patronizes genteel 'lady' authors, such as the plagiarizing 'Miss Lacecap', at the same time as it attacks overreaching male writers, such as 'Dr Scribble', by equating the 'literary' tendency to 'transcend admitted probabilities' with the 'prevalent disposition to question established truths'.[64] The 'new style of writing, or old romance revived' identified by Bisset is said to have 'received its clothing from the literary taylors of Germany', and is irremediably tainted, as a result, by its association with 'modern illuminism'. Radcliffe, by contrast, is depicted in *Modern Literature* as a representative of 'English genius', blessed with the capacity 'so to temper the marvellous with the probable, and so to mingle both with the pleasing and the pathetic, as to hurry on the reader wherever [she chooses]'. Though she accommodated 'the growing taste for the gigantesque', therefore, the 'able and inventive author', in Bisset's terms, admitted it 'with the modifications of judgment in her scenery and machinery' without using it 'as the groundwork of her story'.[65] A similar distinction between forms of the marvellous was later made by Radcliffe herself in a dialogue 'On the Supernatural in Poetry', excerpted from the introduction to *Gaston de Blondeville*, which appeared posthumously in the *New Monthly Magazine* in 1826. In a famous passage, Radcliffe stated that whereas 'Terror', reliant upon obscurity and suggestion, 'expands the soul, and awakens the faculties to a high degree of life', 'Horror', in its naked appeal to the gigantic, 'contracts, freezes, and nearly annihilates' the same faculties, generating a feeling of chaotic disorientation. Predictably enough, Radcliffe sought to underwrite the distinction that informed her work by appealing to Burke's authoritative treatise on the sublime and the beautiful, as well as to the example of Shakespeare and Milton, writers whose 'genius' was protected by their 'better morals'.[66] Radcliffe was still being singled out as a legitimate author even in the 1830s, as in the *Edinburgh Review*'s survey of her work in 1834: though the '"rabble rout"' of imitators had 'laboured to eclipse her in her own field by the simple expedient of crowding wonders and terrors', Radcliffe retained her renown for knowing how 'to relax, as well as to press, the springs of terror and suspense; – to transport the reader, wearied with the darkness visible of Apennine castles, or the scenes of torture in the vaults of the Inquisition, to the moon-illumined streets of Venice, or the sunset dance by the Bay of Naples'.[67] If she was recognized by this time as a writer who sometimes 'copied the marvellous characteristics of the German school', as in Margaret Baron-Wilson's 1839 biography of Lewis, Radcliffe was still credited with having had 'the good taste to reject all of its immoralities'.[68]

What all of these examples point to is the tendency of critics to ground their interpretation of Radcliffe's work on an estimate of her apparently 'feminine' and self-effacing personality. Above all, it seems, what united these critics was their construction of Radcliffe as a political innocent, whose romances somehow transcended the actual or the everyday. Robert Miles's recent study *Ann Radcliffe: The Great Enchantress* has argued that all of Radcliffe's work needs to be seen in the context of her membership of 'the Dissenting, critical, "middling classes"'.[69] A work such as *The Romance of the Forest* (1791), for example, clearly introduces a series of distinctly Whiggish interjections about the miseries of superstition, the horrors of the Bastille, and 'the usual effects of an arbitrary government', and it suggestively makes a villain of a stereotypically libertine French aristocrat, the Marquis de Montalt.[70] Radcliffe's one non-fictional work, *A Journey Made in the Summer of 1794*, also attacks Catholic superstition, pays tribute to 'our glorious WILLIAM' (of Orange), and refers to the city of Liverpool as being 'immersed in the dreadful guilt of the Slave Trade'.[71] Regardless of such markers, though, the occasional topicality of Radcliffe's work seems to have been consistently overlooked by the vast majority of critics and reviewers, who valued her romances precisely because of the refuge they provided from the taint of contemporary politics. The *British Critic*'s review of *The Mysteries of Udolpho*, for example, praised it 'as a place of repose from our severer labours', where readers could 'beguile the hours of weariness and chagrin beneath the shade which fancy spreads around'.[72] This form of praise was further exemplified in a footnote on novels that was added (in 1796) to the opening dialogue of T. J. Mathias's censorious satire *The Pursuits of Literature*. Where the novels of 'Mrs Charlotte Smith, Mrs Inchbald, Mrs Mary Robinson, Mrs &c. &c.' were intermittently 'tainted with democracy', turning 'our girls' heads . . . wild with impossible adventures', the works of 'the mighty magician of . . . UDOLPHO' were divorced from the contemporary altogether and located in a vacuum, their author 'bred and nourished by the Florentine Muses in their sacred solitary caverns, amid the paler shrines of Gothick superstition, and in all the dreariness of inchantment'.[73] Radcliffe was similarly described as transcending the contamination of the contemporary or the modern in Richard Polwhele's poem of 1798 'The Unsex'd Females'. Most famous for its abuse of Mary Wollstonecraft, Polwhele's poem contrasted the overreachers who had 'resign'd [their] power to please' (the same writers as those identified by Mathias) with the writers who maintained the more traditional role of providing 'Poetic feeling and poetic ease', such as Fanny Burney, and Ann Radcliffe.[74] When we read Radcliffe's 'wild and wondrous tales', a contributor to the *New Monthly Magazine* wrote in 1820, 'the world seems shut out, and we breathe only in an enchanted region, where lovers' lutes tremble over placid waters, mouldering castles rise conscious of deeds of blood, and the sad voices of the past echo through deep vaults and lonely galleries': 'her conclusions are lame and impotent almost without example', yet 'while her spells actually operate her power is truly magical'.[75]

Despite the obvious anachronisms in Radcliffean romance (characters in the sixteenth-century setting of *A Sicilian Romance*, for example, play 'the violoncello, . . . the German flute, and . . . the piana-forte'), it seems that few contemporary critics, at least in the 1790s, were interested in subjecting Radcliffe to a historically minded form of criticism.[76] The *Critical*'s review of *Udolpho* stressed that 'the manners do not sufficiently correspond with the aera the author has chosen', and the article on 'Terrorist Novel Writing' in the *Spirit of the Public Journals for 1797* similarly complained that Radcliffe 'affects in the most disgusting manner a knowledge of languages, countries, customs, and objects of art of which she is lamentably ignorant':

she suspends *tripods* from the ceiling by chains, not knowing that a *tripod* is a utensil standing on three feet. She covers the kingdom of Naples with India figs, because *St Pierre* has introduced those tropical plants in his tales, of which the

scene is laid in India, and she makes a convent of monks a necessary appendage
to a monastery of nuns.[77]

Such hostility was rare, though, and the *Critical*'s review of *Udolpho* in
any case qualified the charge it levelled by stating that 'any attempt to
analyse the story . . . would have no other effect than destroying the
pleasure of the reader'.[78] Perhaps the main factor explaining the lack of
critical attention given to Radcliffean anachronism was that she ignored
the more sensitive realm of English history, at least until after *The Italian*,
and concentrated instead upon creating an *aura* of predominantly
Mediterranean pastness. While a work such as *Udolpho*, set in 1584,
sometimes mentions 'the turbulence of that period' or certain
peculiarities of 'that time', these comments seem to be purely concessionary, like the perfunctory scenarios of English travellers abroad
which introduce *A Sicilian Romance* and *The Italian*; as is the case with the
casual reference to the 'Parliamentary Court' records of Guyot de
Pitaval at the start of *The Romance of the Forest*, narrative frames are
rapidly discarded in Radcliffe's work, and are never returned to for the
purposes of closure as they are in the Waverley novels.[79] Whereas in *St
Leon* (1799), for example, Godwin sought to place the Inquisition within
the context of the Counter-Reformation, and the opposition between
institutional authority and concepts of private judgement, Radcliffe by
contrast offered very little to legitimize her recourse to the exoticism of
tribunals and inquisitors. With *The Italian*, indeed, as Scott argued,
Radcliffe '*selected* the new and powerful machinery afforded her by the
Popish religion' (my emphasis) so as to have at her disposal an alluring, if
not completely novel, fictional register of 'monks, spies, dungeons, the
mute obedience of the bigot, the dark and dominating spirit of the crafty
priest – all the thunders of the Vatican, and all the terrors of the
Inquisition'.[80] Even if *The Italian* ultimately defends Catholic institutions,
therefore, it seems fair to say that rather than being concerned about the
accuracy of 'costume', Radcliffe's romances generally appealed instead
to a fund of consumable stereotypes, betraying – with their vagueness
about Catholicism in particular – what Ian Duncan has called 'a
spiritual orientalism in the British Protestant imagination'.[81] The 'scenes' of *The Italian*, as the *British Critic*'s reviewer wrote, 'are laid in a
country highly favourable . . . to the genius and spirit of romance'.[82]

Well into the nineteenth century, indeed, Radcliffe was praised, after
Keats's famous description, as 'mother Ratcliff' – a matronly author-
figure with a unique gift for telling captivating stories.[83] As is still true

today, critics wrote off their misgivings about Radcliffe's work so that they would not interfere with the pleasure she provided. Though Radcliffe's plots 'may be very absurd', and her 'species' of romance 'neither very instructive in its nature, nor so fitted as some other kinds of fictitious writing, to leave agreeable impressions on the mind', as John Dunlop conceded in *The History of Fiction* (1814), 'life perhaps has few things better than sitting at the chimney-corner in a winter evening after a well-spent day, and reading such absurdities': 'romances of this kind', indeed, afford 'a better relaxation than those which approach more nearly to the common business of life'.[84] While 'her descriptions of scenery . . . are vague and wordy', 'her characters are insipid', and 'her story comes to nothing', as Hazlitt claimed in his article 'On the English Novelists', Radcliffe's works nonetheless succeeded in reducing him to a state of child-like dependence: 'Mrs Radcliffe touched the trembling chords of the imagination, making wild music there.'[85]

'The superb absence of any historical sense', Q. D. Leavis wrote in 1932, 'is the saving of The Mysteries of Udolpho.'[86] If Radcliffe was recognized to be ignorant about the countries and periods she referred to, this ignorance in many ways served to underwrite the transport of romance readers, and their (albeit temporary) removal from actuality. According to a contributor to the *Edinburgh Review* in 1823, for example, 'the fair authoress kept herself as much *incognito* as the Author of Waverley; nothing was known of her but her name on the title page. She never appeared in public nor mingled in private society, but kept herself apart, like the sweet bird that sings its solitary notes, shrowded and unseen.'[87] Just as the lives of eighteenth-century peasant poets were used in order to legitimize and locate the authenticity of their work for polite readers, as Morag Shiach has argued, so too were women novelists in this period liable to have their work read and reviewed in the context of their private lives.[88] Critics often attacked Charlotte Smith, for example, because of the way that details about her personal life intruded into novels such as *The Banished Man* (1794).[89] Reviewers of Radcliffe's romances, by contrast, presented apparent facts about her distance from 'the world' in order to prove that her works could be safely consumed by whoever read them.

The main source of biographical information about Radcliffe, Thomas Talfourd's 'Life and Writings of Mrs. Radcliffe', attached to *Gaston de Blondeville* (1826), predicated its praise of her work on the assumption that the author always knew her place. Radcliffe's life was 'a pleasing phenomenon in the literature of her time', indeed, since 'during a period, in which the spirit of personality has extended its influence, till it has rendered the habits and conversations of authors almost as public as their compositions, she confined herself, with delicate apprehensiveness, to the circle of domestic duties and pleasures'.[90] Talfourd actually had very little information about Radcliffe available, but he turned this to his advantage by claiming that the lack of incident in her life only emphasized its 'calm tenor of happiness', and her removal from politics, from 'fashion's idle pastime', and 'controversy's more idle business'.[91] Denying Radcliffe's profile as a more or less professional writer, therefore, the memoir claimed that she had to be cajoled into publishing her work, because 'nothing could tempt her . . . to sink for a moment, the gentlewoman in the novelist'.[92] Radcliffe was averse to 'the very thought of appearing in person as the author of her romances' and 'tremblingly alive to every circumstance which could, by the remotest possibility, raise an inference injurious to the personal character she valued far above literary fame'.[93] Even though – like many male readers – Talfourd complained about the 'impotent conclusions' of her romances, this failure was virtually excused by being attributed to Radcliffe's veneration 'for every species of authority', and her apparent conviction 'that some established canon of romance obliged her to reject real supernatural agency'.[94] Radcliffe's decision to stop writing romances, in the early nineteenth century, was similarly attributed to her consciousness of reputation, since Talfourd speculated that Radcliffe sought to distance herself from the numerous writers who tried to imitate her style. Like so many reviewers in the 1790s, then, Talfourd made an exceptionalist case for the achievement of Radcliffe, the crux of which was that 'she only, of all writers of romance, . . . employed enchantments purely innocent'. Radcliffe was the 'inventor of a new style of romance, 'equally distant from the old tales of chivalry and magic, and from modern representations of credible incidents and living manners', and her works displayed 'the charms of each species of composition; interweaving the miraculous with the probable'.[95]

Well into the nineteenth century, therefore, Radcliffe was celebrated as the author of a uniquely charming and enchanting brand of romance. For all the apparent sincerity of the acclaim Radcliffe received, though, it is important to remain sceptical about the wider significance of such praise, and to recognize the ways in which it was hedged or qualified. In the same way that, according to Ina Ferris, the reputation of the 'proper novel' for prudence 'carried an ambiguous inflection, at once essential and inimical to the values the literary republic sought to affirm', so too was the elevation of Radcliffe's work also somewhat equivocal, since it was so often emphasized that what she wrote was *merely* romance, all but generically trapped, according to the *Critical's* review of *Udolpho*, between 'the trite and the extravagant[,] the Scylla and Charybdis of writers who deal in fiction'.[96] Regardless of the efforts Radcliffe made to dignify her work and set it apart from the mass of escapist fiction, numerous male critics and reviewers made it clear that 'the modern romance' was irremediably inferior to 'the novel' itself, 'the most excellent, but at the same time the most difficult, species of novel-writing'. Though *The Italian* was 'perfect of its kind', and the modern romance might be 'more imposing' than the novel 'on the first perusal', as Arthur Aikin stated in the *Monthly Review*, 'the characteristic which distinguishes it essentially from, and shews its vast inferiority to, the genuine novel, is that, like a secret, it ceases to interest after it can no longer awaken our curiosity; while the other, like truth, may be reconsidered and studied with increased satisfaction'.[97] Coleridge's review of *The Italian* put the matter in a similar light, arguing that even when it was 'supported by the skill of the most ingenious of its votaries', the modern romance 'would soon experience the fate of every attempt to please by what is unnatural, and by a departure from that observance of real life, which has placed the works of Fielding and Smollett . . . among the permanent sources of amusement':

it might for a time afford an acceptable variety to persons whose reading is confined to works of fiction, and who would, perhaps, be glad to exchange dullness for extravagance; but it was probable that, as its constitution (if we may speak) was maintained only by the passion of terror, and that excited by trick, and as it was not conversant in incidents and characters of a natural complexion, it would degenerate into repetition, and would disappoint curiosity. So many cries 'that the wolf is coming', must at last lose their effect.[98]

If Radcliffe was acknowledged as the commanding author of a particular variety of fiction, it was also widely stressed, as in Hugh Murray's *Morality of Fiction* (1805), that the pleasure her work afforded was 'not of a very high order' – and that this pleasure, 'till her time', had been 'confined chiefly to the nursery'.[99] This strictly qualified form of praise became even more common with the ascendancy of Walter Scott and the historical novel. Radcliffe's apparent distance from political controversy was what made her work so attractive for many readers in the first place, as I have argued above, but alongside the example of the Waverley novels, Radcliffean romance was increasingly regarded as naive and ignorant. 'Her style of writing must be allowed to form an era in English romances', as a writer in the *British Review* claimed in 1818, but Radcliffe's 'ignorance was nearly equal to her imagination, and that is saying a great deal'; 'of the modes of life on the continent (where the scenes of all her romances, with the exception of one, are laid) she knew little or nothing'.[100] The frequently acknowledged limitations of Radcliffe's treatment of the supernatural were also reiterated, with Scott's biographer Lockhart stating in *Blackwood's* in 1824 that 'that very clever lady had not brains to exhaust anything – and she no more worked out horror, than she did the scenery of the Apennines'.[101] According to Robert Chambers in 1844, similarly, 'Mrs Radcliffe restricted her genius by an arbitrary rule of composition. She made the whole of her mysterious circumstances resolve into natural causes.' 'No writer has excelled, and few have approached, Mrs Radcliffe' in the 'peculiar province' of rationalizing the supernatural; 'a higher genius, however, would have boldly seized upon supernatural agency as a proper element of romance'.[102]

The extent to which Radcliffe was allocated a relatively minor niche in the unofficial hierarchy of genres is made clear by the overwhelmingly hostile reception of her posthumously published *Gaston de Blondeville, or The Court of Henry III Keeping Festival in Ardenne: A Romance* (1826), an attempt on her part to diversify beyond a widely imitated fictional blueprint. As I argued in the chapter on the Loyalist Gothic romance, *Gaston de Blondeville* is the most overtly conservative of all the works that Radcliffe wrote, not least because it sought to draw attention away from the increasingly sensitive realm of Catholic institutional power which had been exploited by works such as *The Monk*. *Gaston* differs markedly from Radcliffe's previous work in several obvious ways: it is set in England (and is therefore more historically specific than her other romances), it is extensively annotated, probably by her 'biographer' Thomas Talfourd, and – most importantly – it credits the agency of the supernatural. According to the 1834 introduction to Bentley's edition of *The Castle of Otranto*, for example, *Gaston de Blondeville*, if only for its recourse to the supernatural, 'for the poetical grandeur of the being who so awfully "revisits the glimpses of the moon"', was 'entitled to assume a higher rank in romantic fiction than any other which Mrs Radcliffe has produced'.[103] Despite the apparent congeniality of *Gaston* for the critics who represented Radcliffe as a confined author, however, it was dismissed by the vast majority of reviewers as a 'sinking' from the trademark qualities set by her earlier work. As a transparently loyalist romance written in the early 1800s, during a period of protracted conflict, *Gaston* probably seemed to be a dated work by the time that it was actually published in 1826. More tellingly, though, *Gaston* was simply regarded as a work which was too uncharacteristic of the style which had come to be associated with Radcliffe the enchantress. Although the many critics who celebrated Radcliffe's work before *Gaston* also added caveats about her 'impotent' conclusions and her general 'ignorance', therefore, her sole effort to introduce a real ghost and a degree of antiquarian rigour nonetheless met with almost unanimous disapproval. 'Dulness pervades the narrative in *Gaston de Blondeville*', as a critic claimed in the *Ladies' Monthly Museum* in 1826, with 'the writer having copied the style and manner of other novelists, instead of giving the reins to her imagination'; 'if any thing . . . could reconcile us to Mrs Radcliffe's system of explaining every thing by natural causes in her former romances', a writer in the *Edinburgh Review* argued in 1834, 'it would be to see how completely . . . she has failed in the management of a true spirit, for here all her early tact seems to have deserted her'.[104]

In her work before *Gaston*, as Julia Kavanagh wrote in *English Women of Letters* (1863), Radcliffe 'left historical events and the Middle Ages to the past, threw the date of her stories only so far back as to give them a romantic interest, and, far from imitating any who had preceded her, she became, by the thoroughly original method she adopted, the foundress of a new school'.[105] 'Mrs Radcliffe's romances', as Kavanagh claimed, 'fill up the great gap in imaginative literature which lies between Miss Reeve's "English Baron", itself the offspring of "The Castle of Otranto", and Sir Walter Scott's novels.'[106] When Radcliffe attempted to write a more ambitious brand of fiction, however, she succeeded only in betraying her 'imperfect education', and her deficiency 'in character, in penetration, in historical knowledge, [and] in all the minutiae that prove reading, skill, and a cultivated taste'.[107] *Gaston* was 'a singular combination of the Walter Scott and Radcliffe elements', but it ultimately suffered from its author's decision to try and move beyond her true literary domain:

conscious, at last, of her ignorance in archaeology, and vexed, no doubt, that so easy a source of power should have been closed on her so long, she went into the other extreme, and from a complete disregard of historic truth, she indulged herself with an amount of architecture and costume which sat awkwardly on her story, and injured it. Knowledge came too late, and Mrs Radcliffe showed her wisdom in not publishing this tardy attempt. She began by being a disciple of Walpole, and from Walpole to Walter Scott the transition was too great. Her first manner was not good, but it was her best.[108]

Radcliffe's exceptional reputation in the 1790s and early 1800s was at least partly dependent upon the fact that her work was seen to provide a legitimate form of diversion or recreation at a time of obvious national crisis. While this reputation survived well into the nineteenth century, and was invoked against the ambition of her own *Gaston de Blondeville*, though, it is fair to say that Radcliffe's romances were increasingly liable to be judged by more demanding criteria. I want now to conclude this chapter by referring briefly once more to perhaps the most famous piece of Radcliffe criticism, Scott's 1824 introduction to her work for Ballantyne's *Novelist's Library* series. Scott defended Radcliffe from both her 'copyists' and her 'hyper-critics', and he made the outwardly generous gesture of stating that Radcliffe's work should be judged by its own standards alone:

the real and only point is, whether, considered as a separate and distinct species of writing, that introduced by Mrs Radcliffe possesses merit, and affords pleasure; for these premises being admitted, it is as unreasonable to complain of the absence of advantages foreign to her style and plan, and proper to those of another mode of composition, as to regret that the peach-tree does not produce grapes, or the vine peaches.[109]

Scott further praised Radcliffe's work, in the same terms that were often applied to his own novels, by emphasizing both that her romances were morally irreproachable and that they succeeded in unifying an increasingly disparate reading public – appealing to 'every reader . . . from the sage in his study, to the family group in middle life'.[110] Typically, however, Scott also quite clearly indicated where Radcliffe's 'species' of writing came in the hierarchy of genres, and how it was situated in relation to his own work, and he stated, disparagingly, that her brand of romance bore 'nearly the same relation to the novel that the modern anomaly entitled a melo-drama does to the proper drama'.[111] Most famously, of course, as I mentioned earlier, Scott also returned to the issue of Radcliffe's handling of the supernatural. While Scott claimed that Radcliffe's priority was to 'appeal . . . to the passion of fear', her ultimate achievement was limited, even by her own standards, because of the way that she resorted to the rational explanation of her 'mysteries'. 'In this', Scott claimed, 'we do not greatly applaud her art':

A stealthy step behind the arras, may doubtless, in some situations, and when the nerves are tuned to a certain pitch, have no small influence upon the imagination; but if the conscious listener discovers it to be only the noise made by the cat, the solemnity of the feeling is gone, and the visionary is at once angry with his senses for having been cheated, and with his reason for having acquiesced in the deception.[112]

Not only did Radcliffe write within a low genre, therefore, but in exploiting the same formula of resolution not once but four times, she inevitably compromised the force of her appeal to what Scott identified as the reader's 'latent sense of supernatural awe, and curiosity concerning whatever is hidden and mysterious'.[113] Scott's Waverley novels, by contrast, as the next chapter will argue, sought to pre-empt charges either of subliterary status or imaginative stagnation by grounding a fictional superstructure on a historical base. Claiming that 'the true thing will triumph over the brightest inventions of the most ardent imagination', Scott synthesized history and romance so as to provide, as one admiring critic put it, 'the truth of history without the monotony – the interest of romance without its unreality'.[114]

CHAPTER 5

The field of romance: Walter Scott,
the Waverley novels, the Gothic

In 1813, before the appearance of Waverley, if anyone should have
ventured to predict that a writer would arise, who, when every
conceivable form of composition seemed not only to have been
tried, but exhausted, should be the creator of one hitherto unknown, and which, in its immediate popularity, should exceed all
others – who, when we fancied we had drained to its last drop the
cup of intellectual excitement, should open a spring, not only new
and untasted but apparently deep and inexhaustible – that he
should exhibit his marvels in a form of composition the least
respected in the whole circle of literature, and raise the Novel to a
place among the highest productions of human intellect – his
prediction would have been received, not only with incredulity, but
with ridicule

Edinburgh Review, 1832[1]

[Scott] was no genius, merely, as an inspection of Mrs Radcliffe's
novels shows, another Mrs Radcliffe. So he put his novels together
in the easiest way, and his originality consisted in finding new
backgrounds to set off the old conventions, as hers had been

Q. D. Leavis, *Fiction and the Reading Public*, 1932[2]

The previous chapters in this book have argued that the Gothic
romance is a hybrid genre, its diverse affiliations best understood by way
of detailed case studies of authors, works, and publishing events, and via
a focus on the kinds of classification made by contemporary critics and
reviewers. Given my interest in the different ways that writers appealed
to the category of romance and deployed the vocabulary of 'the Gothic',
this final chapter will look much more closely at the work of an
individual who was both a participant in, and a critical surveyor of, the
field of romance – Walter Scott. As the first quotation above illustrates,
Scott was widely acclaimed for transforming the potential of prose

fiction in the writing of the Waverley novels, and credited with effecting a major shift in the status of the novel as a genre. This narrative of Scott's triumphant emergence has been rehearsed many times, of course, but what I want to focus on in particular is the nature of the retrospect that Scott provided on the Gothic romance. Scott corresponded with Lewis and contributed to his *Tales of Wonder*, wrote magazine reviews of works by Godwin, Maturin, and Mary Shelley, discussed the writing of Walpole, Reeve, and Radcliffe in the critical biographies he prepared for Ballantyne's *Novelist's Library*, and frequently alluded to the work of his rivals in the prefaces, postscripts, and notes surrounding the Waverley novels. After a brief discussion of the production and reception of Scott's early work, this chapter will deal with Scott's literary criticism and the different forms of framing material which he used in his writing career, so as to consider the self-reflexive way in which – while attempting to protect his anonymity – he defined a particular set of positions alongside and against the other writers who have been treated so far. Scott forged a role that united the professional and aristocratic or baronial identities of lawyer and laird, and sought to construct an authorial position as a practical man of the world, whose experience extended beyond the literary realm. This chapter will go on to describe the renowned synthesis of history and romance that initially enabled Scott to circumvent the problem of 'repetition' faced by Radcliffe, and in a discussion of three canonical works, *Ivanhoe*, *The Antiquary*, and *The Bride of Lammermoor*, it will then look at the ways in which Scott addressed component features of many 'Gothic' romances: the use of an English medieval setting, the figure of the disguised hero or dispossessed heir, and the sensationalist recourse to supernatural agency. As I will argue, these digressive and rhetorically complex works actually testify to a far more equivocal relation to the Gothic and the category of romance than the received account of Scott's pre-eminence allows. Though the Waverley novels were celebrated with unprecedented enthusiasm as the triumph of real life over romance, and surely hastened the initial decline in critical favour of writers such as Radcliffe, the uncertain tone and identity of Scott's novels and their proximity to the category of romance nonetheless provided the grounds for later critics to conflate the Waverley novels with the works that he had much earlier patronized. In what will serve as a postscript to this book, I will conclude by offering a brief account of the fluctuating reputation of the Gothic romance alongside the Waverley novels in the late nineteenth and early twentieth centuries; while Scott's novels were increasingly relegated to the status of romance or children's literature, 'the Gothic' came to be redefined as a continuous and unified tradition in a way which still exerts a powerful hold today.

Scott began his writing career in the 1790s, during the heyday of the Gothic romance, as the mediator of a largely oral tradition of popular ballads and folk tales, attracted by the recognition being afforded to writers such as Matthew Lewis at the head of the German literary 'invasion'. In his 'Essay on Imitations of the Ancient Ballad' in 1830, Scott described how poetry had been at 'a remarkably low ebb' in Britain in the 1790s, and claimed that the initial success of *The Monk* 'seemed to shew that the prevailing taste in [Germany] might be easily employed as a formidable auxiliary to reviving the spirits of our own'.[3] Scott admitted to writing in the style which had raised the profile of Lewis, but he also projected his early involvement with German literature firmly into the past, and distinguished the nature of his interest from that of all the other translators and imitators by incorporating such a youthful dalliance into an account of his formative literary education. While the 'Essay' obviously represents a retrospective form of self-presentation, Scott in fact seemed to plan the course of his career in poetry from a very early stage, with his first works forming, as Peter Murphy has recently claimed, 'a series, expressive of a sort of apprenticeship'.[4] After a brief spell as a translator (notably of Bürger and Goethe), Scott progressed to the status of editor and imitator, and contributed several annotated tales, founded on Border legends, to Lewis's *Tales of Wonder* (1801). Even before this anthology was published, however, Scott predicted that 'Lewis's stock of horribles' would 'overstock the market', and he clearly distanced himself from the gratuitous sensationalism of many of the tales (though he had used the collection to gain a form of work experience): 'I think the Marvellous in Poetry is ill-timed & disgusting when not . . . ingrafted upon some circumstance of popular tradition or belief which sometimes can give even to the improbable an air of something like probability.'[5] Scott significantly re-inflected the role of the supernatural in his own anthology of poems and tales, *Minstrelsy of the Scottish Border* (1802–3), in which he sought to integrate sensation and folklore, and present 'romantic' ballads founded on local tradition. Even 'before he passed the threshold of authorship', as a result, as Scott's son-in-law and biographer J. G. Lockhart later claimed, he had 'assembled about him . . . almost all the materials on which his genius was destined to be employed for the gratification and instruction of the world'.[6]

When Scott finally appeared as a fully fledged author with *The Lay of the Last Minstrel* (1805), it seems that he was already interested in experimenting with the framing procedures and techniques of synthesis which are now most often associated with the Waverley novels. During the period of his apprenticeship, as Peter Murphy has argued, Scott learnt how to 'give the reader irregularity and remain regular himself'.[7] This ability is evident in the way that *The Lay* presents the Minstrel as a transitional figure or a 'filter' for the distant past. Not only does *The Lay* present the Minstrel straddling ancient and modern worlds, but it also makes the Minstrel responsible for 'the Marvellous', since he – rather than Scott – is the medium for the oral tradition on which the work is based: 'I cannot tell how the truth may be; / I say the tale as 'twas told to me.'[8] Whereas Lewis had stated simply that 'a Ghost or a Witch' was 'a sine-qua-non ingredient in all the dishes, of which I mean to compose my hobgoblin repast',[9] Scott, for his part, clearly distanced *The Lay* from such a casual recourse to supernatural agency, by attempting to supervise 'the Marvellous in Poetry' and give it ethnographic validation as the property of popular tradition or belief. Though many contemporary critics objected to the character of the 'Goblin-Page' serving Lord Cranstoun and the dialogue between the Spirits of the Flood and the Fell (since, as Francis Jeffrey put it, they could have had no 'lawful business . . . at Branksome castle in the year 1550'), the terms used by a critic such as Jeffrey to praise *The Lay* were in fact similar to those he and others later used to praise the Waverley novels.[10] Applauding Scott's 'attempt to transfer the refinements of modern poetry to the matter and the manner of the ancient metrical romance', Jeffrey particularly endorsed *The Lay*'s negotiation of the poetry versus progress trade-off which had been debated so much in the eighteenth century. Rather than even consider this dilemma, Scott – as Jeffrey explained – simply plundered 'the ancient romances' for what they were worth: 'it was evidently Mr Scott's business to retain all that was good, and to reject all that was bad in the models upon which he was to form himself'.[11] If the framing device of the Minstrel is less sophisticated than those to be found in the Waverley novels, it nonetheless allowed Scott, as he put it in the work's preface, to describe both 'scenes highly susceptible of poetical ornament' *and* 'the customs and manners which anciently prevailed on the Borders of England and Scotland'.[12]

What the many favourable reviews of Scott's poetry pointed to was his ability, while remaining in the background himself, to distil or filter for modern consumption the exotic vitality of the primitive, oral past.

Scott's efforts to assimilate 'irregularity' were still liable to generate critical dissent, however, as is most notably clear in Jeffrey's review of *Marmion* (1808) in the *Edinburgh Review*. Where the *Lay* for Jeffrey had circumvented most of the problems attendant upon the revival of 'rudeness', *Marmion*, a poem without the *Lay*'s framing apparatus, in effect re-opened the debate about the nature of Scott's muse, and his relationship with romance. Though Jeffrey's criticism of *Marmion* can partly be attributed to his Whig distaste for the poem's militarism and the Tory position of its introductory elegy, the larger problem to which the review pointed, raised elsewhere by Jeffrey in relation to Byron's *Turkish Tales* and Tom Moore's *Lalla Rookh*, was Scott's apparent loss of a balanced 'stages-of-society' perspective on the attractions of the distant past.[13] Jeffrey emphasized that a second imitation of 'obsolete extravagance' left Scott in danger of appearing as a Quixotic obsessive, 'corrupted by the wicked tales of knight-errantry and enchantment' and displaying 'a taste too evidently unnatural to be long prevalent in the modern world'.[14] Thomas Love Peacock's utilitarian critique of 'The Four Ages of Poetry' (1820) famously accused Scott, along with Byron and the Lake Poets, of 'raking up the ashes of dead savages to find gewgaws and rattles for the grown babies of the age',[15] and perhaps even more seriously, Scott was charged with the imitation of contemporary Gothic romance models. The second canto of *Marmion*, in which the nun Constance is buried alive, caused *The Satirist*'s reviewer, for example, to claim that Scott had drawn 'from the jejune stories of Monk Ghost Lewis, Esq', while Jeffrey similarly likened its 'instruments of knightly vengeance and redress' (the killing of Marmion at Flodden Field) to what might be expected of 'the machinery of a bad German novel'.[16] Jeffrey's review further indicted Scott for 'borrowing' well-worn imagery 'from the novels of Mrs Radcliffe and her imitators', just as Coleridge's contemptuous 'recipe' for Scott's poetry, contained in a letter to Wordsworth in 1810, represented him as a writer who simply added (or in Coleridge's terms, pissed) local detail onto 'the Fable, and the Dramatis Personae' of Radcliffe's work.[17] Many reviews of Scott's later poetry, it is true, acknowledged their virtual impotence in the face of the poems' phenomenal popularity, as when *The British Review*, dealing with *Rokeby* (1813), stated that 'after what Mr Scott has accomplished he may laugh at those critics who deny him the credit of original genius'.[18] Despite the widespread consciousness of a decline in critical authority, it is nonetheless fair to say that reviewers of Scott's poetry frequently queried his recourse to the 'rudeness' of the distant past, and questioned more generally the originality of his perceived formula.

Regardless of his protestations to the contrary, Scott was constantly attentive to the reputation of all of his works, and – having been eclipsed by Byron – went on to divorce himself from his 'attempts in poetry', claiming in a letter to Maria Edgeworth in 1818 that the poems were 'orphans for whom their ostrich parent cares most exceedingly little'.[19] What enabled Scott to distance himself in such a way was the unprecedented commercial *and* critical success initially enjoyed by the productions of 'the Author of *Waverley*'. The varied reception of Scott's poetry makes the widespread, and in some cases almost unqualified, praise accumulated by the novels all the more striking, a contrast nowhere more evident than in the criticism of Francis Jeffrey in the *Edinburgh Review*. Where *Marmion*, in Jeffrey's terms, was a dangerously attractive modern chivalric romance, *Waverley* comfortably transcended the problems attendant upon the revival of rudeness, and had the effect of 'casting the whole tribe of ordinary novels into the shade', by its superiority to 'any thing of the sort which has been offered to the publick for the last sixty years'.[20] Though 'the Author of *Waverley*' remained an anonymous figure to the majority of readers until 1827, Scott's switch to novel-writing, as I will go on to argue, allowed him to create for himself a much more distinct profile in relation to other contemporary writers. *Waverley* as a publishing event supplies further evidence of the way in which Scott advanced claims about the evolutionary development of his career, a process which I will now trace further in a discussion of Scott's negotiation of the field, via both his renowned narrative frames and prefaces and his diverse forms of literary criticism.

'The most remarkable thing about the whole massive paraphernalia of Scott's narrative presentation', Richard Waswo has argued, was 'its incremental appearance throughout his career as a novelist'; in the final years of his life, Scott added still further introductory and documentary material to the novels with the publication of the Magnum Opus collected edition.[21] If there is comparatively little in the way of prefatory material in the works before *Old Mortality* (1816), the self-consciousness of Scott's innovation is nonetheless evident in the first chapter of his first novel. *Waverley* itself has no preface as such, of course (unless the 'Postscript, which should have been a Preface' is counted), but its 'Introductory' opening chapter, a meditation on 'the importance of a title-page', marked the beginning of Scott's efforts to carve a niche for himself in its famous survey of the field of contemporary fiction.[22] What is particularly noticeable in this preamble is the way that the narrator

defines his authorial profile in an overtly negative way, rejecting out-
right 'the example of my predecessors'.[23] Rather than dispute the
ground held by others, Scott sought instead to mark out fictional
territory of his own. While the postscript to *Waverley* admits the work's
emulation, 'in some distant degree', of Maria Edgeworth's 'admirable
Irish portraits',[24] Scott was generally reluctant to credit literary influences, omitting to mention the other women writers who were pioneers of
the so-called national tale, such as Lady Morgan and the Porter sisters.
Scott presented *Waverley* as a fictional *tabula rasa* even though, as Katie
Trumpener has recently stated, the character-name 'Waverley' (or
'Waverly') was itself 'already occupied'.[25] Despite the appearance of
Waverleys in nearly contemporary works by Charlotte Smith and Jane
West, Scott's narrator offers 'WAVERLEY' as an 'uncontaminated
name', thereby implying that the novel cannot be held guilty by association with the 'pages of inanity' that had been produced 'for half a
century past'. Scott's introduction further seeks to establish *Waverley*'s
newness by rejecting a number of different 'supplemental' titles ('"a
Tale of other Days"', '"a Romance from the German"', 'a "Sentimental Tale"', '"A Tale of the Times"'), so avoiding the need to meet the
'preconceived associations' that such subtitles would generate.[26] This
listing of expectations has the effect of reducing these other forms of
contemporary fiction to a formula, and dismissing their claims to
originality, or even interest. The narrator constantly draws attention to
the authority that underwrites such a survey, meanwhile, referring to his
'own intimate knowledge of the particular ingredients necessary to the
composition of romances and novels'; while the narrator is a genial
figure, 'a civil driver' of 'a humble English post-chaise', he also makes it
clear that he is in firm control, as director and supervisor of the journey
into 'more picturesque and romantic country'.[27]

   One initial problem with privileging such a consciously groundbreaking (and often-quoted) passage is that many of Scott's more
detailed references to writers of Gothic romances were, like his reviews
for the *Quarterly*, and his *Novelist's Library* prefaces, ostensibly favourable.
Scott frequently presented a self-deprecating image as a genial and
unpretentious 'sportsman' of an author, indeed, and the veneer of
generosity that characterizes his commentary on contemporaries and
immediate predecessors certainly separates him from writers such as
Walpole and Lewis, who – as I have indicated in previous chapters –
were much more hostile in their reference to competitors. For all the
apparent generosity, though, the praise which Scott gave a work or a

writer was always hedged or qualified in significant ways. In his brief biography of Ann Radcliffe, for example, Scott made it clear that her work was distinct from 'the ordinary meagreness of stale and uninteresting incident' published by the Minerva Press, but as I made clear at the end of the last chapter, he also emphasized that what she wrote was mere 'romance', the relation of which to the novel itself was the same as that of 'the modern anomaly entitled a melo-drama . . . to the proper drama'.[28] Scott defended Radcliffe from 'hyper-critics' by stressing that her work ought to be judged on its own terms, but he also confined the range or the scope of this work, by stating that it was able to do no more than provide 'a solace from the toils of ordinary existence', by 'an excursion into the regions of imagination'.[29] Though Radcliffe was acclaimed for being 'the first to introduce into her prose fictions a beautiful and fanciful tone of natural description and impressive narrative, . . . hitherto . . . exclusively applied to poetry', therefore, this kind of praise was subtly restrictive, since as Fiona Robertson has argued, it chivalrously allowed Radcliffe a role 'not as a novelist but as a "poetess", a dealer in sentiment and gentility'.[30]

Though *The Heart of Midlothian* closes with a homily about the need to follow the 'paths of virtue',[31] Scott clearly distanced many of his novels from the Radcliffean (or stereotypically 'feminine') style of romance closure, even when such a resolution seemed to be structurally integral to a particular plot, as in the final chapter of *Old Mortality* (1816). With the introduction in an advisory capacity of the mantua-maker 'Miss Martha Buskbody', said to be familiar with 'the whole stock of three circulating libraries', Scott via Peter Pattieson quite explicitly projected the desire for 'conventional' plot resolution and 'the marriage of the principal personages' (in this case, Henry Morton and Edith Bellenden) onto a heavily satirized class of women readers.[32] In a similar way, Scott withheld the description of the hero's marriage at the close of *Quentin Durward* (1823), 'leaving it to whom it may please to add farther particulars, after the fashion of their own imagination'.[33] When he referred to writers such as Walpole, Lewis and Maturin, by contrast, it seems as though Scott's praise was chiefly elicited by the 'boldness' and energy which their works were seen to display. Despite the extravagance that he identified in Maturin's *Fatal Revenge* (1807), for example, Scott's review for the *Quarterly* in 1810 claimed that its author's 'powers' still entitled him to 'no common degree of respect', just as Lewis's *The Monk* was said to command the respect of the reader (in Scott's 'Essay on Imitations of the Ancient Ballad'), because 'the author introduced supernatural machinery with a courageous consciousness of his own power to manage its ponderous strength'.[34] This notion of 'respect' similarly informed Scott's discussion of Walpole. In his lives of Walpole and Radcliffe, for example, Scott gendered the distinction between different forms of Gothic romance even more explicitly, by juxtaposing Walpole's 'bold avowal' and Radcliffe's coquettish refusal of 'supernatural machinery'.[35] Not only did Scott appeal to the rhetoric of genius when praising Walpole (for 'that secret and reserved feeling of love for the marvellous and the supernatural', he argued, 'occupies a hidden corner in almost every one's bosom'), but he also claimed that *Otranto*'s 'bold assertion' of the supernatural was in fact far more 'harmonious' with the early medieval setting, and thus more acceptable to the 'gentle reader', possessed of a contractual understanding about what was required to 'humour the deceit'.[36] As I indicated in my first chapter, Scott arguably misread *Otranto* to the extent that he overstated Walpole's historical interest, or projected onto Walpole his own interest, in drawing 'such a picture of domestic life and manners, during the feudal times, as might actually have existed';[37] what this reading of Walpole and Radcliffe revealingly discloses, nonetheless, is Scott's concern to frame the vitalizing energy which he brought to the novel within a narrative of historical plausibility.

This focus on the role of 'gender-constructs' in maintaining the relative position of genres within the field of the novel and romance owes a great deal to Ina Ferris's important work, *The Achievement of Literary Authority*. Building on the premise that 'the Waverley Novels as literary-historical event cannot be understood outside the literary discourse that received them', Ferris argues that male reviewers in the early nineteenth century, including Scott, 'constitute[d] the contemporary novelistic field under female signs of confinement . . . in such a way as to clear a discursive space for another, less confined kind of fiction'.[38] The critical reputation of prose fiction in the early 1800s was largely dependent upon 'moral' rather than 'literary' criteria, and rested upon works meeting certain standards of propriety and utility. In numerous 'male literary reviews' in a politically diverse range of publications, Ferris argues, 'the proper novel typically functioned less as a sign of rationality than as a sign of feminine virtues', and was perceived to represent a falling off from the eighteenth-century tradition of male heavyweights.[39]

As I argued in my account of the reception of Ann Radcliffe's fiction, the discussion of works by women in this period often referred back to the character of their authors: an article in *The New Monthly Magazine* in

1820, for example, 'On the Female Literature of the Present Age', stated that the writings of Mary Brunton displayed 'no very elevated talents, but a singular harmony and proportion in the author's powers', and described the way that the moralist Hannah More looked on humanity 'from a distance, from a height of personal virtue, like a being of another sphere'.[40] Scott implicitly endorsed this view that confinement or removal from society made possible a specifically 'feminine' kind of writing, and – as in his life of Clara Reeve – claimed that 'Gothic' romances by women writers were similarly liable to be restricted in their scope. Though Reeve's work was marked by an exemplary morality, the corollary of this fact, for Scott, was her inability to impress readers in any other way, hence his claim that 'in no part of *The Old English Baron*, or of any other of her works, does Miss Reeve show the possession of a rich or powerful imagination'.[41] Reeve's romance, indeed, was 'sometimes tame and tedious, not to say mean and tiresome', but this was hardly surprising, Scott argued, since,

it was scarce to be expected that the amiable and accomplished authoress, in her secluded situation, and with acquaintance of events and characters derived from books alone, should have rivalled those authors who gathered their knowledge of the human heart from having, like Fielding and Smollett, become acquainted, by sad experience, with each turn of 'many-coloured life'. Nor was it to be thought that she should have emulated in this particular her prototype Walpole . . . a statesman, a poet, and a man of the world, 'who knew the world like a man'.[42]

Scott's agenda was clear even when he was not so dismissive, as his biographical essay on Charlotte Smith illustrates. Though, according to Scott, 'we cannot but remark the number of highly-talented women who have, within our time of novel-reading, distinguished themselves advantageously in this department of literature', their ascendancy was attributed to the feminized nature of the modern novel, 'veiled and clothed with drapery', rather than to their share in the elusive quality of original genius.[43] Even if Scott confessed to the 'sense of temerity' with which he sought to rival the 'brilliant and talented names of Edgeworth, Austen, Charlotte Smith, and others' in the Magnum Introduction to *St Ronan's Well*, it was precisely such a construction of the dominant yet limited fictional orthodoxy which helped to clear a space in which Scott could intervene, and which he could eventually make his own.[44]

One of the most telling accounts of the 'renewal' that Scott effected is offered by his General Preface to the Waverley novels, written in 1829, a retrospective narrative of the stages by which he progressed as a writer of prose fiction. Scott once again sought to underline his mastery of the field in the General Preface, as well as to explain how this knowledge had been initially acquired (when, for example, as a schoolboy, illness made him dependent for amusement upon 'the kingdom of fiction' and the resources of a circulating library in Edinburgh). At the same time, though, Scott projected this waywardness – 'reading without compass or pilot' – firmly into the past, and he described the process by which 'familiar acquaintance with the specious miracles of fiction brought with it some degree of satiety'. The youthful Scott eventually found relief from this unfulfilling gluttony, according to the General Preface, as a result of his gradual engagement with works that offered him a different order of fictional 'license': 'I began, by degrees, to seek in histories, memoirs, voyages and travels, and the like, events nearly as wonderful as those which were the works of imagination, with the additional advantage that they were at least in a great measure true.'[45] After an early attempt at 'a work of imagination in prose' in 'the style of the Castle of Otranto, with plenty of border characters, and supernatural incident' (the fragment 'Thomas the Rhymer'), the next phase in Scott's career, according to the General Preface, saw him attempt to supplement romance with what was conspicuously lacking in the works of Walpole, Reeve, Lewis, or Radcliffe: information about 'customs and manners'.[46] This approach clearly informed Scott's continuation of Joseph Strutt's unfinished work 'Queenhoo-Hall', represented by Scott as a further stage in his progressive 'advance towards romantic composition'.[47] Strutt avowedly subordinated his work almost entirely to the 'purpose of . . . conveying useful instruction',[48] and Scott consequently found it necessary to distance himself from an over-zealous form of antiquarianism which he claimed had little interest for the modern reader. When he finally published his first novel, the General Preface emphasizes, Scott sought to attain the best of both worlds: to focus upon a contested historical period (the 'Forty-Five') which was still highly topical *and* to provide 'a subject favourable for romance' for readers 'living in a civilized age and country' – 'the tincture of manners belonging to an early period of society'.[49]

The perceived innovation effected by Scott's novels was seen to result from the infiltration of the bounded or restricted field of prose fiction – which Scott, of course, helped to define as such – by the more prestigious discourse of historiography, sometimes aligned with 'nature'. Such an identification of history and nature, for example, informed the *Quarterly*'s 1817 review of the first series of *Tales of My Landlord*, a review normally attributed to Scott himself, which distinguished works such as *Old Mortality*, in their 'distinct reality', from 'fancy-pieces' of the imagination.[50] Like so many other critics in the period, Scott represented 'the imitators of Mrs Radcliffe and Mr Lewis' as purveyors of a fictional formula, as in his review of Maturin's *Fatal Revenge*:

> We strolled through a variety of castles, each of which was regularly called Il Castello; met with as many captains of condottieri; heard various ejaculations of Santa Maria and Diabolo; read by a decaying lamp, and in a tapestried chamber, dozens of legends as stupid as the main history; examined such suites of deserted apartments as might fit up a reasonable barrack; and saw as many glimmering lights as would make a respectable illumination.[51]

Where contemporary novels – and especially Gothic romances – were widely seen to be unoriginal, or imitative of each other, Scott opposed this perceived confinement by appealing in his own work to a different order of tradition, and to the inexhaustible resources provided by a combination of folklore, popular belief, and the historical archive. Scott sought to present himself as someone who brought experience to bear upon his writing, and regularly claimed that his credentials as a 'man of the world', along with his professional status as a lawyer, afforded him a unique perspective on the field of literary production. According to Lockhart's *Life*, Scott 'considered literature *per se* as a thing of far inferior importance to the high concerns of political or practical life', and deliberately sought 'the society of men engaged in the active business of the world, rather than that of, so called, literary people', since he felt that 'literature, worthy of the name, was more likely to be fed and nourished by the converse of the former than by that of the latter class'.[52] This contrast between 'active' and 'literary' writers was a productive one for Scott, which he deployed throughout his *Lives of the Novelists*. According to Scott, Daniel Defoe's 'residence at Limehouse, near the Thames, . . . made him acquainted with many of those wild mariners, half privateers, half robbers, whom he must often have heard relate their adventures'.[53] The company which Samuel Richardson kept, by contrast, was 'limited to a little circle of amiable and accomplished persons': 'Sedentary habits . . . had rendered a constitution delicate, which nature had never made strong; and it will be readily believed that the workings of an imagination, constantly labouring in the fields of fiction, increased, rather than relieved complaints, which affected his nerves at an early period.'[54]

As an article in the *Quarterly Review* claimed in 1827, the 'creative genius' of Scott enabled him to alchemize his knowledge and experience in an 'intellectual crucible', and so transform the raw materials of 'tradition and history' into poetic 'gold' or 'treasure'.[55] In the first chapter of *The Heart of Midlothian* (1818), for example, the lawyer Jack Hardie, in conversation with fellow stage-coach passengers Jack Halkit and Peter Pattieson, claims from the perspective of a reader that 'the inventor of fictitious narratives has to rack his brains for means to diversify his tale', so as to avoid becoming reliant upon 'characters or incidents which have . . . been used again and again'.[56] The famous Tolbooth prison, however, a real castle, rather than a mythical or Gothic one, is said to be capable of providing enough anecdotes or examples 'to gorge even the public's all-devouring appetite for the wonderful and the horrible'.[57] Where novels ('Delilahs') seduce but ultimately betray the reader, because all the different forms of plot development have been exhausted, 'the real records of human vagaries' ('the State Trials, . . . the Books of Adjournal') offer 'new pages of the human heart, and turns of fortune far beyond what the boldest novelist ever attempted to produce from the coinage of his brain'.[58] Hardie's theory about the 'romantic' relation of Scottish wildness to English civility is immediately followed, in typically dialogic fashion, by Halkit's dismissive statement about his colleague's willingness to use 'the Commentaries on Scottish Criminal Jurisprudence' as 'a sort of appendix to the half-bound and slip-shod volumes of the circulating library'.[59] The introductory chapter of *The Heart of Midlothian* illustrates, nonetheless, the way that Scott – with an eye on the state of the market – appealed to diverse forms of archival and received material both to distance himself from 'romantic' excess, and to provide *more* impressive and romantic scenes than a mere 'inventor of fictitious narrative' could dream up. 'The true thing', in Hardie's terms, 'will triumph over the brightest inventions of the most ardent imagination' ('the blood of each reader should be curdled, and his epidermis crisped into goose skin'), only with the additional advantage that this pleasurable release is exempt from the stigma usually attached to romance reading.[60]

Though William Godwin had arguably pioneered the synthesis 'Of History & Romance' in his unpublished essay of 1797 and in works such as *St Leon* (1799), Scott was the writer who received the acclaim for 'wedding Fiction and History in delighted union', and for showing 'how history ought to be made available for the purposes of fiction'.[61] Works that called themselves Historical novels 'had existed before', the *Edinburgh* stated in 1832, 'but these were essentially different; they were not historical in the same sense'; unlike certain misnamed 'historical novels', Scott's works did justice to 'the manners, habits, feelings, phraseology, and allusions of other times and other countries', and offered 'new lights' on the past 'which history never gave'.[62] Whereas previous efforts to combine history and fiction, such as Sophia Lee's *The Recess*, had been reviewed with hostility, Scott's novels were widely praised precisely because they synthesized history and romance, and since they were seen to provide what I referred to earlier as 'the best of both worlds': according to the anonymous *Letters to Richard Heber, Esq* (1821), each novel by Scott was 'an essay on the manners and political state of England or Scotland at a given period, as well as a narrative of romantic adventure'.[63] This is not to claim that there was critical unanimity, since many of the historical periods in which Scott set his work, such as the era of the Covenanters in *Old Mortality*, were still contested, and since the genre of the historical romance was still liable to be regarded as a fictional 'mongrel', which offered neither history nor romance.[64] Though the hybrid identity of the Waverley novels was to be much more problematic for critics later in the century, as I will go on to argue, most reviewers of Scott's work during his lifetime nonetheless accepted the coincidence (or at least co-existence) of history and romance in his novels, and endorsed the authorial profile which Scott sought to project: Scott was 'the master of his imagination, rather than the slave', as the *Edinburgh* put it in 1832, a writer of works that were always 'tutored by experience'.[65]

According to James Kerr, the Waverley novels offered 'a counter-genre to the Gothic' which 'defamiliarized and then historicized' the conventions and devices of the Gothic romance.[66] While many of Scott's contemporaries claimed that he digested or displaced the work of his predecessors, however, any account of the Waverley novels which focuses exclusively on their historically minded absorption of romance raw material is liable to neglect both the rhetorical richness of the novels and the weight of the supplementary matter – prefaces, postscripts, notes, and so on – which surrounds them. Even as critics and reviewers celebrated the literary merit of Scott's work, as Ina Ferris has argued, 'they saw the novels as marked by disproportion, absorbed in super-fluities and specificities'.[67] The generic status of individual Waverley novels was a complicated issue from the outset, and as I will argue towards the end of this chapter, the proximity of the Waverley novels to the category of romance was seized upon by many critics, writing later in the century, who sought to downgrade Scott's reputation. In his

discussion of Abbotsford, Scott's re-creation of a baronial Gothic mansion funded by the profits from his writing, Stephen Bann has claimed
that 'Scott's public personality reflected the dualism between ironic
dismissiveness and poetic enthusiasm, at the very point where he engaged with the historical material which he had made his own.'[68]
Drawing an analogy between Abbotsford and the Waverley novels,
Bann suggestively argues that they have in common an 'underlying
rhetoric' which balances 'naiveté against irony'.[69] Just as Abbotsford,
Scott's 'romance in stone', combined modern technological innovation
with a remarkable collection of antiquarian bric-a-brac, so did the
Waverley novels perform what Bann describes as a 'careful balancing
act' in their treatment of romance precursors.[70] In works such as *Ivanhoe*,
The Antiquary, and *The Bride of Lammermoor*, for example, Scott subsumed
Gothic conventions within a historical framework, or set up an opposition between romance and real life in order to relegate the Gothic
romance to the status of a fictional anachronism. Yet in the same novels,
Scott also qualified the rigour with which he assimilated or digested
romance raw material, and – as in *The Antiquary* and *The Bride of
Lammermoor* – complicated the tone and identity of his work by rep-
licating certain Gothic tropes and plot motifs in an apparently faithful
manner.

    Ivanhoe, the first work by Scott to describe itself as a romance, deploys
an English medieval setting, along with a vocabulary – familiar from the
Loyalist Gothic – of castles, barons, knights, and heroines. A close
reading of *Ivanhoe* nonetheless shows that Scott presented this received
material within a historical, rather than an exemplary, framework.
Whereas the military reputation of Richard I had been uncritically
celebrated in the Tory epics of the 1790s, *Ivanhoe* concedes that Richard's
'feats of chivalry' furnished 'themes for bards and minstrels', yet afforded 'none of those solid benefits to his country on which history loves to
pause, and hold up as an example to posterity'.[71] Though the scene of
the tournament at Ashby is described as being 'singularly romantic' (88),
and was indeed widely praised by many reviewers for its pageantry, the
extensive casualties of the conflict, 'including one who was smothered
[to death] by the heat of his armour', are also recorded, and the narrator
offers an aside about the idealization of such ritual violence with the
statement that the tournament came to be known as 'the Gentle and
Joyous Passage of Arms at Ashby' (149). Published just a year after
Scott's judicious 'Essay on Chivalry' first appeared in the Supplement to
the *Encyclopaedia Britannica*, *Ivanhoe* similarly contained its account of

customs and manners within a rigorous presentation of chivalry as an institution. Wilfred of Ivanhoe celebrates chivalry in a famous passage as 'the nurse of pure and high affection – the stay of the oppressed, the redresser of grievances, the curb of the power of the tyrant' (316), but his paean to 'glory' is undercut by the sceptical response of Rebecca, and the terms of his panegyric are qualified in the rest of the work, as Scott repeatedly reminds the reader of the 'licentious' (246) nature of the times and the 'brilliant, but useless, character of a knight of romance' (458). Though the Norman King Richard and Saxon Robin Hood point towards a more harmonious future by recognizing each other as true Englishmen, and Ivanhoe is praised as one of 'the younger race' (465) breaking down cultural barriers, Scott's work nonetheless reminds the reader of 'the dark reality of the horrors of that period': 'It is grievous to think that those valiant barons, to whose stand against the crown the liberties of England were indebted for their existence, should themselves have been such dreadful oppressors, and capable of excesses contrary not only to the laws of England, but to those of nature and humanity' (245).

As I indicated above, however, any discussion of *Ivanhoe*'s relation to romance precursors needs to take account of the way that Scott's work also undermined its pretensions to historical rigour and supplemented its framing of the Loyalist Gothic with a knowing recourse to romance convention. Laurence Templeton's Dedicatory Epistle to *Ivanhoe* valorizes detailed research in referring to the 'hints concerning the private lives of our ancestors' that 'lie scattered through the pages of our various historians' (16), and emphasizes the nature of the constraint under which any writer of historical romance has to operate: he or she 'must introduce nothing inconsistent with the manners of the age' (21). Yet Templeton is also made to consider the accusation that, like the 'unknown author' of *The Antiquary* or 'a second M'Pherson' (14), he is 'intermingling fiction with truth' and 'polluting the well of history with modern inventions' (17). Even after stating that 'the character of the age must remain inviolate' (21), indeed, Templeton signals his debt to an apocryphal authority: 'the singular Anglo-Norman MS, which Sir Arthur Wardour preserves with such jealous care in the third drawer of his oaken cabinet, scarcely allowing any one to touch it, and being himself not able to read one syllable of its contents' (22). This cross-reference to the gullible baronet in *The Antiquary* serves to reconnect *Ivanhoe* with a less rigorous and more ironic relation to the distant past, a move repeated in the footnote at the end of the letter pleading for preferential

postal rates and larger, stronger mailcoaches 'to support the weight of
Antiquarian learning' (504 n.6).

In the course of the work, when Rebecca tends to the wounded
Ivanhoe in the temporary home of her father at Ashby, for example, the
reader is invited to consider his or her knowledge of 'romances and
romantic ballads' and so 'recollect how often the females during the
dark ages – were initiated into the mysteries of surgery' (294). A tone of
bantering digression pervades *Ivanhoe*, and Scott continually returns to a
running joke about Athelstane and the subject of food, so that what is
said to make him particularly resent his captivity at the hands of
Front-de-Boeuf is not so much the infringement of his free-born status as
the fact that the Normans 'put so much garlic into their pottage' (229).
Shortly after the disguised King Richard announces his credentials, as 'a
true English knight', to lead the siege upon Torquilstone Castle, Robin
of Locksley provides another, more bathetic, construction of English
military organization and prowess, cursing the 'Spanish steel-coat'
which protects De Bracy: 'had English smith forged it, these arrows had
gone through, an as if it had been silk or sendal' (332). *Ivanhoe* even
provides a comic episode which seems most reminiscent of a Matthew
Lewis melodrama, when Athelstane recounts how he found himself in
an open coffin after being struck down during the siege of the castle.
Before an audience including King Richard, who claims that 'such a
tale is as worth listening to as a romance' (473), the 'spectre' of Athelstane (472) describes how he 'burst in upon' his captors at Torquilstone:
'the fashion of my grave-clothes, as well as the clanking of my chains,
made me more resemble an inhabitant of the other world than of this'
(475). Scott characteristically added a note to the 1830 edition of *Ivanhoe*,
claiming that he had been 'compelled' to resuscitate Athelstane by the
'vehement entreaties' of his printer, who was 'inconsolable on the Saxon
being conveyed to the tomb' (524 n.55). When considered alongside the
historically minded treatment of chivalry discussed above, or alongside
the Gothic episode in which Ulrica, daughter of Torquil Wolfganger,
describes her rape by the Normans who had murdered her family,
however, this recourse to comic melodrama draws attention to the tonal
ambiguity of the work as a whole. The 'identity' of *Ivanhoe* remains
unresolved at its point of closure, since although the work appears to
offer a unionist allegory of national regeneration, Scott also illustrates,
via the characters of Isaac and Rebecca, the limits of this inclusiveness:
just before Rebecca's fate is decided at the lists, the apparently genial
figure of Friar Tuck describes his idea of a good Christian work as 'the
burning of a witch' (482).[72]

The Antiquary offers an even more complex treatment of 'Gothic' precursors, since it initially distances itself from the formulaic conventions of romance, as embodied in *The Old English Baron*, only to reinstate a less ironic relation to Reeve's work, and replicate the basic outline of her romance's plot. The famous 'Kaim of Kinprunes' episode in the fourth chapter, for example, where Jonathan Oldbuck mistakes a ditch for an ancient defensive fortification, seems at first to establish an opposition between the antiquarian enthusiasm of Oldbuck and the prosaic reality inhabited by characters such as the hero, Edward Lovel, and the mendicant Edie Ochiltree. The way in which Lovel is introduced, by way of allusion to the legitimate heir in *The Old English Baron*, similarly seems to prepare the reader for a knowing and modern perspective on the Gothic romance: 'In short, since the name was fashionable in novel-writing, and that is a great while agone, there never was a Master Lovel of whom so little positive was known, and who was so universally described by negatives.'[73] Lovel, like his host Oldbuck, is initially blasé about the story of the haunted apartment at Monkbarns, and when he spends the night there, he is so consumed by his present concerns, particularly his passion for Isabella Wardour, that he finds it 'difficult to fix his mind upon the stories which had been told him of an apartment, with which they seemed so singularly to correspond', almost regretting the 'absence of those agitated feelings, half fear half curiosity, which sympathise with the old legends of awe and wonder'.[74] Just when the rhetorical opposition between real life and romance seems to have been established, however, Lovel's sleep is 'disturbed by a thousand baseless and confused visions', and the legend of Aldobrand Oldenbuck, with which Grizel Oldbuck had earlier acquainted him, is revived in Lovel's mind. Scott is typically non-committal at this point about what Lovel actually saw, allowing readers to decide for themselves whether it was 'an impression conveyed rather by the eye than by the imagination'.[75] Though the work draws attention to the conventionality of the device it employs, by describing how 'Lovel strove to interrogate this awful person in the form of exorcism proper for the occasion', the effect of the dream episode is ultimately to re-establish the connection between *The Antiquary* and *The Old English Baron*. Where Reeve's Edmund Twyford (later Lovel) is visited by the ghosts of his parents during his trial of courage in the haunted apartment of Lovel Castle, the figure of Lovel in Scott's work is encouraged to 'persevere' by the motto to which Aldobrand Oldenbuck points, 'the words of which appeared to blaze with a supernatural light, and remained riveted upon his memory'.[76] Lovel later emphasizes the potential relevance of the dream to his own circumstances, and although Oldbuck in turn suspects him of romantic excess, Lovel's suspicions are finally confirmed. Following a complicated series of revelations, triggered by Edie Ochiltree's delivery of the prophecy about the grave of 'Malcolm the Misticot', and the death and funeral of the Countess of Glenallan, Lovel recognizes his role in the property plot of the Gothic romance, and emerges as the true heir of the aristocratic Glenallan family: like Edmund Twyford, Lovel had been carried away from his parents shortly after his birth, and brought up to believe himself an illegitimate child. Even if Scott's work subsequently returns to 'real life' by depicting the mobilization of volunteers in response to the threat of invasion, *The Antiquary* nonetheless pays tribute to the romance ending of *The Old English Baron* in its presentation of the marriage of Lovel and Isabella Wardour, and the uniting of their families.

The way that *The Bride of Lammermoor* alludes to Gothic or romance precursors is even harder to classify, since – even more so than *The Antiquary* – it offers what James Kerr has appropriately described as a 'weird amalgam of genres'.[77] Like *Ivanhoe*, *The Bride* in some ways presents itself as a work which subsumes romance within a historical framework. Basing its action on the latent conflict between the dispossessed Edgar Ravenswood, and the new proprietor of his ancestral home, Sir William Ashton, *The Bride* returns this plot to an immediate and resonant social milieu around the time of the Act of Union, so that Ravenswood is presented as someone who had 'espoused the sinking side' in the civil war of 1689, whereas the family of the lawyer Ashton 'had only risen to wealth and political importance' by backing the ascendant faction.[78] Though *The Bride* clearly alludes to the Loyalist Gothic property plot, Scott continually disrupts its schematic opposition between rightful heir and usurper by claiming that 'men spoke differently' (27) about the legitimacy of Ravenswood's grievance, and by suggesting that Ravenswood – like Ashton – is a 'new man', uncomfortable with the legacy of vengeance that he has inherited, and hopeful of seeing 'the day when justice shall be open to Whig and Tory' (101). As is also the case with *Ivanhoe*, however, it is difficult to read *The Bride* simply as a historically minded digestion of romance, since the tone of the work is so often complicated by the digression and the extra detail which it supplies. Scott continually undermines the status of the key players in *The Bride*, employing the figure of the loyal servant Caleb Balderstone, as Ian Duncan has observed, in such a way as to 'drag Edgar's situation down from the tonalities of tragic dignity towards those of farce'.[79] Sir

William Ashton's standing is qualified in a similar way, as when the reader is told about the portrait of Ashton and his wife hanging at the Castle of Ravenswood:

The painter, notwithstanding his skill, overcome by the reality, or, perhaps, from a suppressed sense of humour, had not been able to give the husband on the canvas that air of awful rule and right supremacy, which indicates the full possession of domestic authority. It was obvious, at the first glance, that, despite mace and gold frogs, the Lord Keeper was somewhat henpecked. (192)

Though portraits play an important role during the climax of *The Bride*'s action, when it is noticed that the picture of Ashton's father has been replaced by one of Sir Malise Ravenswood, Scott provides an ironic counterpoint to such portentous symbolism in his references to the work of Dick Tinto, the struggling artist whose notes provide the basis for Peter Pattieson's narrative: 'He particularly shone in painting horses, that being a favourite sign in the Scottish villages; and, in tracing his progress, it is beautiful to observe, how by degrees he learned to shorten the backs, and prolong the legs, of these noble animals, until they came to look less like crocodiles, and more like nags' (15).

   What complicates the identity or tone of *The Bride* above all is the way that it offers competing forms of explanation for the events which it portrays, seeming intermittently both to credit and distance itself from a 'traditional' perspective on the fulfilment of omen and prophecy. *The Bride* refers early on to the story of how Malisius de Ravenswood had recovered his castle and lands from a usurper in the thirteenth century, and the figure of Old Alice subsequently endorses the applicability of the ancient family motto, 'I bide my time' (52), to Edgar's situation. Ravenswood repeatedly strives to refuse the assigned role of avenger, however, and he is said to despise 'most of the ordinary prejudices about witchcraft, omens, and vaticination, to which his country still gave such implicit credit' (252): when Caleb Balderstone repeats Thomas the Rhymer's lines about the final demise of his master's family, for example, Ravenswood dismisses the prophecy as 'nonsense' and 'doggerel' (185). Scott nonetheless re-establishes the connection between *The Bride* and a Gothic romance precursor such as *The Castle of Otranto*, so that when Edgar Ravenswood takes the hand of his adversary's daughter, Lucy Ashton, the apartment in which they stand is 'suddenly illuminated by a flash of lightning', followed by a peal of thunder 'so sudden and dreadful, that the old tower rocked to its foundation, and every inmate concluded it was falling upon them' (125): 'It might seem', the reader is told, 'as if the ancient founder of the castle were bestriding the thunder-storm, and proclaiming his displeasure at the reconciliation of his descendant with the enemy of his house' (126). *The Bride* further alludes to *Otranto*, and especially to the family connection between Theodore and Alfonso the Good, when Henry Ashton is made to notice that Edgar Ravenswood bears a resemblance to the portrait of Sir Malise, 'as like it as if he had loupen out of the canvass' (195). Shortly afterwards, though, *The Bride* plays on this family history in a more obviously knowing way when Edgar, in the company of Lucy Ashton, approaches the hut of Old Alice, who – although blind – recognizes 'the step of a Ravenswood': 'This is indeed . . . an acuteness of organ which I could not have credited had I not witnessed it' (198).

Towards the end of *The Bride*, it appears that the role of prophecy is to be securely framed within a historically minded treatment of popular belief, with the demise of the Ravenswood family presented, as David Brown has argued, both in realistic terms and as it would have appeared to 'the traditional, feudal consciousness – an inexplicable fatal decline'.[80] Just before Ravenswood comes across the apparition of 'old blind Alice' (245–6) at the Mermaiden's Fountain, for example, the narrator intervenes to inform the reader about the provenance of the episode: 'We are bound to tell the tale as we have received it; and, considering the distance of the time, and propensity of those through whose mouths it has passed to the marvellous, this could not be called a Scottish story, unless it manifested a tinge of Scottish superstition' (245). A similar disclaimer is offered at the end of *The Bride*'s penultimate chapter, after Lucy Ashton's death, where the work again legitimizes its presentation of sensational material, by emphasizing its reliance upon the authority of folklore and legend:

By many readers this may be deemed overstrained, romantic, and composed by the wild imagination of an author, desirous of gratifying the popular appetite for the horrible; but those who are read in the private family history of Scotland during the period in which the scene is laid, will readily discover, through the disguise of borrowed names and added incidents, the leading particulars of AN OWER TRUE TALE. (340)

This framing of 'romance' incident is itself undercut in the final chapter, however, when one of 'the three village hags' (341) at the funeral of Lucy Ashton, Ailsie Gourlay, recognizes that Edgar Ravenswood makes 'a thirteenth amang [the mourners] that they ken naething about', predicting that 'if auld freets say true, there's ane o' that company that'll no be lang for this warld' (342). 'Auld freets' or omens are borne out by subsequent events, without further qualification, as Ravenswood goes off to fight a duel with Douglas Ashton and meets his death 'on the Kelpie's flow' (347), in accordance with the terms of Thomas the Rhymer's prophecy. As is well known, Scott's Magnum Opus Introduction of 1830 went on to qualify any idea that *The Bride* endorses a fatalistic construction of events, by offering a clear statement about the role of the mother in the Dalrymple family saga on which the novel is based: 'it is needless to point out to the intelligent reader, that the witchcraft of the mother consisted only in the ascendency of a powerful mind over a weak and melancholy one, and that the harshness with which she exercised her superiority in a case of delicacy, had driven her daughter first to despair, then to frenzy' (10). Yet if such a statement prompts the reader to reconsider the contingency of the events portrayed, the work itself nonetheless refuses to provide a conclusive account of what happened. Rather than subsume the Gothic romance, therefore, *The Bride* arguably displays its kinship with other contemporary Gothic works, such as Hogg's *The Private Memoirs and Confessions of a Justified Sinner*, in allowing different perspectives and orders of explanation to contend with each other.

Some contemporary critics were offended by Scott's apparent willingness to credit prophecy and supernatural agency in the Waverley novels, and this distaste was particularly pronounced in the case of works set close to home in eighteenth-century Scotland, such as *The Bride of Lammermoor*. 'We wish Ailsie Gourlay's prediction had been omitted', Nassau Senior wrote in 1821, since '[l]ike the apparition of Alice Gray, and the prophecy that the last Lord of Ravenswood would stable his steed in the Kelpie's flow, it is a useless improbability'.[81] A 'more serious blemish' still, according to Senior, was the character of Caleb Balderstone:

Of all our author's fools and bores, and we acknowledge we dislike the whole race of them, from Monk Barns down to the Euphuist, he is the most pertinacious, the most intrusive, and, from the nature of his one monotonous note, the least pardonable in his intrusion. His silly buffoonery is always marring, with gross absurdities and degrading associations, some scene of tenderness or dignity.[82]

Yet although Senior criticized *The Bride*'s apparently faithful recourse to romance archaism, and drew attention to the tonal ambiguity consequent upon the 'intrusion' of Caleb, he was nonetheless able to praise

the work as 'a tragedy of the highest order', just as in the same article he
also conceded that *Ivanhoe* was a success, despite being 'formed of the
most peculiar materials': 'Kings, crusaders, knights, and outlaws, Coeur
de Lion, and the Templars, and Robin Hood, and Friar Tuck, and the
Forest of Sherwood, the names, and the times, and the scenes, which are
entwined with our earliest recollections, but which we never hoped to
meet with again in serious narrative.'[83] Though, as I argued above,
Scott's assimilation or digestion of the irregularity of romance was less
complete than some accounts of his triumphant emergence allowed,
most critics absolved Scott from the charge, which Francis Jeffrey had
levelled after the publication of *Marmion*, of an unseemly absorption in
primitive romance models. 'Of the novels produced by the author of
Waverley, there are but two or three, in which some appeal, more or less
forcible, is not directed to our involuntary sympathy with popular
superstition', according to the author of *Letters to Richard Heber* in 1821,
yet at the same time there was no question of Scott himself ever being 'a
serious believer in any of those mysterious phenomena, . . . celebrated in
[his] writings'.[84] Scott's contemporaries generally endorsed his ability to
circumvent the terms of the trade-off between primitivism and progress,
and during his lifetime, at least, most reviewers paid tribute to the
authorial profile which Scott sought to construct, perpetuating his status
as a writer who brought experience to bear upon the field of prose
fiction. According to William Hazlitt, the Waverley novels provided 'a
charming and wholesome relief to the fastidious refinement and "over-
laboured lassitude" of modern readers': 'fresh, as from the hand of
nature', Scott's works proved that 'facts are better than fiction; that
there is no romance like the romance of real life; and that if we can but
arrive at what men feel, do, and say in striking and singular situations,
the result will be "more lively, audible, and full of vent"', than the
fine-spun cobwebs of the brain'.[85] Not only were the Waverley novels in
general widely seen to provide picturesque novelty from sometimes
distant periods and regions, but they were also praised so keenly, and
contrasted with the works which had preceded them, as Hazlitt implied,
because of the way that they were held to reconnect the reader to reality.
While Peacock was one of the most critical readers of Scott's poetry, as I
pointed out at the beginning of this chapter, he recognized Scott, on the
basis of the Waverley novels, as 'perhaps the most universally successful
in his own day of any writer that ever lived', praising the 'Scotch' novels
especially for providing readers with 'great and valuable information'
about the manners of their contemporaries and ancestors.[86] Scott

'demonstrated to more people than ever before in Europe and America as well as in Britain', Gary Kelly has written, 'that the novel had literary potential of the highest order and that it was an ideological discourse of the first importance in constructing a new kind of national culture', capable of uniting in the same pursuit the expanding reading public.[87]

Scott's reputation reached its apex in the 1830s and early 1840s, with the publication of the Magnum Opus edition of his collected works, the appearance of Lockhart's *Life*, and the building of the Scott monument in Edinburgh. During Scott's lifetime, and in the decade or so after his death, the relationship between the Waverley novels and the Gothic romance remained a stable one, since the majority of critics endorsed the view that Scott had 'widened the whole field to an extent of which none that went before him ever dreamed'.[88] A reverential and submissive tone pervaded numerous articles on Scott just as it had often informed earlier praise of the 'mighty magician', Ann Radcliffe, but whereas Radcliffe had been praised for transporting her readers away from the turmoil of the 1790s, Scott was also celebrated for breaking the spell of romance, and ushering his readers instead into the communal space of history and public life.[89] A good example of the way in which Scott was perceived both to have put paid to the Gothic romance and transformed the novel is provided by Margaret Baron-Wilson's *The Life and Correspondence of M. G. Lewis* (1839). In a work primarily devoted to the career of Lewis, the figure of Scott nonetheless hovers in the background to put the author's subject firmly in his place. 'The novels of the "wizard of the north"', according to Baron-Wilson, 'happily annihilated the class of works among which that of Lewis was so prominent', since not only did they sustain 'the deepest and most thrilling interest . . . without the aid of the wild or supernatural', but they gestured back towards the world of the reader with 'historical associations, and ... natural delineations of ordinary life'.[90] This sense of relief at the emergence of the Waverley novels was echoed in an article on 'The Historical Romance' in *Blackwood's Edinburgh Magazine* in 1845. Of 'the novels most in vogue before the immortal creations of Scott', according to the *Blackwood's* reviewer, even the best were distinguished by 'a mawkish sensibility [and] a perpetual sentimentality', and the works of 'Charlotte Smith, Miss Radcliffe, and Miss Burney' in particular were described as being 'wellnigh unreadable' so long after their historical moment. Since these women writers were confined to 'one circle and class of society' (the use of the title 'Miss' to refer to Radcliffe and Burney – both married women – was surely designed to perpetuate this image), they ran out of 'natural ideas' and were consequently 'driven in the search of variety, to the invention of artificial and often ridiculous ones'. The Waverley novels, by contrast, were credited with both 'genuine passion' or 'real genius' *and* fidelity to 'real life'. 'At the very time when literature to all appearance was effete, and invention, for above a century, had run out in the cramped and worn-out channels of imitation', as a result, 'Providence' – acting in the form of the 'Scottish bard' – 'bestowed a new art . . . upon mankind', the historical romance: *Waverley* had an effect akin to 'the sun bursting through the clouds', and 'a new vein of boundless extent and surprising richness was opened as it were under our feet'.[91]

Scott had the unique ability, according to the *Blackwood's* article quoted above, to 'give the truth of history without the monotony – the interest of romance without its unreality'.[92] Yet to privilege such a verdict on the Waverley novels at the end of a study of the Gothic romance is to impose an artificial closure, and to underwrite a simplified and over-stable history of the novel, to the effect that Scott simply superseded his predecessors in the field. Rather than close off the complex question of Scott's relation to the Gothic, I want finally to give a brief account of the reception of Scott's work later in the nineteenth century, so as to make it clear that the relative positions of Scott and the Gothic romance were subject to a significant re-ordering. Scott and his reviewers described the 'evolutionary' impact of the Waverley novels with undeniable force, as I have stressed above, but the apparent critical consensus that Scott's work effected a synthesis of romance and history was nonetheless short-lived. The professionalization of history-writing in the period increasingly led critics to question Scott's expansionist treatment of 'historical' raw material, such that the German historian Leopold von Ranke, proponent of the need to write history 'as it really was', cited Scott as a negative influence in his autobiography, and pledged to avoid 'all imagination' after reading *Quentin Durward* (1823), set in fifteenth-century France.[93] This scepticism about the way in which the Waverley novels dealt with history was shared by an anonymous article published in *Fraser's Magazine* in 1847, 'Walter Scott – Has History Gained by His Writings?', and served to heighten the recognition of the complicity between the Waverley novels and the category of romance. Perhaps more than any other work in the period, Carlyle's essay on Scott, written in 1838, contributed towards undermining the status which Scott had acquired by focusing on the damaging implications of the weight and popularity of his output.[94] Though Carlyle conceded that 'the Author of *Waverley*' had helped to rescue British Literature from 'Werterism, Byronism, and other Sentimentalism', he was nonetheless troubled by the willing participation of Scott and his novels in the commercialized marketplace for fiction: Scott's ultimate concern, Carlyle famously claimed, was 'writing impromptu novels to buy farms with'.[95] Whereas the accounts of Scott's revitalization of the novel to which I referred earlier tended to foreground his repeated recourse to the limitless raw material provided by 'history', many later critics followed Carlyle in focusing upon the fact of repetition alone, inflecting Scott's relationship with the reading public so that he came to be seen as a purveyor of popular romance, catering for an undifferentiated and uncritical mass audience.

This decline in Scott's reputation was even more marked in the second half of the nineteenth century. In a review of Nassau Senior's *Essays in Fiction* in 1864, for example, the young Henry James not only put a negative gloss on the great number of the Waverley novels, but strictly confined the scope of Scott's work (in a manner similar to Scott's reading of Radcliffe forty years earlier) by comparing 'his facility in composition' with 'that of Mrs Henry Wood, of modern repute'.[96] Though James included himself among the readers who still lingered over Scott's 'hasty pages' forty years after they were written, this concession was hardly generous: 'we do it in the full cognizance of the faults which even Mrs Wood has avoided, of foibles for which she would blush'. According to James, the Waverley novels had themselves been superseded by the works of Dickens, Thackeray, and 'twenty other famous writers . . . working in the midst of us', so that 'old-fashioned, ponderous Sir Walter' could only be regarded as an entertainer, a teller of tales: 'Surveying his works, his character, his method, as a whole, we can liken him to nothing better than to a strong and kindly elder brother, who gathers his juvenile public about him at eventide, and pours out a stream of wondrous improvisation.'[97] This characterization of Scott both as a writer of romance and a writer for children was accentuated by Leslie Stephen, writing in the *Cornhill Magazine* in 1871. Stephen singled out *Ivanhoe* as a work which was 'delightful reading for boys' but no longer suitable for men, and he similarly patronized Scott as a charming storyteller: 'if *Ivanhoe* has rightly descended from the library to the schoolroom, we should not be ungrateful to Scott for wasting his splendid talents on what we can hardly call by a loftier name than most amusing nonsense'.[98] Judith Wilt has argued that Scott was a much more 'Victorian' novelist than is often acknowledged, since the

Waverley novels as a publishing phenomenon actually provided 'the enabling environment' for the nineteenth-century novels which were regarded to have displaced Scott's work.[99] If it was still possible for Richard Hutton, writing in 1878, to praise Scott as a writer whose synthesis of private and public concerns reconnected the reader to the outside world,[100] however, the 'best of both worlds' position cultivated by Scott, and endorsed by his first readers, was increasingly redefined by critics who claimed that he wrote neither history nor romance. 'The whole of these historical novels, which once charmed all men, and for which we still have a lingering affection', as Leslie Stephen put it, 'are rapidly converting themselves into mere debris of plaster of Paris': 'Sir F. Palgrave says somewhere that "historical novels are mortal enemies to history", and we shall venture to add that they are mortal enemies to fiction.'[101]

Though Stephen's verdict should be privileged no more than the judgement given by the *Blackwood's* reviewer in 1845, it usefully demonstrates the fluctuation in the critical standing of the Waverley novels in the nineteenth century. A focus on the early reception of the Waverley novels provides an important historical perspective on the waning credibility of the Gothic romance in the first half of the century, since Scott's novels were widely recognized to have put paid to the sensationalist excess of Lewis's work and the 'unreality' of Radcliffean romance. An account of the subsequent reputation of the Waverley novels also serves to frame a contextualizing study of Gothic fiction, however, in that towards the end of the nineteenth century Scott's works were themselves increasingly seen to be complicit with the category of romance, and viewed no more favourably than Gothic works had been viewed by the first critics of the Waverley novels. In the first half of the twentieth century, indeed, as I stated at the beginning of my Introduction, Gothic romances without the historical grounding of Scott's work, labelled and described as part of a unified genre for the first time, began to be revalued precisely because of their perceived unreality. Though it is hard to be certain that the Gothic underwent a revival at the expense of Scott's work, it is fair to say that romances by a writer such as Ann Radcliffe were seen to offer the potential for diversion and escapism in a way that the more hybrid Waverley novels did not, and began to be praised again in terms which were almost identical to those that had been used by conservative critics in the 1790s. While Edith Birkhead's *The Tale of Terror* (1921), for example, still allocated Scott an elevated position as a writer who deployed 'the stuff of real life', and praised

Radcliffe in a defensive manner ('If we scan her romances with a coldly critical eye – an almost criminal proceeding – obvious improbabilities start into view'), her work was nonetheless one of several in the period that helped to set the terms in which the Gothic was redefined and revalued as a genre with a transcendent or universal appeal.[102] According to Birkhead, the Gothic romance satisfies 'the human desire to experience new emotions and sensations, without actual danger': 'Though the title assumes a special significance at the close of the eighteenth century, the tale of terror appeals to deeply rooted instincts, and belongs, therefore, to every age and clime.'[103]

The nature of the impetus behind this revival of the Gothic romance is perhaps clearest in the work of the most famous pioneer in the field of Gothic studies, Montague Summers. In *The Gothic Quest* (1938), Summers – like Birkhead – conceded that 'examples of the most incredible ineptitude might easily be cited' in any discussion of Ann Radcliffe's treatment of Catholicism.[104] Yet to criticize Radcliffe in such a way is to miss the point, according to Summers, since the 'quest' of the reader is precisely for an aura of mystery and remoteness, beyond the constraints of realistic representation:

> To escape thus from humdrum reality is a primitive desire, and, in itself, it is excellent and right. . . . We call our dreams Romance, and it was just this that the Gothic novelists gave to their readers. This, then, is exactly the reason why I think the Gothic novelists, with all their faults and failings, have done us infinite service, and proved themselves true friends to those of us who care to withdraw . . . from the relentless oppression and carking cares of a bitter actuality.[105]

Writing in the late 1930s, Summers claimed that the Gothic romance was 'coming into vogue among the inner circles of the advanced and elect' for the same reason that it had achieved its initial popularity in the late eighteenth century, when 'dark shadows were lowering' and 'the times were difficult, full of anxiety and unrest': readers were 'greedy for "fictional anaesthetics"'.[106] Summers's revaluation of Gothic fiction also needs to be seen in the context of his position as a gentleman-scholar and bibliophile, since – unlike Birkhead – he said little about the 'universal' appeal of romance, and described the Gothic as 'an aristocrat of literature',[107] which offered an antidote to the 'unhealthy and unwholesome rubbish' of twentieth-century popular fiction. Yet while Summers sought to maintain almost proprietorial control over the genre, he nonetheless contributed a great deal towards establishing its respectability, and his account of the refuge which the Gothic provided from the 'bitter actuality' of the modern world was subsequently endorsed by other influential writers such as Devendra Varma, in *The Gothic Flame* (1957): 'if not too restless, too impatient, and too modern', the reader of Gothic fiction 'will find that he is transported back many a long year from this atomic age to a realm of magic and marvels, of knight-errantry and adventure, of combat and love'.[108]

In the last few decades, Georg Lukács's famous study *The Historical Novel*, first translated in 1962, has heralded a revival of academic interest in the work of Scott. Many Scott critics since Lukács have returned to the issue of the synthesis of history and romance in the Waverley novels, in order to present Scott as an innovative historian, whose 'true intellectual background' was as much the Scottish Enlightenment tradition of comparative cultural analysis as it was 'the pre-romantic scene of Gothic novels, primitivism, [or] graveyard poetry'.[109] Interest in the Waverley novels in the twentieth century has largely been confined to the academic community, however, since readers have generally been alienated by the awkward and obtrusive presence of framing conventions and narratorial personae in Scott's work. Scott's prefaces, as Kathryn Sutherland has persuasively argued, anchor the Waverley novels 'within the world of production and exchange', and continually force the reader to acknowledge the process whereby Scott transformed his diverse materials and sources into the valuable commodity of prose fiction.[110] Given the nature of the documentation which surrounds the Waverley novels, along with the novels' renowned deficiency in the portrayal of 'character', it is easy to see why Scott's work has not appealed to readers accustomed to less cumbersome techniques of narration, and to fiction premised upon the exploration of psychological interiority.

Gothic romances, by contrast, have been popular with a wide range of readers in the twentieth century, not least because they lack the 'rootedness' which characterizes the Waverley novels, and display comparatively little in the way of framing material or historical reference. Following the pioneering work of writers such as Birkhead and Summers, the Gothic romance has been praised not only for offering an escape or refuge from modernity, but also as a result of its congruence with a Freudian analysis of character and human nature. Though early-twentieth-century writers had little to say about the 'depth' of the works they discussed, they prepared the ground for later critics to make more expansive claims about the interrogative or transgressive status of the genre as a whole. It has been my contention throughout this book that the larger claims which have been made about the genre fail to do justice either to the variety of the works which are now labelled as 'Gothic' or to the diverse ways in which these works have functioned for their readers. By concluding with a discussion of the shifting relations between Gothic fiction and the Waverley novels, however, I hope to have underlined the claim with which I began my Introduction, that the reputation or status of Gothic works has always been open to contest among both writers and readers. To recognize this is an essential precondition for a historically grounded analysis of the Gothic romance.

Notes

INTRODUCTION

1 David Punter, *The Literature of Terror: A History of Gothic Fictions from 1765 to the Present Day* (London: Longman, 1980), p. 127.
2 Ibid p. 128.
3 Jacqueline Howard, *Reading Gothic Fiction: A Bakhtinian Approach* (Oxford: Clarendon Press, 1994), p. 1.
4 Chris Baldick, Introduction to *The Oxford Book of Gothic Tales* (Oxford University Press, 1992), p. xi.
5 The 'Gothic' label was most commonly used after 1800, and by tales or short stories rather than full-length romances.
6 Ian Duncan, *Modern Romance and Transformations of the Novel: The Gothic, Scott, Dickens* (Cambridge University Press, 1992), pp. 12–13. Complicating the opposition between realism and romance set up by Ian Watt's *The Rise of the Novel*, Duncan argues that romance was not so much superseded as dialectically 'transformed' in this period. See also Michael McKeon, *The Origins of the English Novel 1600–1740* (Baltimore: Johns Hopkins University Press, 1987).
7 Horace Walpole, *The Castle of Otranto: A Gothic Story*, ed. W. S. Lewis (Oxford University Press, 1964), p. 4.
8 Katie Trumpener, *Bardic Nationalism: The Romantic Novel and the British Empire* (Princeton University Press, 1997), p. xv.
9 Gary Kelly, *English Fiction of the Romantic Period 1789–1830* (London: Longman, 1987), p. 49.
10 Clara Reeve, *The Old English Baron*, ed. James Trainer (Oxford University Press, 1977), p. 3.
11 See Howard, *Reading Gothic*, pp. 44–52, for a Bakhtinian theorization of the Gothic's heterogeneity.
12 Cited in Duncan, *Modern Romance*, p. 10.
13 See E. J. Clery, *The Rise of Supernatural Fiction 1762–1800* (Cambridge University Press, 1995), p. 148. Clery identifies 1797 as 'the year in which reviewers and critics began to put a name to the category of fiction we now call Gothic or the fantastic, although the name varied: "modern Romance"; "the *terrible* school", "the Terrorist System of Novel Writing"; "Terrorist Novel

Writing"; "the *hobgoblin-romance*"'. As I will later point out, however, the kinship between writers such as Walpole and Radcliffe was not taken for granted in this period.

14 Elizabeth Napier, *The Failure of Gothic: Problems of Disjunction in an Eighteenth-Century Literary Form* (Oxford: Clarendon Press, 1987), p. 29.

15 See Jerome J. McGann, *The Beauty of Inflections: Literary Investigations in Historical Method and Theory* (Oxford: Clarendon Press, 1985), 17–65 (p. 24).

16 For a brief discussion of the 'neo- and retro-Gothic experiments . . . that swept British fiction in the decade after Waterloo', see Walter Scott, *Ivanhoe*, (Oxford University Press, 1996) ed. Ian Duncan, Introduction, pp. x–xi; for an analysis of 'Irish Gothic', see W. J. McCormack, 'Irish Gothic and After (1820–1945)', *The Field Day Anthology of Irish Writing*, ed. Seamus Deane (Derry: Field Day Publications), 3 vols., II, 831–54; for the emergence of the 'Godwinian' novel, see Pamela Clemit, *The Godwinian Novel: The Rational Fictions of William Godwin, Charles Brockden Brown, and Mary Shelley* (Oxford University Press, 1993).

1. ORIGINS: HORACE WALPOLE AND *THE CASTLE OF OTRANTO*

1 'Anser Pen-Drag-On, Esq', *Scribbleomania, or, The Printer's Devil's Polichronicon. A Sublime Poem* (London, 1815), pp. 137–8.

2 George Saintsbury, *The English Novel* (London: Dent, 1913), p. 155.

3 Rosemary Jackson, *Fantasy: The Literature of Subversion* (London: Methuen, 1981), p. 95.

4 Victor Sage (ed.), Introduction to *The Gothick Novel: A Casebook* (London: Macmillan, 1990), p. 9.

5 Pierre Bourdieu defines the 'field of production' as 'the system of objective relations between . . . agents or institutions and . . . the site of the struggles for the monopoly of the power to consecrate', 'The Production of Belief: Contribution to an Economy of Symbolic Goods', *The Field of Cultural Production: Essays on Art and Literature*, ed. Randal Johnson (Cambridge: Polity Press, 1993), 74–111 (p. 78).

6 Walter Scott, 'Horace Walpole', *The Lives of The Novelists* (London: Dent, 1910), 188–203 (p. 188).

7 See Samuel Kliger's *The Goths in England: A Study in Seventeenth and Eighteenth Century Thought* (Cambridge: Harvard University Press, 1952), and R. J. Smith's *The Gothic Bequest: Medieval Institutions in British Thought 1688–1863* (Cambridge University Press, 1987), along with the works of J. G. A. Pocock.

8 Harriet Guest, 'The Wanton Muse: Politics and Gender in Gothic Theory after 1760', *Beyond Romanticism: New Approaches to Texts and Contexts 1780–1832*, ed. Stephen Copley and John Whale (London: Routledge, 1992), 118–39 (p. 119).

9 James H. Bunn, 'The Aesthetics of British Mercantilism', *NLH* 11 (1980), 303–21 (p. 311).

10 Charles Eastlake, *A History of the Gothic Revival: An Attempt to Show How the Taste for Medieval Architecture Which Lingered in England During the Two Last Centuries Has Since Been Encouraged and Developed* (London, 1872), p. 49.

11 See, for example, Michael McCarthy, *The Origins of the Gothic Revival* (New Haven: Yale University Press, 1987), pp. 1–86.

12 *The World* 12 (1753), pp. 68–9.

13 McCarthy, *Gothic Revival*, p. 1.

14 Dianne S. Ames, 'Strawberry Hill: Architecture of the "as if"', *Studies in Eighteenth-Century Culture* 8 (1978), 351–60 (p. 352). Jerrold Hogle argues that the accumulated 'fragmentary counterfeits' at Strawberry Hill offer a staging of capitalist dynamism: Walpole 'divorces artifacts from their foundations and turns them into *bric-a-brac* signs disjoined from their original substance', 'The Ghost of the Counterfeit in the Genesis of the Gothic', *Gothick Origins and Innovations*, ed. Allan Lloyd Smith and Victor Sage (Amsterdam: Rodopi, 1994), 23–33 (p. 23).

15 Horace Walpole, *A Description of the Villa of Mr Horace Walpole, Youngest Son of Sir Robert Walpole, Earl of Orford, At Strawberry-Hill near Twickenham, Middlesex. With an Inventory of the Furniture, Pictures, Curiosities, & c.* (Strawberry Hill, 1784), p. i.

16 Ames, 'Strawberry Hill', p. 354.

17 Horace Mann to Walpole, 13 Feb. 1750, *The Yale Edition of the Correspondence of Horace Walpole*, ed. W. S. Lewis (New Haven: Yale University Press, 1937–83), xx, 111.

18 Walpole to Henry Conway, 8 June 1747, *Correspondence*, xxxvii, 270; 'Mrs Chevenix's' was a famous hardware shop.

19 Horace Walpole, *Anecdotes of Painting in England; With Some Account of the Principal Artists; And Incidental Notes on Other Arts; Collected by the Late Mr George Vertue; And now Digested and Published from his Original MSS by Mr Horace Walpole*, 3 vols. (Strawberry Hill, 1762–71), i, 108.

20 Walpole to Henry Conway, 12 Feb. 1756, *Correspondence*, xxxvii, 439–40.

21 Eastlake, *Gothic Revival*, p. 43.

22 Walpole to Miss Berry, 17 Oct. 1794, *Correspondence*, xxi, 136–8.

23 'Strawberry Hill', *New Monthly Magazine* 17 (1826), 256–67 (p. 262).

24 Cited in W. S. Lewis, *Horace Walpole's Library* (Cambridge University Press, 1958), p. 2.

25 Walpole to Henry Conway, 23 Sept. 1755, *Correspondence*, xxxvii, 406. For an account of such 'mimicry' in relation to the masked assemblies of the period, see Terry Castle's *Masquerade and Civilization: The Carnivalesque in Eighteenth-Century English Culture and Fiction* (London: Methuen, 1986).

26 Neil McKendrick, 'The Commercialization of Fashion', *The Birth of a Consumer Society: The Commercialization of Leisure in Eighteenth-Century England*, ed. McKendrick and others (London: Hutchinson, 1983), 34–99 (p. 64).

27 'The Works of the Earl of Orford', *Monthly Review* 26 (1798), p. 65.

28 Walpole to George Montagu, 24 Oct. 1758, *Correspondence*, ix, 227.

29 *Gentleman's Magazine* (1812), Peter Sabor (ed.), *Horace Walpole: The Critical*

Heritage (London: Routledge and Kegan Paul, 1987), p. 288.

30 Walpole, *Strawberry Hill*, p. i.

31 Walpole to Thomas Gray, 18 Feb. 1768, *Correspondence*, XIV, 167.

32 Chesterfield, Philip Dormer Stanhope, 4th Earl, *Letters to his Son and Others*, ed. Robert K. Root (London: Dent, 1929), p. 49.

33 Ibid. p. 165.

34 Horace Walpole, *A Catalogue of the Royal and Noble Authors of England, With Lists of their Works*, 2 vols. (Strawberry Hill, 1758), I, p. vii.

35 Walpole, *Anecdotes of Painting*, I, p. vii.

36 Ibid. I, p. viii. A similar relationship informed the initial collaboration between William Beckford and Samuel Henley to produce an annotated edition of *Vathek*.

37 Ibid. I, p. vi and p. viii.

38 *Monthly Review* (1762), Sabor (ed.), *Horace Walpole*, p. 41.

39 Horace Walpole, *Historic Doubts on the Life and Reign of King Richard the Third* (London, 1768), p. xii.

40 Walpole to Thomas Gray, 18 Feb. 1768, *Correspondence*, XIV, 167.

41 Walpole, *Historic Doubts*, p. iii and p. xv.

42 Thomas Pownall, *A Treatise on the Study of Antiquities as the Commentary to Historical Learning* (London, 1782), p. 54.

43 Cited in Thomas Preston Peardon, *The Transition in English Historical Writing 1760–1830* (New York: Columbia University Press, 1933), pp. 144–5.

44 Walpole to George Montagu, 12 Mar. 1768, *Correspondence*, X, 255.

45 Thomas Gray, 'Stanzas to Mr Bentley', Roger Lonsdale (ed.), *Thomas Gray and William Collins: Poetical Works* (Oxford University Press, 1977), p. 45. Walpole to George Montagu, 5 Jan. 1766, *Correspondence*, X, 192.

46 Thomas Babington Macaulay, Review of *Letters of Horace Walpole to Sir Horace Mann*, *Edinburgh Review* 58 (1833), 227–58 (p. 231).

47 Ibid. p. 230.

48 Susan Sontag, 'Notes on "Camp"', *A Susan Sontag Reader* (Harmondsworth: Penguin, 1983), 105–19 (p. 108). Ian Duncan's reader's report helped me to clarify the argument of this paragraph.

49 Timothy Mowl, *Horace Walpole: The Great Outsider* (London: John Murray, 1996), p. 7, p. 6.

50 John Pinkerton, *Walpoliana* (Dublin, 1800).

51 Chesterfield, *Letters*, p. 211.

52 *Monthly Review* 26 (1798), p. 288.

53 Isaac D'Israeli, 'The Pains of Fastidious Egotism', *The Calamities and Quarrels of Authors: With Some Inquiries Respecting their Moral and Literary Characters, And Memoirs for our Literary History* (London, n.d.), 42–51 (p. 46).

54 William Hazlitt, 'Letters of Horace Walpole', *Selected Writings*, ed. Ronald Blythe (Harmondsworth: Penguin, 1970), 418–29 (p. 424).

55 Macaulay, *Edinburgh Review* 58 (1833), p. 227.

56 Archibald S. Foord, '"The Only Unadulterated Whig"', *Horace Walpole: Writer, Politician and Connoisseur. Essays on the 250th Anniversary of Walpole's Birth*,

ed. Warren Hunting-Smith (New Haven: Yale University Press, 1967), 25–44 (p. 33).

57 See, for example, Walpole's *Memoirs of King George II*, ed. John Brooke, 3 vols. (New Haven: Yale University Press, 1985).

58 Walpole to William Mason, 3 Apr. 1775, *Correspondence*, XXVIII, 186.

59 Walpole to George Montagu, 10 July 1766, *Correspondence*, X, 222.

60 Hazlitt, 'Letters of Horace Walpole', *Selected Writings*, p. 419.

61 Cited in Brian Fothergill, *The Strawberry Hill Set: Horace Walpole and his Circle* (London: Faber & Faber, 1983), p. 178.

62 Walpole to George Montagu, 14 Oct. 1756, *Correspondence*, IX, 197. Walpole to William Mason, 24 Oct. 1777, *Correspondence*, XXVII, 339.

63 Macaulay, *Edinburgh Review* (1833), p. 229 and p. 228.

64 Ibid. p. 227.

65 Horace Walpole, *The Castle of Otranto*, p. 4. Future references to this edition will be given in the text.

66 My argument here follows Harriet Guest's 'Wanton Muse', *Beyond Romanticism*, ed. Copley and Whale, p. 122.

67 *Monthly Review* (1765), Sabor (ed.), *Horace Walpole*, p. 72.

68 Scott, 'Horace Walpole', *Lives*, p. 199.

69 Richard Hurd, *Moral and Political Dialogues; With Letters on Chivalry and Romance*, 3 vols. (Farnborough: Gregg International, 1972), III, 193.

70 Walpole to William Mason, 25 June 1782, *Correspondence*, XXIX, 255–6.

71 Walpole to William Mason, 7 Apr. 1774, *Correspondence*, XXVIII, 143.

72 Trumpener, *Bardic Nationalism*, p. 33.

73 See Walpole, *Otranto*, ed. W. S. Lewis, Introduction, p. xi.

74 Napier, *Failure of Gothic*, p. 76.

75 Ibid. pp. 82–3.

76 Walpole to Mme du Deffand, 13 Mar. 1767, *Correspondence*, III, 260.

77 *Critical Review* (1765), Sabor (ed.), *Horace Walpole*, p. 68.

78 *Monthly Review* (1765), ibid. p. 72.

79 Walpole to Mme du Deffand, 13 Mar. 1767, *Correspondence*, III, 261.

80 Walpole to William Cole, 9 Mar. 1765, *Correspondence*, I, 88. See also Napier, *Failure of Gothic*, p. 79.

81 William Warburton, *Works of Alexander Pope*, Sabor (ed.), *Horace Walpole*, p. 75. Walpole to Robert Jephson, 27 Jan. 1780, *Correspondence*, XLI, 410.

82 Walpole to George Montagu, 16 July 1764, *Correspondence*, X, 130. *The Life of Edward Lord Herbert of Cherbury. Written by Himself* (Dublin, 1771), not paginated.

83 Walpole to William Cole, 18 Jan. 1766, *Correspondence*, I, 104. *Monthly Review* (1766), Sabor (ed.), *Horace Walpole*, pp. 107–8.

84 Horace Walpole, *Hieroglyphic Tales* (Strawberry Hill, 1785), pp. vi–vii.

85 Scott, 'Clara Reeve', *Lives*, p. 210.

86 Scott, 'Horace Walpole', *Lives*, pp. 196–7.

87 Walpole to Joseph Warton, 16 Mar. 1765, *Correspondence*, XL, 377.

88 Walpole to William Cole, 28 Feb. 1765, *Correspondence*, I, 85.

89 Walpole to Hertford, 26 Mar. 1765, *Correspondence*, XXXVIII, 525. Walpole to Elie de Beaumont, 18 Mar. 1765, *Correspondence*, XL, 379.

90 Walpole to Horace Mann, 20 Dec. 1764, *Correspondence*, XXII, 271. Walpole to William Cole, 22 Aug. 1778, *Correspondence*, II, 110.

91 Ibid. p. 110.

92 Horace Walpole, 'Postscript' to *Hieroglyphic Tales*, *The Castle of Otranto and Hieroglyphic Tales*, ed. Robert Mack (London: Dent, 1993), p. 137.

93 Thomas Gray to Walpole, 30 Dec. 1764, *Correspondence*, XIV, 137. E. J. Clery has recently claimed that *Otranto*, published shortly after the Cock Lane ghost episode, paid tribute to 'the hedonistic acceptance of ghosts as a fiction', *Rise of Supernatural Fiction*, pp. 17–18. The pleasure experienced by readers such as Gray nonetheless seems to have been predicated on the assumption that other, less enlightened readers took the first edition of *Otranto* seriously.

94 Punter, *Literature of Terror*, p. 52.

95 D'Israeli, 'Pains of Fastidious Egotism', *Calamities*, p. 45.

96 Stephen Bann, 'The Sense of the Past: Image, Text, and Object in the Formation of Historical Consciousness in Nineteenth-Century Britain', *The New Historicism*, ed. H. Aram Veeser (New York: Routledge, 1989), 102 15 (p. 109).

97 Walpole to William Cole, 9 Mar. 1765, *Correspondence*, I, 88.

98 Georg Lukács, *The Historical Novel*, trans. Hannah and Stanley Mitchell (Harmondsworth: Penguin, 1969), p. 15.

99 Walpole, *Otranto*, ed. W. S. Lewis, Introduction, p. xii.

100 John Dunlop, *The History of Fiction: Being a Critical Account of the Most Celebrated Prose Works of Fiction, from the Earliest Greek Romances to the Novels of the Present Age*, 3 vols. (London, 1814), III, 382.

101 Walpole to George Montagu, 5 Jan. 1766, *Correspondence*, X, 192.

102 Walpole, *Otranto*, ed. Robert Mack, Introduction, p. xxii.

103 Walpole to William Cole, 9 Mar. 1765, *Correspondence*, I, 88. John Sitter, 'The Flight from History in Mid-Century Poetry', *Modern Essays on Eighteenth-Century Literature*, ed. Leopold Damrosch (Oxford University Press, 1988), 412–35.

104 Punter, *Literature of Terror*, p. 52. E. J. Clery's *Rise of Supernatural Fiction*, pp. 68–79, also reads *Otranto* as a 'social allegory', which figures the 'contradiction between the traditional claims of landed property and the new claims of the private family' (p. 69 and p. 77).

105 Marilyn Butler, *Romantics, Rebels and Reactionaries: English Literature and its Background 1760–1830* (Oxford University Press, 1981), p. 23.

106 Oliver Goldsmith, 'Letter to the Editor of Lloyd's Evening Post', *Collected Works of Oliver Goldsmith*, ed. Arthur Friedman, 5 vols. (Oxford: Clarendon Press, 1966), III, 195–8 (p. 198).

107 Duncan, *Modern Romance*, p. 29. Caroline Gonda suggests that the fate of Conrad 'embodies Walpole's own predicament as a politician and political historian, attempting to come to terms with the larger-than-life

spectre of his own father, whose opponents had seen him both as a usurper (like Manfred and his forefathers) and too big for his boots (like Alfonso)', *Reading Daughters' Fictions 1709–1834: Novels and Society from Manley to Edgeworth* (Cambridge University Press, 1996), p. 141. Readings of the 'depth' and seriousness of *Otranto* often invoke the incest plot of Walpole's tragedy *The Mysterious Mother* (written in 1768), which was to be influential on Ann Radcliffe's *The Romance of the Forest* and *The Italian*.

108 Reeve, *Old English Baron*, p. 3, pp. 4–5.

109 For a brief summary of the *Modern Anecdote*, often attributed to Lady Elizabeth Craven, see K. K. Mehrotra, *Horace Walpole and the English Novel: A Study of the Influence of the Castle of Otranto 1764–1820* (Oxford: Blackwell, 1934), pp. 64–6.

110 The legacy of *Otranto* to writers such as Beckford and Matthew Lewis, according to Ian Duncan, is 'a "Satanic" dialectic of power, whereby he who most pretends to power turns out to be most powerless', *Modern Romance*, p. 31.

111 Pinkerton, *Walpoliana*, p. xxiii; Anna Barbauld, *The British Novelists; With an Essay and Prefaces, Biographical and Critical*, 50 vols. (London, 1810), XXII, p. i.

112 Anne Grant, *Essays on the Superstitions of the Highlanders of Scotland*, 2 vols. (London, 1811), I, 300–1.

113 William Hazlitt, 'On the English Novelists', *Lectures on the English Comic Writers and Fugitive Writings* (London: Dent, 1967), 127.

114 *The New Monthly Magazine* 16 (1826), 532–6 (pp. 532–3).

115 *Gentleman's Magazine* (1797), cited in Mehrotra, *Horace Walpole*, p. 163. *Monthly Mirror* (1804), Dan J. McNutt (ed.), *The Eighteenth-Century Gothic Novel: An Annotated Bibliography of Criticism and Selected Texts* (New York: Garland, 1975), p. 164.

116 Barbauld, *British Novelists*, XXII, p. ii.

117 Review of *The Poetical Works of Anne Radcliffe*, *Edinburgh Review* 59 (1834), 327–41 (p. 329).

2. THE LOYALIST GOTHIC ROMANCE

1 T. J. Mathias, *The Pursuits of Literature: A Satirical Poem in Four Dialogues. With Notes*, 6th edn (London, 1798), 4th Dialogue, p. 343.

2 James White, *The Adventures of King Richard Coeur de Lion, To Which is Added the Death of Lord Falkland: A Poem*, 3 vols. (London, 1791), I, p. xi and p. xiv.

3 Cited in J. M. S. Tompkins, 'James White, Esq: A Forgotten Humourist', *Review of English Studies* 3 (1927), 146–56 (p. 152). Review of *Earl Strongbow*, *Gentleman's Magazine* 60 (1790), pp. 550–1.

4 *Earl Strongbow: or, The History of Richard de Clare and the Beautiful Geralda*, 2 vols. (London, 1789), I, 91. *Gentleman's Magazine* 60 (1790), p. 551.

5 White, *Earl Strongbow*, I, 1 and 30; I, 151.

6 Ibid. I, 92–3.

7 Ibid. II, 79, II, 35.

8 Ibid. II, 49. White, *The Adventures of John of Gaunt, Duke of Lancaster*, 3 vols. (London, 1791), III, 232.
9 White, *King Richard*, II, 142.
10 Ibid. III, 166.
11 Cited in Duncan, *Modern Romance*, p. 10.
12 William Godwin, *Imogen: A Pastoral Romance from the Ancient British, Damon and Delia, Italian Letters, Imogen*, ed. Pamela Clemit, *Collected Novels and Memoirs of William Godwin*, ed. Mark Philp, 8 vols. (London: William Pickering, 1992), II, p. 173 and p. 196.
13 Ibid. p. 197.
14 Pamela Clemit, 'A Pastoral Romance, from the Ancient British: Godwin's Rewriting of *Comus*', *Eighteenth-Century Fiction* 3 (1991), 217–39 (p. 221).
15 See Jon Mee, *Dangerous Enthusiasms: William Blake and the Culture of Radicalism in the 1790s* (Oxford: Clarendon Press, 1992), pp. 75–120, along with Katie Trumpener, *Bardic Nationalism*, pp. 3–34.
16 Clemit, 'Pastoral Romance', pp. 223–4.
17 See, for example, Henry St John, Viscount Bolingbroke, 'Remarks on the History of England', *Historical Writings*, ed. Isaac Kramnick (University of Chicago Press, 1972), p. 178, and John Cartwright, *Take your Choice!* (London, 1776). Towards the end of the century, radicals generally used the term 'Saxon' rather than 'Gothic', probably because it was more consistent with the theory of the Norman Yoke.
18 J. G. A. Pocock, *The Ancient Constitution and the Feudal Law: A Study of Historical Thought in the Seventeenth Century*, 2nd edn (Cambridge University Press, 1987), p. 380.
19 Jeremy Bentham, *A Fragment on Government*, ed. J. H. Burns and H. L. A. Hart (Cambridge University Press, 1988), p. vi.
20 William Blackstone, *Commentaries on the Laws of England*, 3 vols. (Oxford, 1767–9), III, 268.
21 Reeve, *Old English Baron*, p. 3. Future references to this edition will be given in the text.
22 Walpole to William Cole, 22 Aug. 1778, *Correspondence*, II, 110. Scott, 'Clara Reeve', *Lives*, p. 207.
23 See Mehrotra, *Horace Walpole*, pp. 84–102, for a discussion of the historical romances written between the publication of *Longsword* in 1762 and the early 1790s.
24 *Critical Review* (1762), McNutt (ed.), *Eighteenth-Century Gothic Novel*, p. 98. For a useful listing of eighteenth-century historical romances alongside more familiar 'Gothic' works, see Mehrotra, *Horace Walpole*, Appendix B, pp. 174–84.
25 Clara Reeve, *The Progress of Romance*, 2 vols. (Colchester, 1785), II, 32.
26 Gary Kelly, *Women, Writing, and Revolution 1790–1827* (Oxford: Clarendon Press, 1993), pp. 187–8. Though there is little information available about Reeve's political position, she contended elsewhere for 'a subordination of ranks and degrees of men . . . consistent with the most perfect liberty that

mankind are capable of enjoying', *Plans of Education; With Remarks on the Systems of Other Writers* (London, 1792), p. 213.

27 Gerald Newman, *The Rise of English Nationalism: A Cultural History 1740–1830* (London: Weidenfeld & Nicolson, 1987), p. 112.

28 Elizabeth Carter, *A Series of Letters Between Mrs Elizabeth Carter and Miss Catherine Talbot From the Year 1741 to 1770, To Which Are Added, Letters From Mrs Elizabeth Carter to Mrs Vesey, Between the Years 1763 and 1787*, 2 vols. (London, 1808), II, 195 and 218–19.

29 William Hayley, *An Essay on Epic Poetry; In Five Epistles to the Rev Mr Mason* (Dublin, 1782), p. 40. John Pinkerton, *A Dissertation on the Origin and Progress of the Scythians or Goths, Being an Introduction to the Ancient and Modern History of Europe* (London, 1787), p. xiv. Note the different locations of the 'original' Goths.

30 Richard Hole, *Arthur; or, The Northern Enchantment. A Poetical Romance* (London, 1789), p. iv. *Tales of Terror; With an Introductory Dialogue* (Dublin, 1801), p. 4.

31 John Brewer, *Party Ideology and Popular Politics at the Accession of George III* (Cambridge University Press, 1976), p. 216.

32 Richard Price, *A Discourse on the Love of our Country*, Marilyn Butler (ed.), *Burke, Paine, Godwin, and the Revolution Controversy* (Cambridge University Press, 1984), p. 25.

33 David Cannadine, 'The Making of the British Upper Classes', *Aspects of Aristocracy: Grandeur and Decline in Modern Britain* (Harmondsworth: Penguin, 1995), 9–36 (p. 10).

34 Benedict Anderson, *Imagined Communities: Reflections on the Origins and Spread of Nationalism*, revised edn (London: Verso, 1991), p. 101.

35 Edmund Burke, 'First Letter on a Regicide Peace' (1796), *The Writings and Speeches of Edmund Burke*, series ed. Paul Langford, IX: The Revolutionary War 1794–97; Ireland, ed. R. D. Macdowell (Oxford: Clarendon Press, 1991), 187–264 (p. 253).

36 Cited in Stella Cottrell, 'The Devil on Two Sticks: Francophobia in 1803', *Patriotism: The Making and Unmaking of British National Identity*, ed. Raphael Samuel, 3 vols. (London: Routledge, 1989), I, 259–74 (p. 264). Benedict Anderson's comments on the 'subjective antiquity' of the imagined nation are clearly apposite here, *Imagined Communities*, p. 5.

37 Christopher Hill, 'The Norman Yoke', *Puritanism and Revolution: Studies in Interpretation of the English Revolution of the Seventeenth Century*, rpt. (Harmondsworth: Penguin, 1990), pp. 58–125.

38 H. T. Dickinson, 'Popular Loyalism in Britain in the 1790s', *The Transformation of Political Culture: England and Germany in the Late-Eighteenth Century*, ed. Eckhart Hellmuth (Oxford University Press, 1990), 503–33 (p. 505).

39 John Cartwright, *The Commonwealth in Danger, with an Introduction Containing Remarks on some Late Writings of Arthur Young, Esq* (London, 1795), p. 120; 'An Appeal, on the Subject of the English Constitution' (London, 1797), p. 12; Alice Chandler, *A Dream of Order* (London: Routledge and Kegan Paul,

1971), p. 86. On Turner, see also Clare A. Simmons, *Reversing the Conquest: History and Myth in Nineteenth-Century Literature* (New Brunswick and London: Rutgers University Press, 1990), p. 57.

40 Joseph Cottle, *Alfred, an Epic Poem, in Twenty-Four Books* (London, 1800), p. iv.
41 Ibid. p. vii.
42 Ibid. p. iv and p. 371.
43 Henry James Pye, *Alfred; An Epic Poem, in Six Books* (London, 1801), preface, p. i.
44 Ibid. p. 63.
45 Ibid. p. 61.
46 Ibid. p. 42.
47 Ibid. p. 69.
48 Hurd, 'On the Age of Queen Elizabeth', *Moral and Political Dialogues*, I, 153.
49 Henry James Pye, 'Carmen Seculare for the Year 1800' (London, 1800), no pagination.
50 Ibid.
51 Henry James Pye, 'Ode for the New Year, 1797', in the *Gentleman's Magazine* 67 (1797), p. 60. A note is appended to Pye's poem: 'These last lines were inserted at the desire of the King'.
52 *Gentleman's Magazine* 61 (1791), p. iii.
53 William Gilpin, *Observations on the River Wye, and Several Parts of South Wales, & c., Relative Chiefly to Picturesque Beauty; Made in the Summer of the Year 1770* (Oxford: Woodstock, 1991), p. 14.
54 *Gentleman's Magazine* 68 (1798), p. 1105.
55 William Wordsworth, 'Lowther', in *Poetical Works*, ed. T. Hutchinson, 2nd edn rev. E. De Selincourt (Oxford University Press, 1969), p. 374.
56 *Gentleman's Magazine* 64 (1794), p. 305
57 Ibid. 69 (1799), p. 190.
58 Edmund Burke, 'Letter to a Noble Lord', *The Writings and Speeches of Edmund Burke*, IX, 145–87 (p. 172).
59 Linda Colley, *Britons: Forging the Nation 1707–1837* (New Haven: Yale University Press, 1992), p. 177.
60 *Gentleman's Magazine* 68 (1798), p. 764.
61 Ibid. 69 (1799), pp. 92–4.
62 Ibid. p. 668 - these articles rarely made clear who the 'improvers' actually were. For typical examples of the redefinition of the Gothic in the period, see the references to the 'Gothic and unintelligible burden' of titles and the 'Gothic system of trial by duel' in William Godwin, *Enquiry Concerning Political Justice and its Influence on Modern Morals and Happiness*, ed. Isaac Kramnick (Harmondsworth: Penguin, 1985), p. 477 and p. 641.
63 Richard Polwhele, 'The Old English Gentleman', *Poems*, 5 vols. in one (London, 1810), III, 7 and 15.
64 Ibid. III, 5 and 13; IV, 134 and 136; III, 89.
65 Ibid. III, 3. For a similarly elegiac treatment of rural aristocracy, see Samuel Egerton Brydges, *Arthur Fitz-Albini. A Novel*, 2 vols. (London, 1798).

66 See J. M. S. Tompkins, *The Popular Novel in England 1770–1800* (London: Methuen, 1932), p. 238.

67 Clara Reeve, *Memoirs of Sir Roger De Clarendon: The Natural Son of Edward Prince of Wales, Commonly Called the Black Prince; With Anecdotes of Many Other Eminent Persons of the Fourteenth Century*, 3 vols. (London, 1793), III, p. xxi.

68 Ibid. I, p. x. and III, 228.

69 Ibid. I, p. xii.

70 Ibid. I, 15–16.

71 Ibid. I, 66–7.

72 Ibid. I, 67 and III, 54.

73 Ibid. III, 176.

74 *Monthly Review* (1793), Derek Roper, *Reviewing before the* Edinburgh *1788–1802* (London: Methuen, 1978), p. 163.

75 Richard Warner, *Netley Abbey: A Gothic Story*, 2 vols. (New York: Arno Press, 1974), I, 1 and I, 19; I, 85.

76 Ibid. I, 139.

77 Ibid. I, 177 and I, 106; I, 86.

78 Ibid. II, 190–1.

79 *Mort Castle: A Gothic Story* (London, 1798), p. 24.

80 Ibid. p. 98.

81 Ibid. p. 110 and p. 118.

82 Ibid. p. 190.

83 Ibid. pp. 235–6.

84 Ibid. p. 248.

85 *Netley Abbey*, II, 86. *Mort Castle*, p. 107.

86 Many of the castles used as settings for 'Gothic' romances are discussed in the architectural correspondence of the *Gentleman's Magazine*. See, for example, the description of Raby Castle, the setting for Mary Harley's *St Bernard's Priory; An Old English Tale* (1786), in the *Gentleman's Magazine* 69 (1799), p. 295: 'The exterior of this castle is a striking example of the romantic turn of former days.'

87 Elizabeth Bonhote, *Bungay Castle: A Novel*, 2 vols. (London, 1796), I, pp. vii-viii. For Bonhote's ownership of the land on which her work is set, see Tompkins, *Popular Novel*, p. 225.

88 Stephen Cullen, *The Castle of Inchvally: A Tale – Alas! Too True*, 3 vols. (London, 1796), I, 3.

89 Ibid. I, 3–4. Cullen's preface echoes the story told by Jack Anvil in Hannah More's *Village Politics* (1793), Butler (ed.), *Revolution Controversy*, 179–84 (p. 181). The *Gentleman's Magazine* 73 (1803), p. 327, relates a similar, if more violent, anecdote about a man who was crushed 'to atoms' – 'a due punishment' – while attempting to gain building materials by pulling down Netley Abbey.

90 For a discussion of *Gaston*'s frame narrative, see Trumpener, *Bardic Nationalism*, pp. 103–5.

91 Ann Radcliffe, *Gaston de Blondeville, or The Court of Henry III Keeping Festival in*

Ardenne: A Romance; St Alban's Abbey, A Metrical Tale; With some Poetical Pieces: To Which is Prefixed a Memoir of the Author, with Extracts from her Journals, 4 vols. (London, 1826), I, 82 and I, III.

92 Ibid. III, 21 and III, 39.

93 Ibid. II, 332.

94 In addition to *Caleb Williams* and *The Old Manor House*, see works such as Eliza Fenwick's *Secresy* (1795), Robert Bage's *Hermsprong* (1796), and Mary Wollstonecraft's *The Wrongs of Woman* (1798).

95 See Terry Eagleton, *Heathcliff and the Great Hunger: Studies in Irish Culture* (London: Verso, 1995), pp. 187–94, along with W. J. McCormack, 'Irish Gothic and After'. *Melmoth the Wanderer* offers an instructive counterpoint to the sense of a British manifest destiny outlined by James White's *Earl Strongbow*.

96 *Days of Chivalry: A Romance*, 2 vols. (London, 1797), I, p. ii. See also Jane West, *The Loyalists: An Historical Novel*, 3 vols. (London, 1812), I, 21: 'only anxious to defend and support constitutional principles, I shall plead guilty to many errors in taste, in the construction of the fable, as well as in the style of the narrative'.

97 *British Critic* (1793) and *Critical Review* (1793), Roper, *Reviewing before the Edinburgh*, pp. 163–4.

98 John Ogilvie, *Britannia: A National Epic Poem, in Twenty Books, To Which is Prefixed 'A Critical Dissertation on Epic Machinery'* (Aberdeen, 1801), p. 17.

99 *The Courier* (1818), cited in Louis F. Peck, *A Life of Matthew G. Lewis* (Cambridge: Harvard University Press, 1961), p. 174.

100 David Simpson, *Romanticism, Nationalism, and the Revolt against Theory* (Chicago University Press, 1993), p. 86.

101 Mathias, *Pursuits of Literature*, 4th Dialogue, p. 245.

102 Nathan Drake, *Literary Hours: Sketches Critical and Narrative*, 2nd edn., 2 vols. (London, 1800), I, 146 and 63.

3. GOTHIC 'SUBVERSION': GERMAN LITERATURE, THE MINERVA PRESS, MATTHEW LEWIS

1 'Modern Literature', *Aberdeen Magazine* (1798), cited in André Parreaux, *The Publication of the Monk: A Literary Event 1796–1798* (Paris: Librairie Marcel Didier, 1960), p. 39.

2 'Impartial Strictures on the Poem Called "The Pursuits of Literature": and Particularly a Vindication of the Romance of "The Monk"' (London, 1798), p. 31.

3 Walter Scott, 'Essay on Imitations of the Ancient Ballad', *The Poetical Works of Sir Walter Scott*, IV: Border Minstrelsy (Edinburgh: Adam and Charles Black, 1880), 45. *Critical Review* (1797), Sage (ed.), *The Gothick Novel*, 39–43 (p. 41).

4 Coral Ann Howells, *Love, Mystery, and Misery: Feeling in Gothic Fiction* (London: Athlone Press, 1978), p. 62.

5 William Blake, 'An Island in the Moon', *Complete Writings*, ed. Geoffrey Keynes (Oxford University Press, 1966), 44–63 (p. 53). Reeve, *Progress of Romance*, ii, 70.

6 Scott, 'Ancient Ballad', p. 38.

7 Ibid. p. 36.

8 William Beckford, *Popular Tales of the Germans: Translated from the German*, 2 vols. (London, 1791), i, p. ii.

9 Tompkins, *Popular Novel*, pp. 243–5.

10 Cited in Mary Jacobus, *Tradition and Experiment in Wordsworth's Lyrical Ballads* (Oxford: Clarendon Press, 1976), p. 218.

11 Scott, 'Ancient Ballad', p. 38.

12 Friedrich Schiller, *The Robbers*, trans. Alexander Tytler (Oxford: Woodstock, 1989), p. vii, p. ix and p. x.

13 Peter Teuthold, *The Necromancer: or, The Tale of the Black Forest: Founded on Facts: Translated from the German of Lawrence Flammenberg* (London: Skoob Books, 1989), p. 17.

14 Review of *Albert de Nordenshild, Analytical Review* 24 (1796), p. 404.

15 Coleridge, letter to Southey (3 Nov. 1794), *Collected Letters of Samuel Taylor Coleridge*, ed. Earl Leslie Griggs (Oxford: Clarendon Press, 1956), i, 122.

16 Coleridge, 'To the Author of "The Robbers"', *Poetical Works*, ed. E. H. Coleridge (Oxford University Press, 1969), p. 72.

17 *Analytical Review* (1798), J. R. de J. Jackson (ed.), *Coleridge: The Critical Heritage* (London: Routledge and Kegan Paul, 1970), p. 52. *Critical Review* (1798), Jackson (ed.), *Coleridge*, p. 53.

18 Jackson (ed.), *Coleridge*, p. 60.

19 F. W. Stokoe, *German Influence in the English Romantic Period 1788–1818, with Special Reference to Scott, Coleridge, Shelley and Byron* (Cambridge University Press, 1926), pp. 36–43.

20 Taylor, letter to Southey (Dec. 1798), J. W. Robberds (ed.), *A Memoir of the Life and Writings of the Late William Taylor of Norwich . . . Containing his Correspondence of Many Years with the Late Robert Southey, Esq, and Original Letters from Sir Walter Scott and Other Eminent Literary Men* (London, 1843), pp. 236–7.

21 J. G. Lockhart, *Memoirs of the Life of Sir Walter Scott*, 7 vols. (Edinburgh, 1837–8), i, 295.

22 See Rosemary Ashton, *The German Idea: Four English Writers and the Reception of German Thought 1800–1860* (Cambridge University Press, 1980), p. 7.

23 *The Rovers; or, The Double Arrangement*, George Canning and John Hookham Frere, *Poetry of the Anti-Jacobin* (Oxford: Woodstock, 1991), p. 168.

24 Ibid. p. 162.

25 David Simpson, *Romanticism*, p. 87.

26 Ibid. p. 88.

27 August von Kotzebue, *Lovers' Vows*, adapted by Elizabeth Inchbald (Oxford: Woodstock, 1990), preface.

28 *Anti-Jacobin Review* (1799), cited in Emily Lorraine de Montluzin, *The Anti-Jacobins 1798–1800: Early Contributions to the 'Anti-Jacobin Review'* (Basingstoke:

Macmillan, 1988), p. 117.

29 Jane West, *Poems and Plays*, 4 vols. (London, 1799), I, p. xi.

30 'The Shade of Alexander Pope on the Banks of the Thames. A Satirical Poem. With Notes' (Dublin, 1799), pp. 55–64.

31 See Wordsworth's 'Essay Supplementary to the Preface' of 1815 and Coleridge's renewed attack on Kotzebue in Chapter 23 of the *Biographia Literaria*.

32 'Mauritius Moonshine', 'More Wonders! An Heroic Epistle to M. G. Lewis, Esq M.P.' (London, 1801), p. v; p. 10 and p. 13.

33 Mathias, *Pursuits of Literature*, 4th Dialogue, p. 245. It is interesting to consider the role played by the arch-Tory *Blackwood's Edinburgh Magazine* in reviving the tale of terror in the early nineteenth century.

34 William Preston, 'Reflections on the Peculiarities of Style and Manner in the Late German Writers whose Works Have Appeared in English, and on the Tendency of their Productions' (Dublin, 1801), p. 3.

35 Ibid. p. 31 and p. 7.

36 Preston, 'Reflections', p. 33.

37 Ibid. p. 56. See also Simon Schaffer, 'Natural Philosophy and Public Spectacle in the Eighteenth Century', *History of Science* 21 (1983), pp. 1–43.

38 Stokoe, *German Influence*, p. 49.

39 Preston, 'Reflections', p. 41 and p. 60.

40 Ibid. p. 50.

41 Ibid. p. 17.

42 Wordsworth, 'Preface to the . . . Lyrical Ballads', *Poetical Works*, 734–41 (p. 735).

43 *The Age; A Poem: Moral, Political, and Metaphysical. With Illustrative Annotations. In Ten Books* (London, 1810), p. 208 n.1. Sharon Turner, *Prolusions on the Present Greatness of Britain; on Modern Poetry; on the Present Aspect of the World* (London, 1819), p. 94.

44 Dorothy Blakey, *The Minerva Press 1790–1820* (London: The Bibliographical Society, Oxford University Press, 1939), p. 1.

45 William Lane, 'A Tale Addressed to the Novel Readers of the Present Times' (London, 1795), p. 6.

46 Howells, *Love, Mystery, and Misery*, p. 82.

47 Ina Ferris, *The Achievement of Literary Authority: Gender, History, and the Waverley Novels* (Ithaca: Cornell University Press, 1991), p. 43.

48 Blakey, *Minerva Press*, p. 84.

49 Francis Lathom, *The Impenetrable Secret, Find It Out!*, 2 vols. (London, 1805), I, p. viii.

50 Lathom, prefaces to *Mystery* and *Human Beings*, cited in Montague Summers, *The Gothic Quest* (London: Fortune Press, 1938), p. 309.

51 'Terrorist Novel Writing', *The Spirit of the Public Journals for 1797*, 3rd edn (London, 1802), pp. 227–8.

52 Jon Klancher, *The Making of the English Reading Audiences 1790–1832* (Madison: University of Wisconsin Press, 1987), p. 13.

53 Thomas Carlyle, *London and Westminster Review* (1838), John O. Hayden (ed.), *Scott: The Critical Heritage* (London: Routledge and Kegan Paul, 1970), p. 370.

54 Thomas Trotter, *A View of the Nervous Temperament* (London, 1807), pp. 89–90; p. 165.

55 Wordsworth, 'Preface to the . . . Lyrical Ballads', *Poetical Works*, p. 735.

56 *British Critic* (1797), Ioan Williams (ed.), *The Novel and Romance 1700–1800: A Documentary Record* (London: Routledge and Kegan Paul, 1970), p. 443.

57 See Terry Lovell, *Consuming Fiction* (London: Verso, 1987), p. 49. 'The Projector', *Gentleman's Magazine* 78 (1808), 882–5 (p. 883).

58 Ibid. p. 883.

59 Ibid. p. 884.

60 Ibid. p. 885.

61 Parreaux, *Publication of the Monk*, p. 26.

62 Letter cited in Peck, *Life of Lewis*, p. 118.

63 *The Monk: A Romance*, ed. Howard Anderson (Oxford University Press, 1973), p. 6. Future references to this edition will be given in the text.

64 Syndy M. Conger, *Matthew G. Lewis, Charles Robert Maturin and the Germans: An Interpretative Study of the Influence of German Literature on Two Gothic Novels* (Institut für Englische Sprache und Literatur Universität Salzburg, 1977), p. 12 and p. 89.

65 Ibid. p. 53.

66 Napier, *Failure of Gothic*, p. 126.

67 It is tempting to make more of the obvious similarities between writers such as Walpole, Beckford, Lewis, and Maturin, and position them within their own tradition of 'male Gothic'. Any connection between these writers nonetheless needs to be substantiated rather than simply assumed. There is no substitute for the detailed analysis of individual works, in any case, and it is important to distinguish between, for example, Walpole's 'aristocratic' self-fashioning and Lewis's far more indiscriminate claim on the attention of the reading public.

68 Howard, *Reading Gothic*, p. 184.

69 See Peck, *Life of Lewis*, p. 16. The phrase 'rebellious adolescence' comes from Gary Kelly's discussion of P. B. Shelley's *Zastrozzi*, 'an example of what one could call tearaway Gothic – fiction for and by rebellious adolescence', *English Fiction*, p. 108. Judith Wilt has also referred to *The Monk* as a work which displays the 'adolescent daredevil' habit of 'calling . . . a spade a shovel', *Ghosts of the Gothic: Austen, Eliot, and Lawrence* (Princeton University Press, 1980), p. 43.

70 Howard, *Reading Gothic*, p. 189.

71 *Critical Review* (1797), Sage (ed.), *The Gothick Novel*, p. 40.

72 Duncan, *Modern Romance*, p. 45.

73 Napier, *Failure of Gothic*, p. 118.

74 Howard, *Reading Gothic*, pp. 209–10.

75 Marquis de Sade, 'Reflections on the Novel', in *The 120 Days of Sodom and Other Writings*, trans. Austryn Wainhouse and Richard Seaver (London:

Arrow Books, 1990), 97–116 (p. 114 and p. 109).

76 *Critical Review* (1797), Sage (ed.), *The Gothick Novel*, p. 41.

77 *Analytical Review* (1796), Roper (ed.), *Reviewing before the* Edinburgh, p. 141.

78 Thomas Dutton, 'The Literary Census: A Satirical Poem; with Notes, & c, Including Free and Candid Strictures on the Pursuits of Literature and its Anonymous Author' (London, 1798), p. 73.

79 'Epistle in Rhyme, to M. G. Lewis, Esq M.P. Author of the Monk, Castle Spectre & c.' (London, 1798), p. 1, note.

80 According to Robert Darnton, 'Readers could recognize a sex scene when they saw one, but they expected sex to serve as a vehicle for attacks on the church, the crown, and all sorts of social abuses', 'Sex for Thought', *New York Review of Books* 22 December 1994, 65–74 (p. 66).

81 Thomas Love Peacock, 'An Essay on Fashionable Literature', *Essays, Memoirs, Letters & Unfinished Novels, The Halliford Edition of the Works of Thomas Love Peacock*, ed. H. F. B. Brett-Smith and C. E. Jones (London: Constable, 1934), VIII, 265. Given the short-lived fame of writers such as Lewis and Kotzebue, according to Peacock, 'the condition of a fashionable author' can be seen to differ 'very little in stability from that of a political demagogue' (p. 266).

82 *Literary Memoirs of Living Authors of Great Britain*, 2 vols. (London, 1798), I, 371–2.

83 MS note in Beckford's copy of Thomas Moore's *Letters and Journals of Lord Byron*, cited in Louis Crompton, *Byron and Greek Love. Homophobia in Nineteenth-Century England* (London: Faber & Faber, 1985), p. 142.

84 *Critical Review* (1807), cited in Summers, *Gothic Quest*, p. 279.

85 Cited in Conger, *Lewis, Maturin and the Germans*, p. 11. The 'tales of terror' published by *Blackwood's* in the early nineteenth century similarly seem to have been driven by this principle of competition.

86 Scott, 'Ancient Ballad', p. 46.

87 See, for example, Peter Brooks, *The Melodramatic Imagination: Balzac, Henry James, Melodrama, and the Mode of Excess* (New Haven: Yale University Press, 1976), p. 50.

88 *European Magazine* (1797), cited in Parreaux, *Publication of the Monk*, p. 90. Review of *Santa Maria; or, The Mysterious Pregnancy: A Romance, Gentleman's Magazine* 68 (1798), p. 787.

89 Ronald Paulson, *Representations of Revolution 1789–1820* (New Haven: Yale University Press, 1983), pp. 218–24.

90 Parreaux, *Publication of the Monk*, p. 87.

91 *Monthly Mirror* 2 (1796), p. 98.

92 Mathias, *Pursuits of Literature*, preface to 4th Dialogue, pp. 194–5.

93 *Critical Review* (1797), Sage (ed.), *The Gothick Novel*, pp. 39–40.

94 Ibid. pp. 42–3.

95 *Monthly Review* (1797), McNutt (ed.), *Eighteenth-Century Gothic Novel*, p. 250.

96 *British Critic* (1798), cited in Parreaux, *Publication of the Monk*, p. 8.

97 'On Novels and Romances', *Scots Magazine* 64 (1802), p. 548.

98 Margaret Baron-Wilson, *The Life and Correspondence of M. G. Lewis*, 2 vols. (London, 1839), I, 156.

99 *British Critic* (1797), McNutt (ed.), *Eighteenth-Century Gothic Novel*, p. 252.

100 Matthew Lewis, *The Castle Spectre* (Oxford: Woodstock, 1990), p. iii.

101 Review of *Castle Spectre, Monthly Mirror* 4 (1797), p. 354.

102 Lewis, *Castle Spectre*, p. 41.

103 Ibid. p. 58.

104 Ibid. p. 69. A performance of *The Castle Spectre* was staged at Lewis's Jamaican plantation, and the watching slaves were apparently impressed by the character of Hassan. See *Reminiscences of Michael Kelly, of the King's Theatre, and Theatre Royal Drury Lane, Including a Period of Nearly Half a Century; With Original Anecdotes of Many Distinguished Persons, Political, Literary, and Musical*, 2 vols. (London, 1826), I, 142.

105 'Anser Pen-Drag-On, Esq', *Scribbleomania*, pp. 122–3.

106 *Monthly Visitor* (1797), cited in Parreaux, *Publication of the Monk*, p. 150.

107 Lewis, *Castle Spectre*, p. 102.

108 Ibid. p. 103.

109 *Critical Review* (1798), McNutt (ed.), *Eighteenth-Century Gothic Novel*, p. 254.

110 Cited in Introduction to Jeffrey N. Cox (ed.), *Seven Gothic Dramas* (Athens: Ohio University Press, 1992), p. 38.

111 Ibid. p. 2.

112 Cited in Baron-Wilson, *Life of Lewis*, I, 223.

113 Matthew Lewis, *Adelmorn, The Outlaw; A Romantic Drama, in Three Acts*, 2nd edn (London, 1801), p. iii.

114 Ibid. pp. ix–x.

115 Matthew Lewis, *Adelgitha; or, The Fruits of a Single Error. A Tragedy, in Five Acts* (London, 1806), p. ix.

116 Cited in Peck, *Life of Lewis*, p. 103.

117 Parreaux, *Publication of the Monk*, p. 135.

118 Lewis, *Adelmorn the Outlaw*, epilogue, p. 99.

119 *British Critic* (1801), McNutt (ed.), *Eighteenth-Century Gothic Novel*, p. 256.

120 Lockhart, *Life of Scott*, I, 293. Leigh Hunt, 'A Tale for a Chimney Corner', Peter Haining (ed.), *Great British Tales of Terror. Gothic Stories of Horror and Romance 1765–1840* (Harmondsworth: Penguin, 1973), 350–9 (p. 352).

121 Matthew Lewis, *The Bravo of Venice, A Romance: Translated from the German* (London, 1805), pp. 30–1.

122 Howells, *Love, Mystery, and Misery*, p. 79.

123 See Edith Birkhead, *The Tale of Terror: A Study of the Gothic Romance* (London: Constable, 1921), p. 75: 'The notoriety of Lewis's monk may be estimated by the procession of monks who followed in his train.' Birkhead cites works such as *The New Monk* by 'R. S. Esq', *The Monk of Madrid* by George Moore, and *Manfroné, the One-Handed Monk*, by Mary Anne Radcliffe. It is difficult to find evidence about the impact of *The Monk* upon German writers in this period: see Robert Ignatius Le Tellier, *Kindred Spirits: Interrelations and Affinities Between the Romantic Novels of England and Germany (1790–1820)*

(Institut für Anglistik und Amerikanistik Universität Salzburg, 1982), pp. 57–85.
124 Charlotte Dacre ('Rosa Matilda'), *Confessions of the Nun of St Omer. A Tale*, 3 vols. (London, 1805), I, 1.

4. THE FIRST POETESS OF ROMANTIC FICTION: ANN RADCLIFFE

1 Nathan Drake, *Literary Hours: Sketches Critical and Narrative*, 2nd edn, 2 vols. (London, 1800), I, p. ii.
2 Joseph Fox, *Santa Maria; or, The Mysterious Pregnancy: A Romance*, 3 vols. (London, 1797), I, p. xiv.
3 Mathias, *Pursuits of Literature*, 1st Dialogue, p. 20 n.22.
4 Scott, 'Mrs Ann Radcliffe', *Lives*, p. 224. 'Mrs Radcliffe's Posthumous Romance', *New Monthly Magazine* 16 (1826), 532–6 (pp. 532–3).
5 Ann Radcliffe, *A Sicilian Romance* (Oxford University Press, 1993), ed. Alison Milbank, Introduction, pp. xxvi–xxviii.
6 Sophia Lee, *The Recess; or, A Tale of Other Times*, 3 vols. (New York: Arno Press, 1972), I, 15. See the way that Jeremy Bentham reappropriated Blackstone's famous metaphor of the 'old Gothic castle': 'it is not easier to him to turn the law into a Castle, than it is to the imaginations of impoverished suitors to people it with Harpies', *Fragment on Government*, p. 20, note 'q'.
7 Radcliffe, *Sicilian Romance*, p. 6 and p. 176.
8 See Patricia Meyer Spacks, 'Fathers and Daughters: Ann Radcliffe', *Desire and Truth: Functions of Plot in Eighteenth-Century English Novels* (University of Chicago Press, 1990), pp. 147–74.
9 Ann Radcliffe, *The Mysteries of Udolpho: A Romance*, ed. Bonamy Dobrée (Oxford University Press, 1966), p. 330. Future references to this edition will be given in the text.
10 Marilyn Butler, 'The Woman at The Window: Ann Radcliffe in the Novels of Mary Wollstonecraft and Jane Austen', *Women and Literature* 1 (1980), 128–48 (p. 140). Daniel Cottom makes a similarly recuperative point about the 'bodily rebellion' of Emily St Aubert: 'the swoons, syncopes, and trances that so frequently seize Radcliffe's heroines do make them ludicrous in terms of the style of realism that Austen helped to develop. Nevertheless . . . such behaviour does have meaning. It dramatically expresses a great problem that these heroines face in controlling themselves and in controlling the way they appear to others', *The Civilized Imagination: A Study of Ann Radcliffe, Jane Austen and Sir Walter Scott* (Cambridge University Press, 1985), pp. 51–2.
11 Howard, *Reading Gothic*, p. 126.
12 Ibid. p. 127 and p. 130. See also Robert Miles, *Ann Radcliffe: The Great Enchantress* (Manchester University Press, 1995), p. 152: 'Her heroines' proneness to sensibility – to imaginative excess – created the conditions for what I have called the figural: the inscription of "dream" texts within the

main narrative, texts inscribing meanings alternative to the rational ones of the "explained" supernatural.'

13 Radcliffe, *Sicilian Romance*, p. 4 and p. 20. Ann Radcliffe, *The Romance of the Forest*, ed. Chloe Chard (Oxford University Press, 1986), p. 47; Ann Radcliffe, *The Italian, or The Confessional of the Black Penitents, A Romance*, ed. Frederick Garber (Oxford University Press, 1968), p. 25.

14 Recent critics have insisted, however, that these anti-romances are themselves more rhetorically complex than is often recognized. Jane Spencer argues that *The Female Quixote*, despite its 'conservative moral view', shows that romance can provide a heroine with 'power, importance and a history', *The Rise of the Woman Novelist: From Aphra Behn to Jane Austen* (Oxford: Basil Blackwell, 1986), 187–92 (p. 192). Readings of *Northanger Abbey* often emphasize now that Catherine Morland learns from her reading of the Gothic romance: see Claudia Johnson, *Jane Austen: Women, Politics, and the Novel* (University of Chicago Press, 1988), 28–48.

15 Radcliffe, *Romance of the Forest*, p. 118. Radcliffe, *Italian*, p. 160.

16 Radcliffe, *Italian*, p. 91.

17 Ibid. p. 91.

18 David S. Durant, 'Ann Radcliffe and the Conservative Gothic', *Studies in English Literature* 22 (1982), 519–30 (p. 526).

19 Duncan, *Modern Romance*, p. 13.

20 Jane Austen, *Northanger Abbey*, ed. Anne Ehrenpreis (Harmondsworth: Penguin, 1972), p. 203. Duncan, *Modern Romance*, p. 40.

21 Miles, *Ann Radcliffe*, p. 77. Gary Kelly similarly emphasizes that Radcliffe's heroines are bourgeois or middle class, *English Fiction*, pp. 48–55.

22 Mary Poovey, 'Ideology and *The Mysteries of Udolpho*', *Criticism* 21 (1979) 307–30 (p. 311).

23 Spencer, *Rise of the Woman Novelist*, pp. 181–210.

24 *Monthly Review* (1786), cited in Lee, *Recess*, Introduction, p. xxiii.

25 Lee, *Recess*, I, 4.

26 Ibid. I, 253–4.

27 Rosetta Ballin, *The Statue Room; An Historical Tale*, 2 vols. (London, 1790), I, 9.

28 Eliza Fenwick, *Secresy; or, The Ruin on the Rock* (London: Pandora, 1989), p. 14. Mary Wollstonecraft, *The Wrongs of Woman; or, Maria*, in *Mary and The Wrongs of Woman*, ed. Gary Kelly (Oxford University Press, 1976), p. 73.

29 Ibid. p. 73.

30 Eleanor Ty, *Unsex'd Revolutionaries: Five Women Novelists of the 1790s* (University of Toronto Press, 1993), p. xiv and p. 33.

31 Mary Poovey, *The Proper Lady and the Woman Writer. Ideology as Style in the Works of Mary Wollstonecraft, Mary Shelley, and Jane Austen* (University of Chicago Press, 1984), p. 45.

32 Howard, *Reading Gothic*, p. 64.

33 Scott, 'Mrs Ann Radcliffe', *Lives*, p. 215.

34 Napier, *Failure of Gothic*, pp. 100–1.

35 Ibid. p. 111.

36 Scott, 'Mrs Ann Radcliffe', *Lives*, p. 215.
37 Spacks, *Desire and Truth*, pp. 147–74. Theresa Kelley, *Wordsworth's Revisionary Aesthetics* (Cambridge University Press, 1988), p. 2.
38 Radcliffe, *The Italian*, p. 412. Consider also the influence of Paris on Valancourt in *Udolpho*.
39 Gary Kelly, 'The Limits of Genre and the Institution of Literature: Romanticism between Fact and Fiction', *Romantic Revolutions: Criticism and Theory*, ed. Kenneth R. Johnston and others (Bloomington: Indiana University Press, 1990), 158–75 (p. 170).
40 Radcliffe, *Romance of the Forest*, Editor's note, p. 372 n.18.
41 Austen, *Northanger Abbey*, p. 121 and p. 60.
42 'Pleasures Derived from Objects of Terror', John and Anna Laetitia Aikin, *Miscellaneous Pieces in Prose* (London, 1773). The Aikins' collection also included the 'Gothic' fragment 'Sir Bertrand'.
43 Hugh Murray, *Morality of Fiction; or, An Inquiry into the Tendency of Fictitious Narratives, with Observations on Some of the Most Eminent* (London, 1805), p. 126. Scott, 'Mrs Ann Radcliffe', *Lives*, pp. 213–14.
44 'Count Reginald de St Leon', *St Godwin: A Tale of the 16th, 17th, and 18th Century*, cited in Marie Roberts, *Gothic Immortals: The Fiction of the Brotherhood of the Rosy Cross* (London: Routledge, 1990), p. 48.
45 Kelly, *English Fiction*, p. 54.
46 *Critical Review* (Aug. 1794), *Coleridge's Miscellaneous Criticism*, ed. T. M. Raysor (London: Constable, 1936), p. 366.
47 Drake, *Literary Hours*, I, 359.
48 Wordsworth, 'Preface to . . . "Lyrical Ballads"', *Poetical Works*, pp. 734–41.
49 Radcliffe, *Sicilian Romance*, p. 10.
50 Dunlop, *History of Fiction*, III, 387.
51 Scott, 'Mrs Ann Radcliffe', *Lives*, p. 235.
52 *Monthly Review* (1794), Williams (ed.), *Novel and Romance*, p. 393.
53 Barbauld, *British Novelists*, XLIII, preface, p. iv.
54 *Critical Review* (1794), *Coleridge's Miscellaneous Criticism*, p. 355.
55 Richard Cumberland, *Henry*, Williams (ed.), *The Novel and Romance*, p. 401.
56 Drake, *Literary Hours*, I, 63.
57 Robert Bisset, *Douglas, or, The Highlander – A Novel*, 4 vols. (Dublin, 1800), I, pp. xiii–xv.
58 Cited in Ferris, *Literary Authority*, p. 55.
59 William Beckford, *Azemia, a Novel: Containing Imitations of the Manner, Both in Prose and Verse, of Many of the Authors of the Present Day; With Political Strictures*, 2nd edn (London, 1798), p. 62. Note, however, that – despite the sarcastic references to contemporary women writers – the embedded tale 'Blue-Beard' reads as a non-parodic version of what is often referred to as 'female Gothic'.
60 *Critical Review* (1797), Sage (ed.), *The Gothick Novel*, p. 41.
61 Johnson, *Jane Austen*, p. 34. Radcliffe, *Italian*, p. 121.
62 Radcliffe, *Italian*, p. 87 and p. 211.

63 Ibid. p. 414.
64 Robert Bisset, *Modern Literature: A Novel*, 3 vols. (London, 1804), II, 218.
65 Ibid. II, 220–1.
66 Ann Radcliffe, 'On the Supernatural in Poetry', *New Monthly Magazine* 16 (1826), 145–52 (p. 149).
67 *Edinburgh Review* 59 (1834), p. 329.
68 Baron-Wilson, *Life of Lewis*, I, 173.
69 Miles, *Ann Radcliffe*, p. 3.
70 Radcliffe, *Romance of the Forest*, p. 240.
71 Ann Radcliffe, *A Journey Made in the Summer of 1794, Through Holland and the Western Frontier of Germany, with a Return down the Rhine: To Which Are Added Observations during a Tour to the Lakes* (London, 1795), p. 355 and p. 377. Robert Miles (*Ann Radcliffe*, p. 62) also cites the point in Radcliffe's *Journey* where she visits a monument in Kendal to the Glorious Revolution of 1688: 'At a time, when the memory of that revolution is reviled, and the praises of liberty itself endeavoured to be suppressed by the artifice of imputing to it the crimes of anarchy, it was impossible to omit any act of veneration to the blessings of this event', p. 389.
72 *British Critic* (1794), cited in C. F. McIntyre, *Ann Radcliffe in Relation to her Time* (New Haven: Yale University Press, 1920), p. 41.
73 Mathias, *Pursuits of Literature*, 1st Dialogue, p. 20 n.22.
74 Polwhele, 'The Unsex'd Females: A Poem', *Poems*, II, 39.
75 'On British Novels and Romances', *New Monthly Magazine* 14 (1820), 205–9 (p. 208).
76 Radcliffe, *Sicilian Romance*, p. 22.
77 *Critical Review* (1794), *Coleridge's Miscellaneous Criticism*, p. 357. 'Terrorist Novel Writing', *Spirit of the Public Journals*, p. 227.
78 *Critical Review* (1794), *Coleridge's Miscellaneous Criticism*, p. 357.
79 Radcliffe, *Romance of the Forest*, p. 1.
80 Scott, 'Mrs Ann Radcliffe', *Lives*, p. 217.
81 Duncan, *Modern Romance*, p. 24.
82 *British Critic* (1797), Deborah Rogers (ed.), *The Critical Response to Ann Radcliffe* (Westport: Greenwood Press, 1994), p. 50. 'Italy' offered a congenial setting for extremes of behaviour in numerous 'Gothic' works, such as Charlotte Dacre's *Zofloya* (1806) and Charles Maturin's *Fatal Revenge* (1807).
83 Letter to George and Georgiana Keats, Feb. to May 1819, *The Letters of John Keats*, ed. Maurice Buxton Forman, 3rd edn. (London: Oxford University Press, 1948), p. 300.
84 Dunlop, *History of Fiction*, III, 397.
85 Hazlitt, 'On the English Novelists', *Lectures on the English Comic Writers*, pp. 125–7.
86 Q. D. Leavis, *Fiction and the Reading Public* (London: Chatto & Windus, 1932), p. 139.
87 'The Periodical Press', *Edinburgh Review* 38 (1823) 349–78 (p. 360).
88 See Morag Shiach, *Discourse on Popular Culture: Class, Gender and History in*

Cultural Analysis, 1730 to the Present (Cambridge: Polity Press, 1989), p. 45.

89 Roper, *Reviewing before the* Edinburgh, p. 130.
90 Radcliffe, *Gaston de Blondeville*, I, p. iii.
91 Ibid. I, p. iv.
92 Ibid. I, p. xiii.
93 Ibid. I, p. xc.
94 Ibid. I, p. cxv.
95 Ibid. I, p. cxxxii.
96 Ferris, *Literary Authority*, p. 66.
97 *Monthly Review* (1797), Williams (ed.), *Novel and Romance*, p. 435.
98 *Critical Review* (1798), Rogers (ed.), *Ann Radcliffe*, p. 56.
99 Murray, *Morality of Fiction*, p. 127.
100 Review of *Harrington and Ormond, Tales*, *The British Review and London Critical Journal* 11 (1818), 37–61 (p. 48).
101 *Blackwood's Edinburgh Magazine* (1824), *Lockhart's Literary Criticism*, ed. M. Clive Hildyard (Oxford: Basil Blackwell, 1933), p. 106.
102 *Cyclopaedia of English Literature*, Rogers (ed.), *Ann Radcliffe*, p. 144.
103 *Standard Novels*, XLI: *Vathek, The Castle of Otranto, The Bravo of Venice* (London, 1834), 'Critical Remarks', p. 136.
104 *Ladies' Monthly Museum* (1826), Rogers (ed.), *Ann Radcliffe*, p. 75. *Edinburgh Review* 59 (1834), p. 337.
105 Julia Kavanagh, *English Women of Letters: Biographical Sketches*, 2 vols. (London, 1863), I, 242.
106 Ibid. I, 251.
107 Ibid. I, 254.
108 Ibid. I, 325.
109 Scott, 'Mrs Ann Radcliffe', *Lives*, p. 229.
110 Ibid. p. 215.
111 Ibid. p. 225.
112 Ibid. p. 235.
113 Ibid. p. 244.
114 'The Historical Romance', *Blackwood's Edinburgh Magazine* 58 (1845), 341–56 (p. 346).

5. THE FIELD OF ROMANCE: WALTER SCOTT, THE WAVERLEY NOVELS, THE GOTHIC

1 Review of 'Waverley Novels' and *Tales of My Landlord, Fourth Series, Edinburgh Review* 55 (1832), 61–79 (p. 64).
2 Leavis, *Fiction and the Reading Public*, p. 139.
3 Scott, 'Ancient Ballad', p. 45.
4 Peter Murphy, *Poetry as an Occupation and an Art in Britain 1760–1830* (Cambridge University Press, 1993), p. 141.
5 Letter to Dr Currie (July 1801), cited in Coleman O. Parsons, *Witchcraft and Demonology in Scott's Fiction* (Edinburgh: Oliver and Boyd, 1964), p. 57.

6 Lockhart, *Life of Scott*, I, 382.
7 Murphy, *Poetry*, p. 143.
8 Walter Scott, *The Lay of the Last Minstrel*, *The Poetical Works of Sir Walter Scott*, ed. J. Logie Robertson (London: Henry Frowde, 1909), 1–88 (p. 12).
9 Cited in Peck, *Life of Lewis*, p. 118.
10 *Edinburgh Review* (1805) Francis Jeffrey, *Contributions to the Edinburgh Review* (London, 1853), p. 465.
11 Ibid. p. 455.
12 Scott, *The Lay of the Last Minstrel*, *Poetical Works*, p. 1.
13 See, for example, Jeffrey's review of 'The Corsair: a Tale' and 'The Bride of Abydos: a Turkish Tale', *Edinburgh Review* 23 (1814), pp. 198–229.
14 *Edinburgh Review* (1808), Hayden (ed.), *Scott*, p. 47.
15 Peacock, 'The Four Ages of Poetry', *Essays, Memoirs, Letters*, 1–26 (p. 19).
16 *The Satirist* (1808), cited in Fiona Robertson, *Legitimate Histories: Scott, Gothic, and the Authorities of Fiction* (Oxford: Clarendon Press, 1994), p. 53. *Jeffrey, Edinburgh Review* (1808), Hayden (ed.), *Scott*, p. 38.
17 Jeffrey, *Edinburgh Review* (1808), Hayden (ed.), *Scott*, p. 39. Coleridge, letter to Wordsworth (Oct. 1810), Hayden (ed.), *Scott*, p. 60.
18 *British Review* (1813), Hayden (ed.), *Scott*, p. 66.
19 Scott, letter to Maria Edgeworth, 10 May 1818, *Familiar Letters of Sir Walter Scott*, 2 vols. (Edinburgh: David Douglas, 1894), II, 17.
20 *Edinburgh Review* (1814), Hayden (ed.), *Scott*, p. 79 and pp. 83–4.
21 Richard Waswo, 'Story as Historiography in the Waverley Novels', *ELH* 47 (1980), 304–30 (p. 306). See also Jane Millgate, *Scott's Last Edition: A Study in Publishing History* (Edinburgh University Press, 1987).
22 Scott, *Waverley*, ed. Claire Lamont (Oxford University Press, 1986), p. 4.
23 Ibid. p. 3.
24 Ibid. p. 341.
25 Trumpener, *Bardic Nationalism*, p. 139; Trumpener argues that 'most of the conceptual innovations attributed to Scott were in 1814 already established commonplaces of the British novel', p. 130.
26 Scott, *Waverley*, p. 3.
27 Ibid. p. 4 and p. 24.
28 Scott, 'Mrs Ann Radcliffe', *Lives*, p. 213 and p. 225.
29 Ibid. p. 215.
30 Ibid. pp. 213–14. Robertson, *Legitimate Histories*, p. 16.
31 Scott, *The Heart of Midlothian*, ed. Claire Lamont (Oxford University Press, 1982), p. 507.
32 Scott, *Old Mortality*, ed. Jane Stevenson and Peter Davidson (Oxford University Press, 1993), p. 455 and p. 457.
33 Scott, *Quentin Durward*, ed. Susan Manning (Oxford University Press, 1992), p. 501.
34 *Quarterly Review* (1810), *Sir Walter Scott on Novelists and Fiction*, ed. Ioan Williams (London: Routledge and Kegan Paul, 1968), p. 207; Scott, 'Ancient Ballad', p. 46.

35 Scott, 'Mrs Ann Radcliffe', *Lives*, p. 232.
36 Scott, 'Horace Walpole', *Lives*, pp. 196–7 and p. 199.
37 Ibid. p. 197.
38 Ferris, *Literary Authority*, p. 15 and p. 71.
39 Ibid. p. 55.
40 'On the Female Literature of the Present Age', *The New Monthly Magazine* 14 (1820), 271–5 (pp. 273–4).
41 Scott, 'Clara Reeve', *Lives*, p. 207.
42 Ibid. p. 209.
43 Scott, 'Charlotte Smith', *Lives*, p. 334.
44 Scott, Magnum Opus Introduction to *St Ronan's Well*, Walter Scott, *The Prefaces to the Waverley Novels*, ed. Mark A. Weinstein (Lincoln: University of Nebraska Press, 1978), p. 200.
45 Scott, 'General Preface', appended to *Waverley*, p. 350.
46 Ibid. p. 351.
47 Ibid. p. 353.
48 Joseph Strutt, *Queenhoo-Hall, a Romance: and Ancient Times, a Drama*, 4 vols. (Edinburgh, 1808), I, p. i.
49 Scott, 'General Preface', *Waverley*, p. 352.
50 *Quarterly Review* (1817), Hayden (ed.), *Scott*, 113–43 (pp. 113–14).
51 *Quarterly Review* (1810), *Scott on Novelists and Fiction*, ed. Williams, p. 207.
52 Lockhart, *Life of Scott*, IV, 194–5.
53 Scott, 'Daniel De Foe', *Lives*, p. 365.
54 Scott, 'Samuel Richardson', *Lives*, p. 9, and p. 14.
55 'Historical Romance', *Quarterly Review* 35 (1827), 518–66 (p. 521).
56 Scott, *Heart of Midlothian*, p. 21.
57 Ibid. p. 20.
58 Ibid. pp. 21–2.
59 Ibid. p. 23.
60 Ibid. p. 22 and p. 23.
61 *Blackwood's Edinburgh Magazine* (Oct. 1817), Jackson (ed.), *Coleridge*, p. 331. *Edinburgh Review* 55 (1832), p. 65.
62 *Edinburgh Review* 55 (1832), p. 65.
63 *Letters to Richard Heber, Esq. Containing Critical Remarks on the Series of Novels Beginning with 'Waverley', and an Attempt to Ascertain their Author* (London, 1821), p. 147.
64 *Eclectic Review* (1820), Hayden (ed.), *Scott*, p. 193.
65 *Edinburgh Review* 55 (1832), p. 73.
66 James Kerr, *Fiction against History: Scott as Storyteller* (Cambridge University Press, 1989), p. 5 and p. 6.
67 Ina Ferris, 'The Indefatigable Word: Scott and the Comedy of Surplusage', *Scott in Carnival: Selected Papers from the Fourth International Scott Conference, 1991* ed. J. H. Alexander and David Hewitt (Aberdeen: Association for Scottish Literary Studies, 1993), 19–26 (p. 19): 'Scott's narrative was thus linked to the romance matrix of surplus and errancy even as it was valorised in terms

of the manliness and health that distinguished it from the debased femininity . . . of ordinary romance' (p. 19).

68 Stephen Bann, *The Clothing of Clio: A Study of the Representation of History in Nineteenth-Century Britain and France* (Cambridge University Press, 1984), p. 106.

69 Ibid. p. 96 and p. 106.

70 The phrase 'romance in stone' comes from John Buchan's *Sir Walter Scott* (1932), cited in John Sutherland, *The Life of Walter Scott: A Critical Biography* (Oxford: Blackwell, 1995), p. 273. Bann, *Clothing of Clio*, p. 106. Scott himself deployed the architectural analogy in Laurence Templeton's Dedicatory Epistle to *Ivanhoe*: 'I may share in the ill-deserved applause of those architects, who, in their modern Gothic, do not hesitate to introduce without rule or method, ornaments proper to different styles and different periods of the art', Scott, *Ivanhoe*, p. 21.

71 Scott, *Ivanhoe*, pp. 458–9. Future references to this edition will be given in the text.

72 See Ian Duncan's Introduction for a fuller discussion of the way that *Ivanhoe* 'dwells on the limits and exclusions of . . . imperial cultural nationalism', Scott, *Ivanhoe*, p. xx.

73 Walter Scott, *The Antiquary*, ed. David Hewitt (Edinburgh University Press, 1995), p. 35.

74 Ibid. p. 76.

75 Ibid. p. 78.

76 Ibid. p. 79. In contrast to the role of Oldbuck's German ancestor, Dousterswivel is presented both as a comedy German and a sinister mystic.

77 Kerr, *Fiction against History*, p. 90.

78 Walter Scott, *The Bride of Lammermoor*, ed. Fiona Robertson (Oxford University Press, 1991), p. 27. Future references to this edition will be given in the text.

79 Duncan, *Modern Romance*, p. 138.

80 David Brown, *Walter Scott and the Historical Imagination* (London: Routledge and Kegan Paul, 1979), p. 136.

81 *Quarterly Review* (1821), Hayden (ed.), *Scott*, 215–55 (p. 230).

82 Ibid. p. 231.

83 Ibid. p. 228 and p. 235.

84 *Letters to Richard Heber*, p. 186.

85 William Hazlitt, *Lectures on English Poets* and *The Spirit of the Age* (London: Dent, 1910), pp. 227–8.

86 Peacock, 'An Essay on Fashionable Literature', *Essays, Memoirs, Letters*, p. 266 and p. 275.

87 Kelly, *English Fiction*, p. 140. See also, by the same author, 'The Limits of Genre', *Romantic Revolutions*, ed. Johnston and others, pp. 158–75. Kelly draws upon Benedict Anderson's influential thesis about the role of the newspaper and the novel in the formation of 'imagined communities'.

88 Review of *Lives of the Novelists*, *Quarterly Review* 34 (1826), 349–78 (p. 376).

89 See Ina Ferris, 'The Reader in the Rhetoric of Realism: Scott, Thackeray, and Eliot', *Scott and his Influence: The Papers of the Aberdeen Scott Conference, 1982*, ed. J. H. Alexander and David Hewitt (Aberdeen: Association for Scottish Literary Studies, 1983), pp. 382–92.

90 Baron-Wilson, *Life of Lewis*, I, 175.

91 'The Historical Romance', *Blackwood's Edinburgh Magazine* 58 (1845), 341–56 (pp. 345–6).

92 Ibid. p. 346.

93 See Bann, *Clothing of Clio*, p. 23.

94 Ina Ferris's much fuller account of the decline of Scott's reputation, to which my own is indebted, argues that Carlyle's essay 'set in place the terms in which Scott's critical decline later in the century (and virtual erasure in our own) would be registered', *Literary Authority*, p. 248.

95 Thomas Carlyle, *London and Westminster Review* (1838), Hayden (ed.), *Scott*, p. 350 and p. 371.

96 Henry James, *North American Review* (1864), Hayden (ed.), *Scott*, p. 428.

97 Ibid. p. 428 and p. 431.

98 Leslie Stephen, *Cornhill Magazine* (1871), Hayden (ed.), *Scott*, p. 453 and p. 455.

99 Wilt argues that the model of the relationship between the novel and the mass audience provided by Scott's works was 'utterly necessary to liberate the moral energy behind the fictions of the great Victorians', Judith Wilt, *Secret Leaves: The Novels of Sir Walter Scott* (University of Chicago Press, 1985), p. 3.

100 According to Hutton 'no man can read Scott without becoming more of a public man, whereas the ordinary novel tends to make him less of one than before', *Sir Walter Scott* (London, 1878), p. 102.

101 Stephen, *Cornhill Magazine* (1871), Hayden (ed.), *Scott*, p. 456.

102 Birkhead, *Tale of Terror*, p. 156 and p. 42.

103 Ibid. p. 221 and p. 15.

104 Summers, *Gothic Quest*, p. 196.

105 Ibid. p. 198.

106 Ibid. p. 11 and p. 13.

107 Ibid. p. 397.

108 Devendra Varma, *The Gothic Flame, Being a History of the Gothic Novel in England: Its Origins, Efflorescence, Disintegration, and Residuary Influences* (London: Arthur Barker, 1957), p. 230.

109 P. D. Garside, 'Scott, the Romantic Past and the Nineteenth Century', *The Review of English Studies* 23 (1972), 147–61 (p. 150).

110 K. Sutherland, 'Fictional Economies: Adam Smith, Walter Scott and the Nineteenth-Century Novel', *ELH* 54 (1987), 97–127 (p. 104).

Bibliography

WORKS PUBLISHED BEFORE 1850

Aikin, John, and Aikin, Anna Laetitia (Anna Barbauld), *Miscellaneous Pieces in Prose*, London, 1773.

ANONYMOUS

The Age; A Poem: Moral, Political, and Metaphysical. With Illustrative Annotations. In Ten Books, London, 1810.

Days of Chivalry: A Romance, 2 vols., London, 1797.

'Epistle in Rhyme to M. G. Lewis, Esq M.P. Author of the Monk, Castle Spectre & c.', London, 1798.

'Historical Romance', *Quarterly Review* 35 (1827), 518–66.

'The Historical Romance', *Blackwood's Edinburgh Magazine* 58 (1845), 341–56.

'Impartial Strictures on the Poem Called "The Pursuits of Literature": and Particularly a Vindication of the Romance of "The Monk"', London, 1798.

Letters to Richard Heber, Esq. Containing Critical Remarks on the Series of Novels Beginning with 'Waverley', and an Attempt to Ascertain their Author, London, 1821.

Literary Memoirs of Living Authors of Great Britain, 2 vols., London, 1798.

Modern Anecdote of the Ancient Family of the Kinkvervankotsdarsprakengotchderns: A Tale for Christmas, London, 1779.

Mort Castle: A Gothic Story, London, 1798.

'Mrs Radcliffe's Posthumous Romance', *New Monthly Magazine* 16 (1826), 532–6.

'On British Novels and Romances', *New Monthly Magazine* 14 (1820), 205–9.

'On the Female Literature of the Present Age', *New Monthly Magazine* 14 (1820), 271–5.

'On Novels and Romances', *Scots Magazine* 64 (1802), 545–8.

'The Periodical Press', *Edinburgh Review* 38 (1823), 349–78.

Reminiscences of Michael Kelly, of the King's Theatre, and Theatre Royal Drury Lane, Including a Period of Nearly Half a Century; With Original Anecdotes of Many Distinguished Persons, Political, Literary, and Musical, 2 vols., London, 1826.

'The Shade of Alexander Pope on the Banks of the Thames. A Satirical Poem. With Notes', Dublin, 1799.

'Some Remarks on the Use of the Preternatural in Works of Fiction', *Blackwood's Edinburgh Magazine* 3 (1818), 648–50.

'Strawberry Hill', *New Monthly Magazine* 17 (1826), 256–67.
Tales of Terror; With an Introductory Dialogue, Dublin, 1801.
'Terrorist Novel Writing', *The Spirit of the Public Journals for 1797*, 3rd edn, London, 1802, 227–9.
'Anser Pen-Drag-On Esq', *Scribbleomania, or, The Printer's Devil's Polichronicon. A Sublime Poem*, London, 1815.
Ballin, Rosetta, *The Statue Room; An Historical Tale*, 2 vols., London, 1790.
Barbauld, Anna Laetitia, *The British Novelists; With an Essay and Prefaces, Biographical and Critical*, 50 vols., London, 1810.
Baron-Wilson, Margaret, *The Life and Correspondence of M. G. Lewis*, 2 vols., London, 1839.
Beckford, William, *Azemia, a Novel: Containing Imitations of the Manner, Both in Prose and Verse, of Many of the Authors of the Present Day; With Political Strictures*, 2nd edn, London, 2 vols., 1798.
  Modern Novel Writing; or The Elegant Enthusiast; And Interesting Emotions of Arabella Bloomville: A Rhapsodical Romance: Interspersed with Poetry, 2 vols., London, 1796.
  Popular Tales of the Germans: Translated from the German, 2 vols., London, 1791.
Bird, John, *The Castle of Hardayne. A Romance*, 2 vols., London, 1795.
Bisset, Robert, *Douglas, or, The Highlander: A Novel*, 4 vols., Dublin, 1800.
  Modern Literature: A Novel, 3 vols., London, 1804.
Blackstone, William, *Commentaries on the Laws of England*, 3 vols., Oxford, 1767–9.
Bonhote, Elizabeth, *Bungay Castle: A Novel*, 2 vols., London, 1796.
Brydges, Samuel Egerton, *Arthur Fitz-Albini. A Novel*, 2 vols., London, 1798.
Carter, Elizabeth, *A Series of Letters Between Mrs Elizabeth Carter and Miss Catherine Talbot From the Year 1741 to 1770, To Which Are Added, Letters From Mrs Elizabeth Carter to Mrs Vesey, Between the Years 1763 and 1787*, 2 vols., London, 1808.
Cartwright, John, 'An Appeal, on the Subject of the English Constitution', London, 1797.
  The Commonwealth in Danger, with an Introduction Containing Remarks on some Late Writings of Arthur Young, Esq, London, 1795.
  Take your Choice!, London, 1776.
Cottle, Joseph, *Alfred, an Epic Poem, in Twenty-Four Books*, London, 1800.
Cullen, Stephen, *The Castle of Inchvally: A Tale – Alas! Too True*, 3 vols., London, 1796.
Curties, T. J. Horsley, *Ethelwina, or the House of Fitz-Auburne. A Romance of Former Times*, 3 vols., London, 1799.
Dacre, Charlotte, *Confessions of the Nun of St Omer. A Tale*, 3 vols., London, 1805.
D'Israeli, Isaac, *The Calamities and Quarrels of Authors: With Some Inquiries Respecting their Moral and Literary Characters, And Memoirs for our Literary History*, London, no date.
Drake, Nathan, *Letters to Richard Heber, Esq. Containing Critical Remarks on the Series of Novels Beginning with 'Waverley' and an Attempt to Ascertain their Author*, London, 1821.
  Literary Hours: Sketches Critical and Narrative, 2nd edn, London, 1800.

Dunlop, John, *The History of Fiction: Being a Critical Account of the Most Celebrated Prose Works of Fiction, from the Earliest Greek Romances to the Novels of the Present Age*, 3 vols., London, 1814.

Dutton, Thomas, 'The Literary Census: A Satirical Poem; with Notes, & c., Including Free and Candid Strictures on the Pursuits of Literature and its Anonymous Author', London, 1798.

Fox, Joseph, *Santa Maria; or, The Mysterious Pregnancy: A Romance*, 3 vols., London, 1797.

Gentleman's Magazine, London, 1731–1907.

Grant, Anne, *Essays on the Superstitions of the Highlanders of Scotland*, 2 vols., London, 1811.

Hayley, William, *An Essay on Epic Poetry; In Five Epistles to the Rev Mr Mason*, Dublin, 1782.

Hole, Richard, *Arthur; or, The Northern Enchantment. A Poetical Romance*, London, 1789.

Lane, William, 'A Tale Addressed to the Novel Readers of the Present Times', London, 1795.

Lathom, Francis, *The Impenetrable Secret, Find it Out!*, 2 vols., London, 1805.
The Unknown; or, The Northern Gallery. A Romance, 3 vols., London, 1808.

Leland, Thomas, *Longsword, Earl of Salisbury. An Historical Romance*, 2 vols., London, 1762.

Lewis, Matthew, *Adelgitha; or, The Fruits of a Single Error. A Tragedy, in Five Acts*, London, 1806.
Adelmorn, The Outlaw; A Romantic Drama, in Three Acts, 2nd edn, London, 1801.
The Bravo of Venice, A Romance: Translated from the German, London, 1805.
Romantic Tales, 4 vols., London, 1808.
Tales of Wonder; Written and Collected by M. G. Lewis, 2 vols., London, 1801.

Lockhart, J. G., *Memoirs of the Life of Sir Walter Scott*, 7 vols., Edinburgh, 1837–8.

Macaulay, Thomas Babington, Review of *Letters of Horace Walpole to Sir Horace Mann*, *Edinburgh Review* 58 (1833), 227–58.

Mathias, T. J., *The Pursuits of Literature: A Satirical Poem in Four Dialogues. With Notes*, 6th edn, London, 1798.

Maturin, Charles, *Fatal Revenge, or, The Family of Montorio. A Romance*, 3 vols., London, 1807.

'Moonshine, Mauritius', 'More Wonders! An Heroic Epistle to M. G. Lewis, Esq M.P.', London, 1801.

Murray, Hugh, *Morality of Fiction; or, An Inquiry into the Tendency of Fictitious Narratives, with Observations on Some of the Most Eminent*, London, 1805.

Ogilvie, John, *Britannia: A National Epic Poem, in Twenty Books, To Which is Prefixed 'A Critical Dissertation on Epic Machinery'*, Aberdeen, 1801.

Pinkerton, John, *A Dissertation on the Origin and Progress of the Scythians or Goths, Being an Introduction to the Ancient and Modern History of Europe*, London, 1787.
Walpoliana, 2 vols., Dublin, 1800.

Polwhele, Richard, *Poems*, 5 vols. in one, London, 1810.

Pownall, Thomas, *A Treatise on the Study of Antiquities as the Commentary to Historical Learning*, London, 1782.

Preston, William, 'Reflections on the Peculiarities of Style and Manner in the Late German Writers Whose Works Have Appeared in English, and on the Tendency of their Productions', Dublin, 1801.

Pye, Henry James, *Alfred; An Epic Poem, in Six Books*, London, 1801.

'Carmen Seculare for the Year 1800', London, 1800.

Radcliffe, Ann, *Gaston de Blondeville, or The Court of Henry III Keeping Festival in Ardenne: A Romance; St Alban's Abbey, A Metrical Tale; With some Poetical Pieces: To Which is Prefixed a Memoir of the Author, with Extracts from her Journals*, 4 vols., London, 1826.

A Journey Made in the Summer of 1794, Through Holland and the Western Frontier of Germany, with a Return down the Rhine: To Which Are Added Observations during a Tour to the Lakes, London, 1795.

'On the Supernatural in Poetry', *New Monthly Magazine* 16 (1826), 145–52.

Reeve, Clara, *Memoirs of Sir Roger De Clarendon: The Natural Son of Edward Prince of Wales, Commonly Called the Black Prince; With Anecdotes of Many Other Eminent Persons of the Fourteenth Century*, 3 vols., London, 1793.

Plans of Education; With Remarks on the Systems of Other Writers, London, 1792.

The Progress of Romance, 2 vols., Colchester, 1785.

REVIEWS

Review of *Albert de Nordenshild; or The Modern Alcibiades. A Novel. Translated from the German*, *Analytical Review* 24 (1796), 404.

Review of *The Castle Spectre*, *Monthly Mirror* 4 (1797), 354–60.

Review of 'The Corsair: A Tale' and 'The Bride of Abydos: A Turkish Tale', *Edinburgh Review* 23 (1814), 198–229.

Review of *Harrington and Ormond, Tales*, *The British Review and London Critical Journal* 11 (1818), 37–61.

Review of *The Italian*, *Analytical Review* 25 (1797), 516–20.

Review of *Ivanhoe: A Romance*, *Edinburgh Review* 33 (1820), 1–54.

Review of Sir Walter Scott, *Lives of the Novelists*, *Quarterly Review* 34 (1826), 349–78.

Review of *The Monk*, *Monthly Mirror* 2 (1796), 98.

Review of *The Poetical Works of Anne Radcliffe*, *Edinburgh Review* 59 (1834), 327–41.

Review of 'Waverley Novels' and *Tales of My Landlord, Fourth Series*, *Edinburgh Review* 55 (1832), 61–79.

Richards, George, *Poems*, 2 vols., Oxford, 1804.

Robberds, J. W. (ed.), *A Memoir of the Life and Writings of the Late William Taylor of Norwich . . . Containing his Correspondence of Many Years with the Late Robert Southey, Esq, and Original Letters from Sir Walter Scott and Other Eminent Literary Men*, London, 1843.

Scott, Walter, *Letters on Demonology and Witchcraft, Addressed to J. G. Lockhart, Esq*, London, 1830.

The Miscellaneous Prose Works of Sir Walter Scott, Bart., 3 vols., Edinburgh, 1841.

Standard Novels, XLI: *Vathek, The Castle of Otranto, The Bravo of Venice*, London, 1834.

Strutt, Joseph, *Queenhoo-Hall, a Romance: and Ancient Times, a Drama*, 4 vols., Edinburgh, 1808.

Trotter, Thomas, *A View of the Nervous Temperament*, London, 1807.

Turner, Sharon, *The History of the Anglo-Saxons, from their First Appearance above the Elbe, to the Norman Conquest*, 4 vols., London, 1799–1802.

  Prolusions on the Present Greatness of Britain; on Modern Poetry; on the Present Aspect of the World, London, 1819.

Walpole, Horace, *Anecdotes of Painting in England; With Some Account of the Principal Artists; And Incidental Notes on Other Arts; Collected by the Late Mr George Vertue; And now Digested and Published from his Original MSS by Mr Horace Walpole*, 3 vols., Strawberry Hill, 1762–71.

  A Catalogue of the Royal and Noble Authors of England, With Lists of their Works, 2 vols., Strawberry Hill, 1758.

  A Description of the Villa of Mr Horace Walpole, Youngest Son of Sir Robert Walpole, Earl of Orford, At Strawberry-Hill near Twickenham, Middlesex. With an Inventory of the Furniture, Pictures, Curiosities, & c., Strawberry Hill, 1784.

  Hieroglyphic Tales, Strawberry Hill, 1785.

  Historic Doubts on the Life and Reign of King Richard the Third, London, 1768.

  The Life of Edward Lord Herbert of Cherbury. Written by Himself, Dublin, 1771.

Warton, Thomas, *The History of English Poetry, from the Close of the Eleventh to the Commencement of the Eighteenth Century. To which are Prefixed, Two Dissertations. I. On the Origin of Romantic Fiction in Europe. II. On the Introduction of Learning into England*, 3 vols., 1774–81.

West, Jane, *The Loyalists: An Historical Novel*, 3 vols., London, 1812.

  Poems and Plays, 4 vols., London, 1799.

White, James, *The Adventures of John of Gaunt, Duke of Lancaster*, 3 vols., London, 1791.

  The Adventures of King Richard Coeur de Lion, To Which is Added the Death of Lord Falkland: A Poem, 3 vols., London, 1791.

  Earl Strongbow: or, The History of Richard de Clare and the Beautiful Geralda, 2 vols., London, 1789.

The World, for the Year 1753, London, 1753.

WORKS PUBLISHED AFTER 1850

Ames, Dianne S., 'Strawberry Hill: Architecture of the "as if"', *Studies in Eighteenth-Century Culture* 8 (1978), 351–60.

Anderson, Benedict, *Imagined Communities: Reflections on the Origin and Spread of Nationalism*, revised edn, London: Verso, 1991.

Andrews, Malcolm, *The Search for the Picturesque: Landscape Aesthetics and Tourism in Britain, 1760–1800*, Aldershot: Scolar Press, 1989.

Ashton, Rosemary, *The German Idea: Four English Writers and the Reception of German Thought 1800–1860*, Cambridge University Press, 1980.

Austen, Jane, *Northanger Abbey*, ed. Anne Ehrenpreis, Harmondsworth: Penguin, 1972.

Bage, Robert, *Hermsprong, or Man as He Is Not*, ed. Peter Faulkner, Oxford University Press, 1985.

Baldick, Chris (ed.), *The Oxford Book of Gothic Tales*, Oxford University Press, 1992.

Bann, Stephen, *The Clothing of Clio: A Study of the Representation of History in Nineteenth-Century Britain and France*, Cambridge University Press, 1984.

'The Sense of the Past: Image, Text, and Object in the Formation of Historical Consciousness in Nineteenth-Century Britain', *The New Historicism*, ed. H. Aram Veeser, New York: Routledge, 1989, 102–15.

Barrell, John, *English Literature in History: An Equal, Wide Survey*, London: Hutchinson, 1983.

Barrett, Eaton Stannard, *The Heroine, or Adventures of a Fair Romance Reader*, London: Henry Frowde, 1909.

Beckford, William, *Vathek*, ed. Roger Lonsdale, Oxford University Press, 1970.

Beer, Gillian, *Romance*, London: Methuen, 1970.

Bentham, Jeremy, *A Fragment on Government*, ed. J. H. Burns and H. L. A. Hart, Cambridge University Press, 1988.

Birkhead, Edith, *The Tale of Terror: A Study of the Gothic Romance*, London: Constable, 1921.

Blake, William, *Complete Writings*, ed. Geoffrey Keynes, Oxford University Press, 1966.

Blakey, Dorothy, *The Minerva Press 1790–1820*, London: The Bibliographical Society, Oxford University Press, 1939.

Bolingbroke, Henry St John, Viscount, *Historical Writings*, ed. Isaac Kramnick, University of Chicago Press, 1972.

Botting, Fred, *Gothic*, London: Routledge, 1996.

Bourdieu, Pierre, *The Field Of Cultural Production: Essays on Art and Literature*, ed. Randal Johnson, Cambridge: Polity Press, 1993.

Brewer, John, *Party Ideology and Popular Politics at the Accession of George III*, Cambridge University Press, 1976.

The Pleasures of the Imagination: English Culture in the Eighteenth Century, London: HarperCollins, 1997.

Brooks, Peter, *The Melodramatic Imagination: Balzac, Henry James, Melodrama, and the Mode of Excess*, New Haven: Yale University Press, 1976.

Brown, David, *Walter Scott and the Historical Imagination*, London: Routledge and Kegan Paul, 1979.

Bunn, James H., 'The Aesthetics of British Mercantilism', *NLH* 11 (1980), 303–21.

Burke, Edmund, *A Philosophical Enquiry into the Origin of our Ideas on the Sublime and Beautiful*, ed. Adam Phillips, Oxford University Press, 1990.

Reflections on the Revolution in France, ed. Conor Cruise O'Brien, Harmondsworth: Penguin, 1968.

The Writings and Speeches of Edmund Burke (General Series Editor, Paul Langford), IX: I. The Revolutionary War; II. Ireland, ed. R. D. Macdowell, Oxford: Clarendon Press, 1991.

Butler, Marilyn, *Romantics, Rebels and Reactionaries: English Literature and its Background 1760–1830*, Oxford University Press, 1981.

'The Woman at the Window: Ann Radcliffe in the Novels of Mary Wollstonecraft and Jane Austen', *Women and Literature* 1 (1980), 128–48.

(ed.), *Burke, Paine, Godwin, and the Revolution Controversy*, Cambridge University Press, 1984.

Cannadine, David, 'The Making of the British Upper Classes', *Aspects of Aristocracy: Grandeur and Decline in Modern Britain*, Harmondsworth: Penguin, 1995, 9–36.

Canning, George and Frere, John Hookham, *Poetry of the Anti-Jacobin*, Oxford: Woodstock, 1991.

Castle, Terry, *Masquerade and Civilization: The Carnivalesque in Eighteenth-Century English Culture and Fiction*, London: Methuen, 1986.

'The Spectralization of the Other in *The Mysteries of Udolpho*', *The New Eighteenth Century: Theory, Politics, English Literature*, ed. Felicity Nussbaum and Laura Brown, London: Methuen, 1987, 231–53.

Chandler, Alice, *A Dream of Order*, London: Routledge and Kegan Paul, 1971.

Chesterfield, Philip Dormer Stanhope, 4th Earl, *Letters to his Son and Others*, ed. Robert K. Root, London: Dent, 1929.

Clark, Kenneth, *The Gothic Revival: An Essay in the History of Taste*, 3rd edn, London: John Murray, 1962.

Clemit, Pamela, *The Godwinian Novel: The Rational Fictions of William Godwin, Charles Brockden Brown, and Mary Shelley*, Oxford University Press, 1993.

'A Pastoral Romance, From the Ancient British: Godwin's Rewriting of *Comus*', *Eighteenth-Century Fiction* 3 (1991), 217–39.

Clery, E. J., *The Rise of Supernatural Fiction 1762–1800*, Cambridge University Press, 1995.

Coleridge, S. T., *Coleridge's Miscellaneous Criticism*, ed. T. M. Raysor, London: Constable, 1936.

Collected Letters of Samuel Taylor Coleridge, ed. Earl Leslie Griggs, 6 vols., Oxford: Clarendon Press, 1956–71.

Poetical Works, ed. E. H. Coleridge, Oxford University Press, 1969.

Colley, Linda, 'The Apotheosis of George III: Loyalty, Royalty and the British Nation 1760–1820', *Past and Present* 102 (1984), 94–129.

Britons: Forging the Nation 1707–1837, New Haven: Yale University Press, 1992.

'Whose Nation? Class and National Consciousness in Britain 1750–1830', *Past and Present* 113 (1986), 97–117.

Conger, Syndy M., *Matthew G. Lewis, Charles Robert Maturin and the Germans: An Interpretative Study of the Influence of German Literature on Two Gothic Novels*, Institut für Englische Sprache und Literatur Universität Salzburg, 1977.

Cottom, Daniel, *The Civilized Imagination: A Study of Ann Radcliffe, Jane Austen and Sir Walter Scott*, Cambridge University Press, 1985.

Cottrell, Stella, 'The Devil on Two Sticks: Francophobia in 1803', *Patriotism: The Making and Unmaking of British National Identity*, ed. Raphael Samuel, 3 vols., London: Routledge, 1989, 1, 259–74.

Cox, Jeffrey N., (ed.), *Seven Gothic Dramas*, Athens: Ohio University Press, 1992.

Crompton, Louis, *Byron and Greek Love: Homophobia in Nineteenth-Century England*,

London: Faber & Faber, 1985.

Dacre, Charlotte, *Zofloya, or The Moor*, ed. Kim Ian Michasiw, Oxford University Press, 1997.

Darnton, Robert, 'Sex for Thought', *New York Review of Books*, 22 December 1994, 65–74.

Davis, Lennard J., *Factual Fictions: The Origins of the English Novel*, New York: Columbia University Press, 1983.

De Montluzin, Emily Lorraine, *The Anti-Jacobins 1798–1800: Early Contributions to the 'Anti-Jacobin Review'*, Basingstoke: Macmillan, 1988.

Dickinson, H. T., *Liberty and Property: Political Ideology in Eighteenth-Century Britain*, London: Methuen, 1979.

'Popular Loyalism in Britain in the 1790s', *The Transformation of Political Culture: England and Germany in the Late-Eighteenth Century*, ed. Eckhart Hellmuth, Oxford University Press, 1990, 503–33.

Duncan, Ian, *Modern Romance and Transformations of the Novel: The Gothic, Scott, Dickens*, Cambridge University Press, 1992.

Durant, David S., 'Ann Radcliffe and the Conservative Gothic', *Studies in English Literature* 22 (1982), 519–30.

Eagleton, Terry, *Heathcliff and the Great Hunger: Studies in Irish Culture*, London: Verso, 1995.

Eastlake, Charles, *A History of the Gothic Revival: An Attempt to Show How the Taste for Medieval Architecture Which Lingered in England During the Two Last Centuries Has Since Been Encouraged and Developed*, London, 1872.

Edgeworth, Maria, *Castle Rackrent: An Hibernian Tale*, ed. George Watson, Oxford University Press, 1964.

Ellis, Kate Ferguson, *The Contested Castle: Gothic Novels and the Subversion of Domestic Ideology*, Urbana: University of Illinois Press, 1989.

Fenwick, Eliza, *Secresy; or, The Ruin on the Rock*, London: Pandora, 1989.

Ferris, Ina, *The Achievement of Literary Authority: Gender, History, and the Waverley Novels*, Ithaca: Cornell University Press, 1991.

'The Indefatigable Word: Scott and the Comedy of Surplusage', *Scott in Carnival: Selected Papers from the Fourth International Scott Conference, 1991*, ed. J. H. Alexander and David Hewitt, Aberdeen: Association for Scottish Literary Studies, 1993, 19–26.

'The Reader in the Rhetoric of Realism: Scott, Thackeray, and Eliot', *Scott and his Influence: The Papers of the Aberdeen Scott Conference, 1982*, ed. J. H. Alexander and David Hewitt, Aberdeen: Association for Scottish Literary Studies, 1983, 382–92.

Foord, Archibald S., '"The Only Unadulterated Whig"', *Horace Walpole: Writer, Politician and Connoisseur. Essays on the 250th Anniversary of Walpole's Birth*, ed. Warren Hunting-Smith, New Haven: Yale University Press, 1967, 25–44.

Fothergill, Brian, *The Strawberry Hill Set: Horace Walpole and his Circle*, London: Faber & Faber, 1983.

Garside, P. D., 'Scott, the Romantic Past and the Nineteenth Century', *The*

Review of English Studies 23 (1972), 147–61.

Gilpin, William, *Observations on the River Wye, and Several Parts of South Wales, & c., Relative Chiefly to Picturesque Beauty; Made in the Summer of the Year 1770*, Oxford: Woodstock, 1991.

Godwin, William, *Caleb Williams*, ed. David McCracken, Oxford University Press, 1982.

Damon and Delia, Italian Letters, Imogen, ed. Pamela Clemit, *Collected Novels and Memoirs of William Godwin*, ed. Mark Philp, 8 vols., London: William Pickering, 1992, II.

Enquiry Concerning Political Justice and its Influence on Modern Morals and Happiness, ed. Isaac Kramnick, Harmondsworth: Penguin, 1985.

St Leon, ed. Pamela Clemit, Oxford University Press, 1994.

Goldsmith, Oliver, 'Letter to the Editor of Lloyd's Evening Post', *Collected Works of Oliver Goldsmith*, ed. Arthur Friedman, 5 vols., Oxford: Clarendon Press, 1966, III, 195–8.

Gonda, Caroline, *Reading Daughters' Fictions 1709–1834: Novels and Society from Manley to Edgeworth*, Cambridge University Press, 1996.

Grosse, C. F. A., *Horrid Mysteries*, trans. P. Will, 2 vols. in one, London: Robert Holden, 1927.

Guest, Harriet, 'The Wanton Muse: Politics and Gender in Gothic Theory after 1760', *Beyond Romanticism: New Approaches to Texts and Contexts 1780–1832*, ed. Stephen Copley and John Whale, London: Routledge, 1992, pp.118–39.

Haining, Peter (ed.), *Great British Tales of Terror: Gothic Stories of Horror and Romance 1765–1840*, Harmondsworth: Penguin, 1973.

Harley, Mary, *St Bernard's Priory; An Old English Tale*, 2 vols., New York: Arno Press, 1977.

Hayden, John O. (ed.), *Scott: The Critical Heritage*, London: Routledge and Kegan Paul, 1970.

Hazlitt, William, *Lectures on English Poets* and *The Spirit of the Age*, London: Dent, 1910.

Lectures on the English Comic Writers and *Fugitive Writings*, London: Dent, 1967.

Selected Writings, ed. Ronald Blythe, Harmondsworth: Penguin, 1970.

Hill, Christopher, 'The Norman Yoke', *Puritanism and Revolution: Studies in Interpretation of the English Revolution of the Seventeenth Century*, rpt., Harmondsworth: Penguin, 1990, 58–125.

Hogle, Jerrold E., 'The Ghost of the Counterfeit in the Genesis of the Gothic', *Gothick Origins and Innovations*, ed. Allan Lloyd Smith and Victor Sage, Amsterdam: Rodopi, 1994, 23–33.

Howard, Jacqueline, *Reading Gothic Fiction: A Bakhtinian Approach*, Oxford: Clarendon Press, 1994.

Howells, C. A., *Love, Mystery, and Misery: Feeling in Gothic Fiction*, London: Athlone Press, 1978.

Hume, Robert D., 'Gothic Versus Romantic: A Revaluation of the Gothic Novel', *PMLA* 84 (1969), 282–90.

Hurd, Richard, *Moral and Political Dialogues; With Letters on Chivalry and Romance*, 3 vols., Farnborough: Gregg International, 1972.

Hutton, Richard, *Sir Walter Scott*, London, 1878.

Jackson, J. R. de J. (ed.), *Coleridge: The Critical Heritage*, London: Routledge and Kegan Paul, 1970.

Jackson, Rosemary, *Fantasy: the Literature of Subversion*, London: Methuen, 1981.

Jacobus, Mary, *Tradition and Experiment in Wordsworth's Lyrical Ballads*, Oxford: Clarendon Press, 1976.

Janowitz, Anne, *England's Ruins: Poetic Purpose and the National Landscape*, Oxford: Basil Blackwell, 1990.

Jeffrey, Francis, *Contributions to the Edinburgh Review*, London, 1853.

Johnson, Claudia, *Jane Austen: Women, Politics, and the Novel*, University of Chicago Press, 1988.

Kavanagh, Julia, *English Women of Letters: Biographical Sketches*, 2 vols., London, 1863.

Keats, John, *The Letters of John Keats*, ed. Maurice Buxton Forman, 3rd edn, London: Oxford University Press, 1948.

Kelley, Theresa, *Wordsworth's Revisionary Aesthetics*, Cambridge University Press, 1988.

Kelly, Gary, *English Fiction of the Romantic Period 1789–1830*, London: Longman, 1987.

'The Limits of Genre and the Institution of Literature: Romanticism between Fact and Fiction', *Romantic Revolutions: Criticism and Theory*, ed. Kenneth R. Johnston and others, Bloomington: Indiana University Press, 1990, 158–75.

Women, Writing, and Revolution 1790–1827, Oxford University Press, 1993.

Kelly, Isabella, *The Abbey of St Asaph: A Novel*, 3 vols., New York: Arno Press, 1977.

Kerr, James, *Fiction against History: Scott as Storyteller*, Cambridge University Press, 1989.

Ketton-Cremer, R. W., *Horace Walpole: A Biography*, 3rd edn, London: Methuen, 1964.

Kiely, Robert, *The Romantic Novel in England*, Cambridge: Harvard University Press, 1972.

Klancher, Jon, *The Making of the English Reading Audiences 1790–1832*, Madison: University of Wisconsin Press, 1987.

Kliger, Samuel, *The Goths in England: A Study in Seventeenth and Eighteenth Century Thought*, Cambridge: Harvard University Press, 1952.

Kotzebue, August von, *Lovers' Vows*, adapted by Elizabeth Inchbald, Oxford: Woodstock, 1990.

Langford, Paul, *A Polite and Commercial People: England 1727–1783*, Oxford University Press, 1992.

Lathom, Francis, *The Midnight Bell, A German Story, Founded on Incidents in Real Life*, London: Skoob Books, 1989.

Leavis, Q. D., *Fiction and the Reading Public*, London: Chatto & Windus, 1932.

Lee, Sophia, *The Recess; or, A Tale of Other Times*, 3 vols., New York: Arno Press, 1972.
Lennox, Charlotte, *The Female Quixote*, ed. Margaret Dalziel, Oxford University Press, 1989.
Le Tellier, Robert Ignatius, *Kindred Spirits: Interrelations and Affinities Between the Romantic Novels of England and Germany (1790–1820)*, Institut für Anglistik und Amerikanistik Universität Salzburg, 1982.
Levinson, Marjorie, and others, *Rethinking Historicism. Critical Readings in Romantic History*, Oxford: Basil Blackwell, 1989.
Lewis, Matthew, *The Castle Spectre*, Oxford: Woodstock, 1990.
The Monk: A Romance, ed. Howard Anderson, Oxford University Press, 1973.
Lewis, W. S., *Horace Walpole's Library*, Cambridge University Press, 1958.
Horace Walpole: The A. W. Mellon Lectures in the Fine Arts, 1960, New York: Pantheon, 1961.
Lockhart, J. G., *Lockhart's Literary Criticism*, ed. M. Clive Hildyard, Oxford: Basil Blackwell, 1933.
Lonsdale, Roger (ed.), *Thomas Gray and William Collins: Poetical Works*, Oxford University Press, 1977.
Lovell, Terry, *Consuming Fiction*, London: Verso, 1987.
Lukács, Georg, *The Historical Novel*, trans. Hannah and Stanley Mitchell, Harmondsworth: Penguin, 1969.
McAndrew, Elizabeth, *The Gothic Tradition in Fiction*, New York: Columbia University Press, 1979.
Macaulay, James, *The Gothic Revival 1745–1845*, Glasgow: Blackie, 1975.
McCalman, Iain, *Radical Underworld: Prophets, Revolutionaries, and Pornographers in London, 1795–1840*, Cambridge University Press, 1988.
McCarthy, Michael, *The Origins of the Gothic Revival*, New Haven: Yale University Press, 1987.
McCormack, W. J., 'Irish Gothic and After (1820–1945)', *The Field Day Anthology of Irish Writing*, ed. Seamus Deane, 3 vols., Derry: Field Day Publications, 1991, II, 831–54.
McGann, Jerome J., *The Beauty of Inflections: Literary Investigations in Historical Method and Theory*, Oxford: Clarendon Press, 1985.
McIntyre, C. F., *Ann Radcliffe in Relation to her Time*, New Haven: Yale University Press, 1920.
McKendrick, Neil, 'The Commercialization of Fashion', McKendrick and others (eds.), *The Birth of a Consumer Society: The Commercialization of Leisure in Eighteenth-Century England*, London: Hutchinson, 1983, 34–99.
McKeon, Michael, *The Origins of the English Novel 1600–1740*, Baltimore: Johns Hopkins University Press, 1987.
McNutt, Dan J. (ed.), *The Eighteenth-Century Gothic Novel: An Annotated Bibliography of Criticism and Selected Texts*, New York: Garland, 1975.
Maturin, Charles, *Melmoth The Wanderer*, ed. Douglas Grant, Oxford University Press, 1968.
Mee, Jon, *Dangerous Enthusiasms: William Blake and the Culture of Radicalism in the*

1790s, Oxford: Clarendon Press, 1992.

Mehrotra, K. K., *Horace Walpole and the English Novel: A Study of the Influence of the Castle of Otranto 1764–1820*, Oxford: Blackwell, 1934.

Miles, Robert, *Ann Radcliffe: The Great Enchantress*, Manchester University Press, 1995.

Gothic Writing: A Genealogy 1750–1820, London: Routledge, 1993.

Millgate, Jane, *Scott's Last Edition: A Study in Publishing History*, Edinburgh University Press, 1987.

More, Hannah, *Strictures on the Modern System of Female Education*, 2 vols., New York: Garland, 1974.

Mowl, Timothy, *Horace Walpole: The Great Outsider*, London: John Murray, 1996.

Murphy, Peter, *Poetry as an Occupation and an Art in Britain 1760–1830*, Cambridge University Press, 1993.

Nairn, Tom, *The Enchanted Glass: Britain and Its Monarchy*, London: Radius, 1988.

Napier, Elizabeth, *The Failure of Gothic: Problems of Disjunction in an Eighteenth-Century Literary Form*, Oxford: Clarendon Press, 1987.

Newman, Gerald, *The Rise of English Nationalism: A Cultural History 1740–1830*, London: Weidenfeld & Nicolson, 1987.

Parreaux, André, *The Publication of the Monk: A Literary Event 1796–1798*, Paris: Librairie Marcel Didier, 1960.

Parsons, Coleman O., *Witchcraft and Demonology in Scott's Fiction*, Edinburgh: Oliver and Boyd, 1964.

Paulson, Ronald, *Representations of Revolution 1789–1820*, New Haven: Yale University Press, 1983.

Peacock, T. L., *Essays, Memoirs, Letters & Unfinished Novels, The Halliford Edition of the Works of Thomas Love Peacock*, ed. H. F. B. Brett-Smith and C. E. Jones, 10 vols., London: Constable, 1924–34, vol. 8.

Peardon, Thomas Preston, *The Transition in English Historical Writing 1760–1830*, New York: Columbia University Press, 1933.

Peck, Louis F., *A Life of Matthew G. Lewis*, Cambridge: Harvard University Press, 1961.

Pocock, J. G. A., *The Ancient Constitution and the Feudal Law: A Study of English Historical Thought in the Seventeenth Century*, 2nd edn, Cambridge University Press, 1987.

Virtue, Commerce, and History: Essays on Political Thought and History, Chiefly in the Eighteenth Century, Cambridge University Press, 1985.

Poovey, Mary, 'Ideology and *The Mysteries of Udolpho*', *Criticism* 21 (1979), 307–30.

The Proper Lady and the Woman Writer. Ideology as Style in the Works of Mary Wollstonecraft, Mary Shelley, and Jane Austen, University of Chicago Press, 1984.

Punter, David, *The Literature of Terror: A History of Gothic Fictions from 1765 to the Present Day*, London: Longman, 1980.

Radcliffe, Ann, *The Castles of Athlin and Dunbayne: A Highland Story*, ed. Alison Milbank, Oxford University Press, 1995.

The Italian, or The Confessional of the Black Penitents, A Romance, ed. Frederick

Garber, Oxford University Press, 1968.

The Mysteries of Udolpho: A Romance, ed. Bonamy Dobrée, Oxford University Press, 1966.

The Romance of the Forest, ed. Chloe Chard, Oxford University Press, 1986.

A Sicilian Romance, ed. Alison Milbank, Oxford University Press, 1993.

Railo, Eino, *The Haunted Castle: A Study of the Elements of English Romanticism,* London: Routledge, 1927.

Reeve, Clara, *The Old English Baron,* ed. James Trainer, Oxford University Press, 1977.

Roberts, Marie, *Gothic Immortals: The Fiction of the Brotherhood of the Rosy Cross,* London: Routledge, 1990.

Robertson, Fiona, *Legitimate Histories: Scott, Gothic, and the Authorities of Fiction,* Oxford: Clarendon Press, 1994.

Rogers, Deborah D. (ed.), *The Critical Response to Ann Radcliffe,* Westport: Greenwood Press, 1994.

Roper, Derek, *Reviewing before the* Edinburgh *1788–1802,* London: Methuen, 1978.

Sabor, Peter (ed.), *Horace Walpole: The Critical Heritage,* London: Routledge and Kegan Paul, 1987.

Sade, D. A. F., Marquis de, *The 120 Days of Sodom and Other Writings,* trans. Austryn Wainhouse and Richard Seaver, London: Arrow Books, 1990.

Sadleir, Michael, *The Northanger Novels: A Footnote to Jane Austen,* Oxford University Press, 1927.

Sage, Victor (ed.), *The Gothick Novel: A Casebook,* London: Macmillan, 1990.

Saintsbury, George, *The English Novel,* London: J. M. Dent, 1913.

Schaffer, Simon, 'Natural Philosophy and Public Spectacle in the Eighteenth Century', *History of Science* 21 (1983), 1–43.

Schiller, Friedrich, *The Robbers,* trans. Alexander Tytler, Oxford: Woodstock, 1989.

Scott, Walter, *The Antiquary,* ed. David Hewitt, Edinburgh University Press, 1995.

The Bride of Lammermoor, ed. Fiona Robertson, Oxford University Press, 1991.

'Essay on Imitations of the Ancient Ballad', *The Poetical Works of Sir Walter Scott,* IV: Border Minstrelsy, Edinburgh: Adam and Charles Black, 1880.

Familiar Letters of Sir Walter Scott, 2 vols., Edinburgh: David Douglas, 1894.

The Heart of Midlothian, ed. Claire Lamont, Oxford University Press, 1982.

Ivanhoe, ed. Ian Duncan, Oxford University Press, 1996.

The Lives of the Novelists, London: Dent, 1910.

Old Mortality, ed. Jane Stevenson and Peter Davidson, Oxford University Press, 1993.

The Poetical Works of Sir Walter Scott, ed. J. Logie Robertson, London: Henry Frowde, 1909.

Quentin Durward, ed. Susan Manning, Oxford University Press, 1992.

Redgauntlet, ed. Kathryn Sutherland, Oxford University Press, 1985.

Waverley, ed. Claire Lamont, Oxford University Press, 1986.

The Prefaces to the Waverley Novels, ed. Mark A. Weinstein, Lincoln: University of Nebraska Press, 1978.
Sir Walter Scott on Novelists and Fiction, ed. Ioan Williams, London: Routledge and Kegan Paul, 1968.
Shelley, P. B., *Zastrozzi and St. Irvyne*, ed. Stephen C. Behrendt, Oxford University Press, 1986.
Shiach, Morag, *Discourse on Popular Culture: Class, Gender and History in Cultural Analysis, 1730 to the Present*, Cambridge: Polity Press, 1989.
Simmons, Clare A., *Reversing the Conquest: History and Myth in Nineteenth-Century British Literature*, New Brunswick and London: Rutgers University Press, 1990.
Simpson, David, *Romanticism, Nationalism, and the Revolt against Theory*, Chicago University Press, 1993.
Sitter, John, 'The Flight from History in Mid-Century Poetry', *Modern Essays on Eighteenth-Century Literature*, ed. Leopold Damrosch, Oxford University Press, 1988, 412–35.
Smith, Charlotte, *The Old Manor House*, ed. Anne Ehrenpreis, Oxford University Press, 1989.
Smith, R. J., *The Gothic Bequest: Medieval Institutions in British Thought 1688–1863*, Cambridge University Press, 1987.
Sontag, Susan, *A Susan Sontag Reader*, Harmondsworth: Penguin, 1983.
Southey, Robert, *Poems of Robert Southey*, London: Henry Frowde, 1909.
Spacks, Patricia Meyer, *Desire and Truth: Functions of Plot in Eighteenth-Century English Novels*, University of Chicago Press, 1990.
Spencer, Jane, *The Rise of the Woman Novelist: From Aphra Behn to Jane Austen*, Oxford: Basil Blackwell, 1986.
Stafford, Fiona J., *The Sublime Savage: A Study of James Macpherson and the Poems of Ossian*, Edinburgh University Press, 1988.
Stewart, Keith, 'Ancient Poetry as History in the Eighteenth Century', *Journal of the History of Ideas* 19 (1958), 335–47.
Stokoe, F. W., *German Influence in the English Romantic Period 1788–1818, with Special Reference to Scott, Coleridge, Shelley and Byron*, Cambridge University Press, 1926.
Summers, Montague, *The Gothic Quest*, London: Fortune Press, 1938.
Sutherland, John, *The Life of Walter Scott*, Oxford: Basil Blackwell, 1995.
Sutherland, Kathryn, 'Fictional Economies: Adam Smith, Walter Scott and the Nineteenth-Century Novel', *ELH* 54 (1987), 97–127.
Tales of Terror from Blackwood's Magazine, ed. Robert Morrison and Chris Baldick, Oxford University Press, 1995.
Teuthold, Peter, *The Necromancer: or, The Tale of the Black Forest: Founded on Facts: Translated from the German of Lawrence Flammenberg*, London: Skoob Books, 1989.
Tompkins, J. M. S., 'James White, Esq: A Forgotten Humourist', *Review of English Studies* 3 (1927), 146–56.
The Popular Novel in England 1770–1800, London: Methuen, 1932.

Trumpener, Katie, *Bardic Nationalism: The Romantic Novel and the British Empire*, Princeton University Press, 1997.

Ty, Eleanor, *Unsex'd Revolutionaries: Five Women Novelists of the 1790s*, University of Toronto Press, 1993.

Varma, Devendra, *The Gothic Flame, Being a History of the Gothic Novel in England: Its Origins, Efflorescence, Disintegration, and Residuary Influences*, London: Arthur Barker, 1957.

Walpole, Horace, *The Castle of Otranto*, ed. W. S. Lewis, Oxford University Press, 1964.

 The Castle of Otranto and Hieroglyphic Tales, ed. Robert Mack, London: Dent, 1993.

 Memoirs of King George II, ed. John Brooke, 3 vols., New Haven: Yale University Press, 1985.

 The Yale Edition of the Correspondence of Horace Walpole, ed. W. S. Lewis and others, 48 vols., New Haven: Yale University Press, 1937–83.

Warner, Richard, *Netley Abbey: A Gothic Story*, 2 vols., New York: Arno Press, 1974.

Waswo, Richard, 'Story as Historiography in the Waverley Novels', *ELH* 47 (1980), 304–30.

Watt, Ian, *The Rise of the Novel: Studies in Defoe, Richardson and Fielding*, London: Chatto & Windus, 1957.

Williams, Ioan (ed.), *The Novel and Romance 1700–1800: A Documentary Record*, London: Routledge and Kegan Paul, 1970.

Wilt, Judith, *Ghosts of the Gothic: Austen, Eliot, and Lawrence*, Princeton University Press, 1980.

 Secret Leaves: The Novels of Sir Walter Scott, University of Chicago Press, 1985.

Wollstonecraft, Mary, *Mary* and *The Wrongs of Woman*, ed. Gary Kelly, Oxford University Press, 1976.

Wordsworth, William, *Poetical Works*, ed. T. Hutchinson, 2nd edn rev. E. De Selincourt, Oxford University Press, 1969.

Index

CAMBRIDGE STUDIES IN ROMANTICISM

GENERAL EDITORS
MARILYN BUTLER, *University of Oxford*
JAMES CHANDLER, *University of Chicago*